mediating
modernity

mediating
modernity

german literature
and the "new" media,
1895–1930

the pennsylvania state university press
university park, pennsylvania

Reprinted by permission of North Point Press, a division of Farrar, Straus and Giroux, LLC:

"The Panther" and "Portrait of My Father as a Young Man" from *New Poems* (1907) by Rainer Maria Rilke, a bilingual edition translated by Edward Snow. Translation copyright © 1984 by Edward Snow. Excerpt from "Black Cat" from *New Poems: The Other Part* (1908) by Rainer Maria Rilke, translated by Edward Snow. Translation copyright © 1987 by Edward Snow.

Portions of Chapter 2 appeared in *New German Critique* 99 (Fall 2006): 121–49.

Library of Congress Cataloging-in-Publication Data

Harris, Stefanie, 1968–
   Mediating modernity : German literature and the "new" media, 1895–1930 / Stefanie Harris.
   p.   cm. — (Refiguring modernism)
Includes bibliographical references and index.
Summary: "An interdisciplinary examination of the responses of literary authors in Germany, from 1895–1930, to the emerging media of image and sound recording"—Provided by publisher.
ISBN 978-0-271-03511-6 (pbk. : alk. paper)
1. German literature—20th century—History and criticism.
2. German literature—19th century—History and criticism.
3. Mass media and literature—Germany—History.
4. Mass media in literature.
5. Modernism (Literature)–Germany. I. Title.

PT405.H3445   2009
830.9'355—dc22
2009000978

Copyright © 2009 The Pennsylvania State University
All rights reserved
Printed in Canada by Friesens
Published by The Pennsylvania State University Press,
University Park, PA 16802-1003

The Pennsylvania State University Press is a member of the Association of American University Presses.

It is the policy of The Pennsylvania State University Press to use acid-free paper. Publications on uncoated stock satisfy the minimum requirements of American National Standard for Information Sciences—Permanence of Paper for Printed Library Material, ANSI Z39.48–1992.

for APOSTOLI

contents

	Acknowledgments	ix
1	Introduction: Print in the Age of Edison	1
2	Exposures: Rilke, Photography, and the City	21
3	Kinetic Writing and Kino-Books	54
4	Crisis of the Novel: Döblin's Media Aesthetic	95
5	From Wordminded to Eyeminded: John Dos Passos's Image-Text	133
	Notes	165
	Bibliography	187
	Index	195

Acknowledgments

This book has been a while in the making, and the list of people to whom I owe thanks could probably make up its own volume. I have been mentored, challenged, taught, and befriended by people both inside and outside the university, and it is my greatest pleasure to talk, to watch movies, to think, and to learn with and from them.

I would like to thank especially some of my earliest and most demanding readers. John Johnston is an invaluable teacher, colleague, and friend, and I am grateful to him for helping me launch this project and for his continued support and advice throughout. I have learned so much from and my book is the better for my conversations with Elissa Marder. I would also like to thank Max Aue and Robin Blaetz. And I am deeply indebted to Dalia Judovitz for her intellectual and personal generosity.

I am grateful to my valued colleagues at Northwestern. My heartfelt thanks especially to Peter Fenves for helping me to shape and to present my work; I will always be grateful for the unflagging support. Sam Weber, Rainer Rumold, and Helmut Müller-Sievers graciously read and commented on early drafts. Franziska Lys always had an open door and an open ear. Thanks, finally, to Scott Durham for reminding me that the life of the mind is a life in the world.

This book was written with support from a University Research Grant from Northwestern University and the Alice Berline Kaplan Center for the Humanities at Northwestern. I have benefited enormously from the many conferences at which early stages of my work were presented and the invaluable feedback from colleagues in my field.

I would like to thank Sandy Thatcher at Penn State University Press for his early support of the book and to Laura Reed-Morrisson and Patty Mitchell for seeing it through to the end. Andrew Lewis provided invaluable advice for improving my prose. Many thanks, as well, to the anonymous reviewers from the press who steered me to improvements on the book.

I am fortunate to have a large network of family and friends who have listened to me, read for me, and supported me throughout the process of writing this book. To my parents, Erna and David Harris, my love and my thanks. To friends back east, abroad, and on the third coast, you inspire and challenge me. Finally, this book could never have been written without Apostolos Vasilakis, whose calm, wit, and brilliance always carry the day.

one

Introduction: Print in the Age of Edison

"Edison" is the slogan of the times.... The torchbearers of culture hasten to new heights, while the people below greedily listen to the clattering of the movies and put a new waltz on the phonograph.

FRANZ PFEMFERT, "FILM AS EDUCATOR" (1911)

In the first issue of the leading expressionist journal, *Die Aktion,* the journal's founder Franz Pfemfert still maintained that the high arts could be designated as such because they were literally above the media fray. As the traditional arts of literature, theater, and painting soared to ever greater aesthetic heights, the masses below were abandoned to the corrupting influences of entertainment technologies. In a trajectory stemming from the romantic tradition, Pfemfert's idealist poetics continued to insist on the distance between art and life, the artist and the masses, the aesthetic and the functional—that is, on transcendent claims to truth and beauty and their communicability. Pfemfert was, of course, not alone in his criticism of the new media emerging at the beginning of the twentieth century. Indeed, the rhetoric of this period often foreshadows the dystopian prophecies that accompany our current state of technological transition at the start of the twenty-first century: the loss of a privileged world of books and learning, the distracting and agitating effects of the proliferation of images, a lack of unified meaning and coherence. With his statement, however, Pfemfert indicates (albeit unwittingly) an even greater shift than that of the perceived split between so-called high and low culture. For he concludes his essay by referring to the traditional arts in terms of their lofty aims and signification and by criticizing film and the phonograph in terms of the material effects of their functioning—the clatter of the projector and the scratches and hisses of the phonograph player. In other words, he concludes his essay by drawing attention to their status as media, specifically as mass media, which he insists will never sate the greedy appetites of an overstimulated public. The loss of aura is already foretold in the allusion to mere surface effects and mechanistic functioning. With this move, however, the author already indicates that even the so-called high arts were always also the product of specific, which is to say limited, means of recording, transmission, and reception. For these flickering images on film and the raspy sounds of the phonograph are the recording of real physical effects that the symbolic mediation of print had never been able to encode, thus permitting a data stream to be perceived by a public consciousness that would be forever altered in its wake.

Questions concerning the relationship between contemporary technology and the arts are not uncommon today. The pages of newspapers, news magazines, books, scholarly journals, and the internet resonate with this at times ferocious debate. How does or will new media affect how we read books, present ideas, learn, and interact with each other? How do various media shape and influence how we experience the world, record that experience, and communicate it to others? These questions, however, were not formulated for the first time with the advent of television, the computer, and other digital media. The shock of new media is itself not new. Rather, one finds very similar questions being formulated around the beginning of the twentieth century by poets, novelists, and philosophers, during the nascent stages of mechanical technologies of reproduction that changed the manner in which we perceive and understand the natural world. The interrogation by these literary authors of what I will call the *mediascape* of the early twentieth century is twofold: the term "mediascape" both refers to the traditional and new media of the period for the recording and transmission of knowledge as a collective whole and suggests a relationship to the world as constituted or conditioned by those media through which we perceive, experience, and represent our world. In other words, it is through the various and differentiable media that our relations to oneself, to others, and to the world are shaped and created. What then is the position of the print medium—specifically, the novel and narrative discourse—in this emerging media environment? For it is important to recognize that literature, too, is not only a medium, delimiting a particular mode of selection, combination, transmission, and reception of data, but further, depends on evolving technologies of production—namely, the letter, paper, print, or other means by which it is composed.[1] The alteration or introduction of new media by necessity changes the composition and perspective of other, already ubiquitous media, and further, introduces the possibility that traditional conceptions of literature may no longer be able to contain this increasingly hypermediated world. In the pages of many of these early twentieth-century writers, we read the beginning of a poetics of media that still informs our relation to the mediascape over a century later.

WRITING TECHNOLOGIES

Etymologically, *medium* denotes a midpoint, a middle state or position, or something that is in-between. In physics, a medium is an intervening substance, such as air or water, through which a force acts or an effect is produced. In spiritualism the medium was a living person through which a supernatural agency was believed to manifest itself. Both uses of the term suggest a transparent, open channel to any and all information passing through it. However, a medium can also be the means or instrument used to accomplish something. We are using it in this sense when we refer to an artist's medium as oil, or watercolor, or egg tempera. The broad terms *media* or *mass media* as they are employed today are generally associated with communications technologies, such as radio, television, film, or the internet, and printed matter with a wide circulation and including blogs and electronic communications in addition to traditional (now "old") print media. The term *medium* must thus be understood simultaneously in two senses: not only as a position or a place, but also a particular means or material by which positionings and placings are manifested through the specific manner in which information is stored, transmitted, and received. Marking a place, the idea of media is revealed as a stubbornly historic or contingent concept, inseparable from the material means of its functioning. In this way, any abstract *theory of media* is rendered impermanent and always already obsolete by multiple specific and physical occurrences.

As Marshall McLuhan stated in *Understanding Media*, the basic function of media may be "to store and to expedite information,"[2] but by definition, the medium employed presupposes an act of selection of that information, and further, organizes the information thus stored and transmitted in a particular way. A medium thus implies technical differentiation, for through various media, information flows are separated into incompatible data channels with differently formatted data (one might think, for example, of visual images as opposed to sound recordings). We can read this perhaps as an updated version of McLuhan's by now ubiquitous if poorly understood dictum, "The medium is the message," for as McLuhan plainly stated, "It is the medium that shapes and controls the scale and form of human association and action."[3] A medium, then, does not merely imply the selection and formatting of information in a delimitated fashion, but by means of this selection and formatting, organizes how we perceive and understand that information, and as a result, establishes both one's position in and relationship to time and space, altering sense ratios and patterns of perception. In other words, media produce real and varied physical effects in those interacting with them and this in a way that may even take priority over the content of the information being communicated. At the far end of this argument, one can conclude that the term *medium* does not merely delimit a particular technology of communication but serves as the historical *a priori* of the organization of perception itself.[4] As a result, we find, historically, a very close relationship between technical standards for information storage and transmission, the change in perceptual modes, and formulations of a theory of media. New media that challenge traditional patterns of sensibility impact other media that were very much invested in those same experiential modes. The various means for the processing, storage, and transmission of data are determined by the technological possibilities of a particular period. Differing media do not merely transfer any and all information (the model of a transparent and open channel), rather the term *medium* refers to that system or network through which information is, or just as important, is not, available for selection. Media map out the grid of intelligibility, and with the appearance of new media, this grid is altered. With the increasing digitization of media, the notion of different and exclusive data streams may appear quaint to us now, but I will argue that it is precisely this technologically outmoded concept of media thresholds that explains why the literature of the early twentieth century is in a privileged position to register these effects, and serves as the site on which is registered the alteration or restructuration of this grid of intelligibility.

The meditations on technology and media by literary authors of the early twentieth century can function as a way of reflecting on these changes in the mediascape. For contrary to the frequent depiction of the modernist author in self-isolation, the expanding mediascape of the late nineteenth and early twentieth centuries did not go unnoticed or unrecorded. The works I examine span roughly the dates 1895 to 1930—from the year in which the first moving pictures were screened before public audiences in Berlin to the approximate end of the silent era—and include novels, short stories, screenplays, theoretical and philosophical essays, and cultural critiques of the period. At one level, the texts serve to document and register the technology of the turn of the century, and in this sense we might consider them as records of our own technological prehistory. One notes in their pages, for example, the many references to photographs, films, phonograph records, radio, typewriters, the telegraph, and the telephone. These texts do not reference these technologies merely to mark their historical appearance, however, nor are new technologies employed solely as symbolic shorthand for industrial, social, or economic modernization. Rather, they serve as a means of literary self-reflection on prose narrative within the multiple modes of inscription and reproduction that were beginning to saturate the perceptual field.

The period in question records for us the moment in which writing, which is based on the symbolic mediation of language, is positioned against media like photography, film, the radio, and phonography, which are techniques for recording and transmitting physical effects. This would be one way, for example, to formulate the problem of the referent that is such a hallmark of modernist literature, and certainly the question of reference emerges as a marked difference between prose writing with its linguistic code and other media that record the direct physical effects of light and sound waves. A central issue of the debate between literature and other media will be, paradoxically enough, the perceptual *im*-mediacy of these new forms.[5] However, the question of reference, or the power of words to adequately represent, is certainly not a new one, and was posed long before the advent of moving images (and will be raised again, as we will see, as a challenge to the aesthetic viability of film). More important, what is introduced with the new media, and the modernization which they both announce and represent, is a radically new relationship to time and space, a relationship that is marked by an inability to keep time (in both senses of the word) or to order space in a unified fashion. It is through this apparent impasse and the literary strategies provoked by hyperstimulation, fragmentation, simultaneity, the lived experience of daily life, or any other of the many spatial and temporal "disorders" described during this period, that we can look to what literature can tell us about the role of the new media in the construction of a particularly modern subject and the relationship of that subject to the world, to others, and to the self.[6]

Although literary historians have analyzed problems of perception, memory, and language in the literary texts of modernity, because they have restricted their focus to the texts alone, or at least as an alternative to and distinct from mass media, what has not yet been understood is how the literature of this period engages with the larger mediascape of which it is a part. In other words, one cannot reflect specifically on writing or on broader questions of the work of art without theorizing about media. Himself no stranger to multimedia events, Bertolt Brecht once reflected on the relationship between cinematic and literary discourse:

> The old forms of communication do not remain unaffected by the development of new ones, nor do they survive alongside them. The filmgoer develops a different way of reading stories. But the man who writes the stories is a filmgoer too. The mechanization of literary production cannot be thrown into reverse. Once instruments are used, even the novelist who makes no use of them is led to wish that he could do what the instruments can: to include what they show (or could show) as part of that reality which constitutes his subject-matter; and above all, to assume the attitude of somebody using an instrument.[7]

As a result, literature is affected not only by its own material means of production but also by the media with which it competes. The texts I examine in the following chapters present their authors as assuming the attitude of somebody using an instrument. For the writer, encountering other media, such as film, profoundly affects the act of literary production itself. These texts articulate their authors' recognition that literature has been impacted by technologies that have introduced new temporal and spatial organizations, thus leading the author to question traditional values of poetic art and to experiment with a new type of writing that takes these technological effects into account. If the communication of experience traditionally presupposed a unified consciousness or a continuous, circumscribed, and autonomous subject in time and space, the interference of technology in the social dynamic and the noise and cacophony of varying information networks forces us to formulate a new theory of consciousness. The early twentieth century witnessed the transformation of the novel into a medium whose communicative structure was challenged by the advent of the unremitting immediacy of new media that reorganized the networks through which information was transmitted and presented. One way of understanding the experimental and fragmented nature of what is often called the "modern" novel is as a recording of a certain asynchrony between literature and the mediascape in which it is situated.

DN 1900: SOUND-IMAGE-PRINT

The idea of a perceptual and intelligible shift brought about in conjunction with developments in new media echoes the epistemic breaks that Michel Foucault outlines in *The Order of Things* (1966) when he describes the discontinuities in forms of discourse and the field of knowledge at particular historical moments. In his study, Foucault sought to "reveal a *positive unconscious* of knowledge: a level that eludes the consciousness of the scientist and yet is part of scientific discourse."[8] To employ, to analyze, or to write about discourse is already to imply rules for its use. The "order of discourse," therefore, not only describes discursive practices, but more broadly the conceptual terrain in which knowledge is formed and produced. The *episteme*—those discursive rules and categories that constitute discourse and therefore knowledge—may remain unvoiced and unthought, but as the space or condition of possibility for all thinking, it is impossible to think outside the *episteme*. The entry "Foucault, Michel, 1926–" in the 1984 edition of the *Dictionnaire des philosophes* describes the philosopher's work as "an analysis of the conditions under which certain relations between subject and object are formed or modified, to the extent that these relations are constitutive of a possible knowledge."[9] And in *The Order of Things,* Foucault analyzes these conditions of possibility in the modern sciences of linguistics, biology, and political economy. In his review of Foucault's text, Georges Canguilhem clarifies what is introduced with Foucault's analysis: "The idea that language is a grid for experience is not new. But the idea that the grid itself calls for decoding still had to be formulated."[10]

Almost twenty years after the publication of *The Order of Things,* the German literary and media theorist Friedrich Kittler borrowed from Foucault's methodological approach to write *Discourse Networks, 1800/1900* (1985), in which he delineates regimes of knowledge through their respective and distinct epistemologies. Like Foucault, Kittler contrasts clearly delineated epochs in order to describe their distinguishing characteristics. Foucault had identified epistemic breaks occurring between the sixteenth and seventeenth centuries (the classical period) and the eighteenth and nineteenth centuries (the modern period). Kittler likewise marks two epistemological breaks. The first, which he argues occurred in 1800, corresponds to Foucault's modern period. The second, which Foucault only alludes to in the final chapter of *The Order of Things* as possible and in the future, occurred, according to Kittler, at the start of the twentieth century. Kittler believes that Foucault overlooked this break because he focused his analysis on text for the most part, whereas Kittler argues that discourse networks or systems are not limited to the print medium—at least, not after 1900. In his lecture "Literatur und Literaturwissenschaft als Word Processing" (Literature and Literary Studies as Word Processing), Kittler remarks that while focusing his analysis on the rationality of systems of knowledge, Foucault largely ignored the rationality of technologies through which human knowledge is acquired, stored, and transmitted. What Kittler adds to the conversation, then, is that varying discourses of knowledge, science, and truth have not only been subject to radical shifts or discontinuities over the past two centuries, but that these shifts are in no small part occasioned by the particular technological means at one's disposal for the production of knowledge in general. Kittler thus clarifies the condition under which, in Foucault's words, "something can become an object of a possible knowledge," in his statement: "Media determine our situation" [*Medien* bestimmen unsere *Lage*].[11] As we know, Foucault's work includes analyses of systems of knowledge, not merely in terms of what is said, but more frequently, in terms of what is *not* said, or at least not said in the public arena, and in terms of the relationship between various discourse regimes and institutional policies: What is rational? Who is allowed to speak? What are the determining conditions under which a discourse can be employed? What is considered true? What we do not get in Foucault, or at most very rarely, however, is an analysis of the *techniques* of a system of discourse.[12] For example, Foucault and Kittler will both stress the role of education in determining the conditions under which discourse can be employed and in determining who is a legitimate agent of this discourse. However, Kittler extends this notion further with his claim that educational processes, reading practices, theories of reading, and the practice of literary analysis itself are determined by specific technologies of the letter. Indeed the title of Kittler's own lecture, "Literature and Literary Studies as Word Processing," reveals the extent to which its author has completely abandoned the hermeneutic model as untenable: literature is just a particular means of data processing through the medium of print and the materiality of the letter.

Like the group that Franz Pfemfert identified, "Edison!" could also be the slogan of Kittler's groundbreaking work on the impact of the emerging media environment on the discursive regimes of the early twentieth century. If in Pfemfert's view, however, the emergence of new media widens the chasm between so-called high culture and low, Kittler's deployment of the term often assumes a technological determinism against which the artist can offer no resistance. In December 1877, Edison presented to the public the prototype of what would become the phonograph (in Germany, this instrument went by the trademark name *Gramophone*); and in February 1892, Edison patented the kinetoscope, which when combined with the projection devices developed by the Lumière brothers in France and the Skladanowsky brothers in Germany, would become what we know today as cinema. With these two inventions, acoustic and optical effects could be recorded in time. Before Edison, in Kittler's decidedly linear formulation, literature was the only medium for recording not only linguistic but also visual and audible data flows as temporal or serial data. When fully internalized through the practices of silent reading that rely on perfect alphabetization (Kittler's term for what we might think of as a literacy of transparency), the mental sound movie of print allowed all readers to participate in a life-world that literature of the time described and that philosophy and poetry ratified. With the invention of sound and image recording, however, acoustic and optical effects could be recorded in so-called real time. The recording of other forms of data (namely, sounds and images) meant that the materiality of the text as itself an object of data processing could no longer be ignored. Thus literature could be seen as just another imperfect and limited medium and displaced from its position of absolute sovereignty (in an inversion of Pfemfert's metaphor of cultural peaks and valleys). The "torchbearers" literally pre-date electric light and can only allude to a romantic-classical tradition that has long since ceased to exist.

Kittler's *Discourse Networks, 1800/1900* investigates the metamorphosis or systems shift denoted by the two dates of his title, when literature, which had once operated as an autonomous sphere for the totalization of human experience, began to compete with other media for the inscription of reality. Kittler took his German title—*Aufschreibesysteme*—from the early twentieth-century memoirs that Senate President Daniel Paul Schreber wrote to prove his sanity. These are the same memoirs that Freud analyzed as a case study of paranoia. Schreber's exhaustive and redundant writings are the product of an *Aufschreibesystem*, or literally *writing-down-system*, under which he is commanded and compelled to write by distant forces. Kittler uses Schreber's term as a critical concept to describe what is inscribed by a particular culture at a particular time, or as he states, to "designate the network of technologies and institutions that allow a given culture to select, store, and process relevant data."[13] In other words, Kittler alludes to Schreber to understand the rigid and normative systems of cultural production within a given network. With contemporary developments in more complex digital technologies operating through sophisticated coding to which the user has no access, Kittler will argue elsewhere that these networks are decidedly authoritarian.[14] Critical to Kittler's reappraisal of Foucault's discourse analysis, as we see here, is the fact that the discourse network is not limited to language stored in the archive of print. The title of Kittler's subsequent book, *Gramophone Film Typewriter* (1986), is one way of announcing the death of the hegemony of the book itself.

According to the first half of *Discourse Networks*, "1800," poetry occupied a privileged status in the discourse network of the nineteenth century precisely because it was not considered a medium. As Kittler notes: "The other arts were defined by their respective media (stone, color, building material, sound); the medium of poetry, however—language or tone, language as tone, but certainly never language as letters—disappears beneath its content so that . . . the spirit can appear directly to the spirit."[15] Poetry alone does not constitute the entirety of the discourse network, however, but is part of a triad with philosophy and the state, for these authors are themselves produced under the influence of the state apparatus in compulsory education, the homogenization of writing, and the new discipline of silent reading. Kittler argues in detail that the 1800s saw a shift in language learning in German schools from complete words and phrases to the phonetic unit that is voiced inwardly in the act of reading, thereby echoing the voice of the Mother from whom the romantic poets first gained access to language. Consequently, the poet's pen on paper is conceived as a continuous translation of these inner soundings of the spirit, and literature appears to function as a transparent channel in which words tremble with sensuality and memory, and the reader hallucinates a prelinguistic meaning between the letters and the lines of the printed text.

Kittler reads the traces of these discursive effects through close analysis of a variety of texts, starting with the scene of writing in Goethe's *Faust*. He finds a privileged example of the exalted position of literature in the elusive quest for the blue flower of Novalis's literary double Heinrich von Ofterdingen. As Ofterdingen admits, "I long to catch sight of the blue flower. It is always on my mind and I can write and think of nothing else."[16] Poetry serves here as the means of obtaining this vision, through its ability to transform words into flowers and flowers into words, since poetic words "liquidate material media."[17] In other words, poetry established itself as a medium that denied its own functioning as a medium. This is why Novalis can write in one of the fragments of his *Allgemeinen Brouillons*, "If one reads correctly, then a real, visible world unfolds itself in us internally according to the words."[18] Here Novalis seems to provide a perfect interpretation of interpretation in general—readers do not see letters, but hallucinate a perfect signified. Poetry translates the other arts into a nonmaterial and universal medium that is called Imagination, that marvelous sense, as Novalis once wrote, that can replace all our senses.

In the nineteenth century, poetic writing was so general and absolute a medium that the term *medium* did not encompass it, but Kittler argues that the discourse network of the early twentieth-century was the product of the technical differentiation of written, optical, and acoustic data flows through the typewriter, film, and the phonograph, and the concurrent sciences of and experimentation on the body that led to their invention. These new media are important at many different levels, but primarily in their differing functions *as* media. In other words, they delineate distinct and separable channels of information and data processing. As a result the discourse network of 1900 is one of division and deviation. For with the introduction of new media, written, optical, and acoustic data flows are separated from each other and rendered autonomous. Indeed, this technical differentiation—the separation of data flows—becomes the very definition of a medium in this historical context. Against a background of noise, each individual medium can only channel a select and limited amount of information. The clattering of film reels and whistling and scratching of phonograph records give evidence to the wealth of information and noise that no symbolic writing could ever encode. In other words, they draw attention to the existence of alternate data flows that must be organized through different channels. Texts are only a specific form of data processing, and as long as no film or phonograph, no computer or word processor, existed to break the textual monopoly, the literary sciences could ignore the materiality of their object of study and assume sense and meaning, content and form. With this differentiation, the materiality of discourse, as opposed to the transparent meaning of the word, is made explicit, thus bringing the hermeneutic project to an end. Interpretation of the text is subordinated to the identification of its medium of transmission. In the absence of a universal reference, discourses make *sense* only with the support of other discourses. Signals received and amplified are employed to close a given network's loop, and it is only an anthropocentric illusion that maintains that books present themselves to theoretical eyes whose freedom (from discourse) then allows them to discover meaning. Or as Nietzsche, the first "mechanized philosopher,"[19] once wrote in a letter, "Our writing tools are also working on our thoughts."[20]

With the invention of the phonograph, technical sound recording renders explicit the materiality of language, and a methodological and distinct separation is drawn between the real physical effects of sound recording and the symbolic notation of phonetics and phonology. It is within this historical context, Kittler argues, that the possibility of a structural linguistics, in which words become symbols with only an arbitrary relation to the real, emerges. And it is not only the phonograph that contributes to this event—the typewriter will also play a major (indeed, determining) role, for the typewriter effects the dislocation of language from the individual body or subject engaged in the production of writing. As Mark Seltzer notes in his book, *Bodies and*

Machines: "The typewriter, like the telegraph, replaces, or pressures, that fantasy of continuous transition with recalcitrantly visible and material systems of difference: with the standardized spacing of keys and letters; with the dislocation of where the hands work, where the letters strike and appear, where the eyes look, if they look at all."[21] We note that in his attempt to explain the nonreferential value of the linguistic sign, Saussure resorted to a comparison with writing—a comparison that is telling indeed because the point is more strongly made with typing than with writing longhand. "We shall use writing to draw some comparisons that will clarify the whole issue. . . . The value of letters is purely negative and differential. The same person can write *t*, for instance, in different ways: [the text reproduces here three different handwritten variations of the letter *t*]. The only requirement is that the sign for *t* not be confused in his script with the signs used for *l, d*, etc. Values in writing function only through reciprocal opposition within a fixed system that consists of a set number of letters."[22] The letter is void of significant content—its meaning is pure difference. In his analysis of the technologies of the early twentieth century, Kittler focuses much of his attention on the typewriter and its specific mode of production. Indeed, typewriters were not only finding increasing use because of their speed but also their enhanced legibility—both of which were requirements in the information boom of the early twentieth century. We find not only the increased use of typewriters, but a general interest as well in the simplification of typefaces, which were subjected to extensive experimentation in order to rate their varying degrees of legibility. The letters that the typewriter produces are not autonomous vessels bearing meaning, rather the letters are what they are only through the contrast of distinct black figures on white paper. The problem with Saussure's example of the *t* written in longhand is that this *t* is only differentiable from every other letter produced by the same hand. In this case, each individual would constitute only his own system of differentiation. With the typewriter, however, the system of differentiation becomes collective, which was, in fact, Saussure's point. In other words, with the typewriter, the separation between letters becomes visible. In order for letters to exist as signs, however, they must stand on a background that no mechanism can record or store, meaning that the medium of print must always simultaneously indicate its own threshold.

In *Discourse Networks, 1800/1900,* Kittler refrains from naming the periods designated by the two dates of his title, or what is most commonly referred to in German literary history as romanticism and modernism. Instead, he selects a mathematical formula to serve as an epigraph to each section:

1800: $e^{ix} = \cos x + i \sin x$ *Leonhard Euler*
1900: $y = (+a) + (-a) + (+a) + (-a) + \ldots$ *Bolzano*[23]

As David Welbery instructs Kittler's presumably mathematically challenged readers, the first formula "can be interpreted as an algorithm of 'growth,' the movement of progressive augmentation that characterizes the discourse network of 1800. The second formalizes the pulse of differential alternation that permeates the modernist discourse network."[24] By refusing to give names to the periods in question, Kittler not only reveals his persistent fascination with engineers and mathematicians, but further hopes to deflect the reader's traditional presuppositions associated with the terms "Romantic" and "Modern" (or any other name they have been given in the history of interpretive discourse). Nevertheless, the substitution of these words by formulas does present a question that Kittler does not pursue, namely, what kind of medium is the language of mathematics? The deployment of mathematical formulas suggests that all elements of cultural production are subject to the same abstract, unyielding rules. In other words, in this historically mathematical view, the media landscape is rigid and fixed rather than constantly in play, and hybrid or fluid forms are either rejected from the outset or normalized. Bolzano's formula becomes, within the context of Kittler's argument, a blueprint that dictates not only how literature and newer media but also economics, politics, education, social policy, and so on, are perceived and comprehended. I will show, however, that a close examination not just of the media but of the early theories of media produced during this period suggests that the terrain is hardly this straightforward. The system does not alternate with such perfect symmetry.

THE BLUE FLOWER: FROM POETRY TO FILM

It is not surprising that Kittler situates not only literature but also the evolution of psychoanalysis (more specifically, the constitutive elements of a Freudian vis-à-vis a Lacanian perspective)[25] within a technologically determined narrative, as if the effects of media were inscribed directly onto the unconscious. What is omitted from this narrative, however, is a sense of the interruption and disruption of a monolithic network. In other words, in this period, the explicit meditations by literary authors on image-based and sound-based technologies and their attempts to come to terms with a perceived disconnect between the inherited literary tradition and the world in which they lived reveal an important resistance to these new technologies that cannot be overlooked. One way this anxiety is verbalized is within various iterations of the question, how can one go on writing in the reconfigured mediascape? By engaging in a structural analysis of the larger mediascape—and by focusing on literature as an intrinsic element in that system—I have sought to highlight (rather than ignore) the fluidity that permeates the relationship between the actual media with which we record and transmit knowledge and the construction of the subject and the subject's relation to the world as constituted by those media. In other words, in this period the relationship of the subject to these new media was one of constant renegotiation, and often not without recourse to media technologies that may, in this brave new world, have already seemed anachronistic.

When McLuhan stated that the contents of one medium are always other media, he was only echoing what Walter Benjamin had already made clear in what is perhaps the most widely cited essay in media, and particularly film, studies, "The Work of Art in the Age of Mechanical Reproduction": "Traditional art forms in certain phases of their development strenuously work toward effects which later are effortlessly attained by the new ones."[26] The essay marks a pivotal moment in twentieth-century aesthetics because Benjamin shifts the then current question of whether or not film should be considered art to the question of how the technical reproducibility of film forces us to rethink our assumptions concerning the work of art in general. Benjamin does not merely marvel over the technological wonder of the moving image, but instead uses his meditation on this technology to reflect on among other things how our previous assumptions about art become shifted. For example, our criterion of authenticity is useless when it comes to a work of art designed for reproducibility, such as the photograph or a film. As the essay makes clear, a change has transpired in what constitutes the essence or nature of art (to say nothing of the notion of *essence* itself), for the technical reproduction of art is inseparable from the technologies that have created it. Norbert Bolz has thus correctly drawn our attention to the fact that Benjamin's insight was to analyze film not as an art form but as a medium, with a specific and delimited mode of recording, transmission, and reception.[27] We find in Benjamin's writing a relationship between technical standards and changes in perception, between cultural production and a constantly evolving understanding of the concept of *media* itself. "During long periods of history," Benjamin wrote, "the mode of human sense perception changes with humanity's entire mode of existence. The manner in which human sense perception is organized, the medium in which it is accomplished, is determined not only by nature but by historical circumstances as well."[28] Media do not merely delimit a particular technology of communication but serve as the historical apriori of the organization of perception itself. One need only consider Benjamin's pronouncement on the decline of the "aura" of the unique artwork as a result of its having been photographed and disseminated; the loss of "aura" is a direct function of the upsetting of traditional spatial and temporal relations, and that has everything to do with the manner in which the work stores and transmits information. In other words, it has everything to do with the placement of the work within a network.

We should not be surprised, then, to discover that after 1900, Novalis's blue flower turns up in a new setting, namely, in Benjamin's description of the specificity of the cinematic medium:

> In the film studio, the equipment has penetrated so deeply into reality that its pure aspect freed from the foreign substance of equipment is the result of a special technical procedure, namely, the shooting by the specially adjusted camera and the mounting of the shot together with similar ones. The equipment-free aspect of reality here has become the height of artifice, and the sight of immediate reality has become the blue flower in the land of technology.[29]

Benjamin's allusion to one of the preeminent symbols of German romanticism suggests that film has taken over a function that was once the domain of the romantic poet—the blue flower that was once hallucinated from the words of the written page is now transferred to countless film screens, which is to say that the image appears to be presented directly, although its relationship to "reality" must be heavily scrutinized. With this choice of phrase, Benjamin indicates the extent to which the functions of the universal medium of the previous century (poetry) have been separated into various domains. One does not have to "read correctly," as Novalis once wrote, in order to see the blue flower, although the media literacy of the public will have important sociopolitical consequences. Benjamin clearly argues that one's reception of that blue flower is a direct function of the *technical* means by which film records, programs, and transmits information. New technologies of representation force us to rethink the notion of representation in general.

In her essay, "Benjamin, Cinema, and Experience: 'The Blue Flower in the Land of Technology,'" Miriam Hansen indicates that the "blue flower" would at first glance appear an odd choice of allusion to be used in conjunction with film, if for no other reason than its status as a preeminent poetic metaphor of the unattainable object, the incarnation of desire. Its "aura" would appear at odds with the very technologies of reproduction that Benjamin tells us have contributed to its decline. Hansen proposes that Benjamin's allusion to the "blue flower" may have been part of a larger argument in which cinema "could be redeemed . . . as a medium of experience."[30] However, this reading suggests that what might be recouped with the screen image of the "blue flower" is the secure and stable position of the individual subject to the work, which is at odds with the "shock effect" of the cinematic medium as it is otherwise described in the essay. Rather than looking back to a previous discursive model, Benjamin's reference to the "blue flower," particularly when taken in conjunction with the position of the reference in one of the more explicitly technical portions of the essay, likely indicates the extent to which Benjamin dramatically underscores the perceptual shift of modern consciousness as a result of the intervention of technology, and as a result, one's increasing inability to conceive of the blue flower *except* as an image on the screen. In other words, the flower (as poetry) no longer signifies the liquidation of all media, which is to say their perfect translatability or what Benjamin called "pure language" in "The Task of the Translator,"[31] but reveals itself as firmly embedded within a particular media-specific network of storage, transmission, and reception.

Samuel Weber's essays on Benjamin in the collection *Mass Mediauras* make clear the extent to which the recording of the technical apparatus is doubled by reception as a technical effect, for as he points out, the German verb *aufnehmen* is used by Benjamin to designate both the technical procedure of cinematic recording and its reception by the spectator.[32] In English, *aufnehmen* translates literally as "to take up." This doubling is clear in the quotation from "The Work of Art in the Age of Mechanical Reproduction"; the "equipment-free aspect of reality"—that is to say, what we see on the screen—is only perceptible from the position of the camera. In other words, with film, we see ourselves seeing; the film records our own processes of perception. However, just as the film is the product of certain media effects, so too our perception of the world around us is informed by other components of the mediascape. Even the reception of film in a state of distraction and the shock effect of disconnected and disorienting images only doubles the technical condition of cinematic production itself. Bolz seems to say as much in his own analysis of the essay when he writes: "The conclusive media-technical condition of the decline of the aura is the mass reproduction of images which, in their endless doubling of reality, absorb reality itself. In a fully aestheticized world, in which reality coincides with its own image, there can be no discriminating transcendence of art."[33] An aesthetics that moors the work of art to fractured space and time, to circumstance, to contingency, to the moment, is not easily or seamlessly incorporated into prevailing views of the duration and permanence of the artwork and its unique experience by an individual. The media technologies of the early twentieth century radically changed the manner in which art was conceived, produced, and experienced.

With the end of the media monopoly of print, what happens, to paraphrase Kittler, when the acoustic and optical realms *stop not writing themselves*? In other words, what happens to the writing of a printed text when the phonograph and cinematograph—and both names refer, not accidentally, to writing—are able to fix the hitherto unwritable data flow of time and the visual image? Another critical part of the question, however, is how do examinations of mechanical media lead to an examination of the literary arts themselves? It is in congruence with this larger mediascape and other narrative modes (and not merely a reaction against or a slavish imitation of them) that the early twentieth-century author begins to redefine poetry, the novel, the essay, and other forms of writing. The boundaries between media are not permeable—despite calls for cinematic writing and the like—but are defined by technological thresholds. And this incompatibility becomes, for many, grounded in a more general anxiety surrounding the split between word and image as vehicles for representation. The so-called *image-text* therefore becomes a highly unstable site for thinking through the question of art.[34] Further, these distinct channels—print, image, sound—suggest differences in communicative media that are in excess of their mutual translatability. As such, the discourse on literature and the "new" media at the beginning of the century is an interrogation of the limits and boundaries of differentiated media.

LITERATURE AS MEDIA

A reconfigured understanding of the modern novel and related literary modes emerges from a sustained examination of the interactions between literary history and the history of media technologies. The multiple inscriptions of print, image, and sound in the modern mediascape give rise to ways of thinking about, producing, and reading literature that take up the modes of recording and reproduction that were beginning to saturate the perceptual field in the late nineteenth and early twentieth centuries. Over the course of this book, I examine four texts that give evidence of the changing status of the literary text and the way in which authors understand their own medium. In selecting from a combination of greater and lesser known works, and from German and American examples, I further show how these reflections on the aesthetic and social shifts in the new mediascape do not themselves remain static but are constantly in flux. If modernism is commonly understood as a retreat from mass culture and modernization, I intend to show how this sweeping claim does not take into account the many detailed examinations of new media taken up by even the most stalwart members of this canon, and to argue that the period can not be properly understood without a consideration of the literary turn to concerns about media.

I begin with an examination of the work produced by Rainer Maria Rilke during his Paris period, revealing how the emerging media environment at the beginning of the century, and the corresponding technological training of the sensorium, is a frequent preoccupation of his letters and essays and is inscribed in the pages of his literary record. Tellingly, both in his novel *Die Aufzeichnungen des Malte Laurids Brigge* (*The Notebooks of Malte Laurids Brigge*, 1910) and in the poems and other writings of the period, Rilke makes explicit reference to photography, particularly in relation to his anxiety over the city and the act of writing, leading one to inquire into the ontological and epistemological stakes of the photograph such that poetic writing, or at least a certain notion of poetic writing, becomes problematized. Rilke employs the language of photography to examine questions of framing, perception, temporality, memory, and the relationship to death—questions that permeate not only his reflections on the mediascape at the beginning of the century, but those of all of the authors I discuss. Mindful of the possibilities of the new technologies, Rilke does not cede any ground to them but instead argues for the continued relevance and necessity of the work of art in the age of its technical reproducibility.

With the introduction of film, pictures of course became both mechanical and *moving*. Kurt Pinthus's *Kinobuch* (1913), a collection of screenplays by a variety of young German expressionist authors, opens a discussion of non-novelistic considerations of film by literary authors. Strikingly, a number of these screenplays are built around a scene of writing or reading. I develop the argument that early film criticism in Germany and Austria—at least that practiced by members of the literary community, and including Hugo von Hofmannsthal, Robert Musil, and Thomas Mann—was a formulation of the changing terrain of the literary medium within a mediascape in which aesthetic reception was increasingly programmed by mechanical forms of recording and representation. In other words, I examine how the notion of writing itself was changed by how people were beginning to think about photography and film.

Almost every emerging technology from the end of the nineteenth and beginning of the twentieth centuries is accounted for in Alfred Döblin's novel *Berlin Alexanderplatz* (1929). Unlike Rilke, for whom technological models of representation presented a crisis to his understanding of poetic language (as articulated through his literary double, Malte), Döblin explicitly employs alternative media to expand literary discourse. *Berlin Alexanderplatz* thus not only records other, nonliterary discourses, but further, adopts strategies, such as cinematic and phonographic techniques, from the media it concorporates. I posit that early twentieth-century literature is part of the assemblage of the differentiation of media that occurs with the invention of technologies such as film and the phonograph which record and transmit alternate information flows. I pay specific attention to Döblin's earlier works—his short stories, screenplays, and particularly, essays that either directly or indirectly address the mediascape—in order to show the development of ideas that are later worked out and refined in *Berlin Alexanderplatz*.

Like Döblin's *Berlin Alexanderplatz,* John Dos Passos's *Manhattan Transfer* exploits alternative media to construct a text about a city that reveals the extent to which the city is defined by the competing networks of media found in it. In other words, Dos Passos's works reflect on their own possibility and restrictedness within the grid of intelligibility constituted by the new media. In his later *U.S.A.* trilogy, these separable media flows are made explicit, delimiting the boundaries and gaps where the media are not seamless. By focusing particularly on the mode of writing Dos Passos termed the Camera Eye, a concept that brings literary representation together with photographic technology, we revisit the questions Rilke posed some twenty years earlier, but this time from the position of the photographer as successful poet, not that of the poet as failed photographer. Rilke struggled with the question of how the medium of photography problematizes the presuppositions of poetic writing, but Dos Passos used the Camera Eye, and by extension a theorization of photographic recording, to show how one can employ the epistemological considerations introduced by the fact of photography precisely in order to go on writing. By concluding with this American author, it is my intention to put the German response to the new media into a broader context, drawing out both the continuities and singularities in the shifted media aesthetic of the beginning of the century.

The crisis of representation brought about by the new media, or even more specific technological interventions into the literary domain, did not, of course, spell the end of the book—despite dire predictions to the contrary. Rather, at the limit of narrative representation, the books of the early twentieth century record their own changing status as a medium. By reading against the established notion of the literary creation of autonomous and poetically ideal realms, we can see how the history of literature intersects with the history of media, especially image- and sound-based recording. The texts I examine help show how their authors use the encounter with mechanical media to address the changing conditions of human experience and the problem of communicating that experience through their work. Of foremost concern, then, are not thematic considerations of media (for example, Franz Biberkopf's trip to the cinema in Döblin's novel), but rather stylistic experiments within prose and poetry, the reproduction of, say, cinematic effects within the literary text, and, especially, the explicit meditation on media in the letters and essays of these authors. In this way, both familiar and less familiar writers can be seen not only as deeply engaged with the question of the position of literature in the emerging mediascape but also as early media theorists. Contrary to Pfemfert's early pronouncement in *Die Aktion,* "Edison!" is the slogan of the times precisely because the emerging technological environment and the corresponding technological training of the human sensorium are implicit and necessary characteristics of the very notion of modernity itself.

In closing the book, I consider how we might productively consider the relevance of the relationship of literature to "new media" around 1900 to our own current moment. For even a brief survey of postwar and postmodern literary works will show that authors of literary prose continue to interrogate, examine, and analyze both emerging digital media and what is now usually referred to as "traditional" media (photography, film, television, and audio recording). Are questions of medial specificity simply transposed to the digital age or have a different set of concerns emerged? I offer that in the postwar period, the shock and novelty of the "new" media abated so that questions concerning spatial and temporal experience, subjectivity, agency, and memory are taken up especially in relation to the role of media in the apparatus of power relations. For these later generations of writers, the literary experimentation of the authors of the modern mediascape will be less compelling than the writings of someone like Walter Benjamin and his prescient analyses of the sociopolitical repercussions of the new media.

two

Exposures: Rilke, Photography, and the City

This time, Paris was just what I had expected: difficult. And I feel like a photographic plate that has been exposed too long, in that I remain forsaken to this powerful influence.... Out of fright I went right off Sunday to Rouen. An entire cathedral is necessary to drown me out.... Would you believe that the glance of a woman passing me in a quiet lane in Rouen so affected me that I could see almost nothing afterward, could not collect myself? Then gradually the beautiful cathedral was finally there, the legends of her densely filled windows, where earthly events shine through and one sees the blood of its colors.

RAINER MARIA RILKE TO LOU ANDREAS-SALOMÉ,
OCTOBER 21, 1913

The German poet Rainer Maria Rilke first arrived in Paris on August 28, 1902, at the age of twenty-six. He lived in the city, with frequent extended journeys throughout Europe, until the beginning of World War I. The letter quoted in the epigraph was posted to his former lover and lifelong confidante, Lou Andreas-Salomé, within days of his return to the city after an absence of approximately five months. In it, one notes a familiar theme of Rilke's letters: his ambivalent attitude toward Paris. Whenever he mentions his adoptive city, he describes only its chaos, noise, and crowds, and his own resulting anxiety, although after every departure he always wished to return. He was in Paris for less than a week in October 1913 before he fled to Rouen. What makes this passage particularly striking, however, is how Rilke describes the two environments with two very different techniques of image production—the one mechanically produced (the photograph), the other handcrafted by artisans (the stained-glass window). Rilke leaves Paris, a city he associates with the photograph, for the comfort of Rouen, a smaller town dominated by its famous cathedral. In the Cathedral Poems of his *New Poems,* Rilke associates the cathedral with strength, permanence, and eternity in contrast to the random accidents and chance occurrences on the streets below.[1] And in a letter to his wife, Clara Rilke, dated less than one month before the October trip to Rouen, Rilke writes that he has been spending time in the Bibliothèque Nationale looking at images of twelfth- and thirteenth-century cathedrals: "They [the cathedrals] are isolation and stillness, escape and quiet from the changing impressions and hubbub of these streets. They are the future, just as they are the past; everything else moves, flows, runs, and tumbles . . . they tower over and wait."[2] In other words, the cathedrals are removed from and unaffected by the flow of time. The recording of the lived experience of passing moments is, however, precisely the domain of photography.

In addition to the temporal disjuncture of photographs and stained-glass windows, Rilke positions himself differently to them, as either coexistent with or distinct from the image. In this manner, he articulates a distinction not only in production but also in reception. That is, the nature of vision itself is presented here through two different models. Observing the stained-glass windows, Rilke writes that he "sees" them and, in seeing, responds to the fullness of the legends communicated directly through the play of light and color. However, with respect to the photographic plate, one cannot say that Rilke properly "sees," for the camera's shutter never closes. As a result, the images continue to inscribe themselves directly onto him without stopping. There is no separation between himself as a subject and the objects observed. This leads one inevitably to ask: why does Rilke employ the modality of the camera, and a malfunctioning one at that, in order to describe his experience of the city?

The word *photograph* is, of course, derived from the Greek words for *light* and *writing.* A photograph is literally an image written with light onto specially prepared paper or metal plates. Over one hundred years of writing on photography—from William Henry Fox Talbot's famous "pencil of nature" to Susan Sontag's description of photography as "the registering of an emanation"[3]—has emphasized this indexical relationship. In the photographic image, the data stream of light reflected off objects is itself materially encoded. In Rilke's own formulation, this encoding process seems to take place directly onto him, without his own intervention. However, the data thus recorded always remain fragmented and incomplete, severed from the temporal flow in which they are simultaneously embedded. With the stained-glass window, on the other hand, light does not create or reproduce an image; it brings an already existing and fixed image into visibility by shining through multiple pieces of colored glass carefully pieced together by human hands. Rilke's description suggests that the windows are transparent on both the physical and the representational levels: "One sees the blood of its colors." And he explicitly draws attention to the legends that are both the content of the cathedral's windows and the texts in which one could read about the lives of the saints. These legends were not merely images but stories. As the light passes through the window, the text "shines through"—the once earthly happenings become transparent and meaningful to the observer below, within the cathedral's silent, closed walls.

Rilke's position inside the cathedral is strangely akin to that of a spectator inside a camera obscura. Light enters through a small pinhole and projects inside the camera an image of the reality outside. The cathedral in which Rilke is standing seems to function in a similar manner in his description. The interior is dark, and the light coming through the windows projects an external reality that the observer inside the space can perceive only as a result of this light. As Rilke notes, "Earthly happening becomes transparent" or "shines through." By positing Rilke's perception of the stained glass as similar to the act of perception one experiences inside the camera obscura, one would seem to posit the image techniques Rilke refers to—photography and stained-glass—as comparable. Indeed, most histories of photography begin with a chapter on the camera obscura as its precursor. Here, however, Rilke describes two radically different experiences that exemplify distinct temporal, perceptual, and representational models.

In this sense, Rilke articulates a distinction between these two visual techniques that is the extended subject of Jonathan Crary's insightful study of image production and reception in the nineteenth century, *Techniques of the Observer*. Crary's intention is to extricate the camera obscura "from the evolutionary logic of a technological determinism":

> The camera obscura and the photographic camera, as assemblages, practices, and social objects, belong to two fundamentally different organizations of representation and the observer, as well as of the observer's relation to the visible. By the beginning of the nineteenth century the camera obscura is no longer synonymous with the production of truth and with an observer positioned to see truthfully. The regularity

of such statements ends abruptly. The assemblage constituted by the camera breaks down and the photographic camera becomes an essentially dissimilar object, lodged amidst a radically different network of statements and practices.[4]

The discourse surrounding both the camera obscura and a theory of vision underscores a fundamental understanding of an image as an image of the world and thus distinct from it, whereas through the photographic apparatus the image coincides with the world. In the organization of the camera obscura, therefore, the observer is distinct from the visible world that is observed, while in the organization of the photographic camera the observer is inseparable from the visible and is embodied in discrete temporal and spatial moments.

As Crary demonstrates, scientific and psychological discourses of the nineteenth-century break with the paradigm of decorporealized vision modeled through the camera obscura and are reflected in alternate visual technologies, including the photograph. For example, by focusing on "specific nerve energies" (Johannes Müller) and the internal projection of afterimages, one begins to conceive of perception as uncoupled from a necessarily external referent. Observation is thus no longer "the inspection of an inner space or a theater of representations" but is increasingly "exteriorized; the viewing body and its objects begin to constitute a single field on which inside and outside are confounded."[5] And because observation is radically tied to the body, "temporality and vision become inseparable. The shifting processes of one's own subjectivity experienced in time became synonymous with the act of seeing, dissolving the Cartesian ideal of an observer completely focused on an object."[6] Hence the act of seeing is tied to the body not merely in terms of the physiological makeup of the retina and optic nerve but also in terms of the body's particular location in time and space. In other words, if the mechanics of the camera obscura prevented the observer from realizing his or her own position as part of the representation, the discourse surrounding nineteenth-century technologies revealed the intersubjective element always inherent in this act. Whereas the model of vision offered by the camera obscura promotes a transparency of representation and direct observation of a transcendent image as a representation of some external and atemporal (even eternal) truth, the model offered by photography and other nineteenth-century developments effaces the distinction between observer and object observed and radically temporalizes and subjectifies the act of seeing. Thus the move from camera obscura to photography is not a progressive one but exemplifies a radical redefinition of how we not only observe but know the world and experience our position in it.

In Paris, as if penetrated by light waves, Rilke is recorded with (and becomes a recording of) the sensory data received through the eye. The exterior and the interior are no longer distinguishable. And he is without protection from these influences—the city is being recorded on him and in him nonstop. This overload of the image frightens him and leads him to interrupt the task for which he returned to Paris, namely, to write. It is not just that the city as such becomes an inopportune place for Rilke to write: the particular medium he associates with the city is, in a sense, not compatible with his project of writing. But what is at stake in the photograph that problematizes poetic writing? What we discover in this brief passage is not only a distinction between two types of image production and between two geographical locations (Paris and Rouen), but also a conflict between two types of representation, the one a ceaseless opening to the present and the other atemporal and transcendent. Because the aperture of the photographic apparatus Rilke describes never closes, the image cannot endure. And for Rilke this is in conflict with his understanding of the function of art, described in the context of his admiration for the sculptor Auguste Rodin's work: "The object [that serves as a model for art] is definite, the art object must be even more definite; withdrawn from all chance, removed from all obscurity, lifted out of time and given to space, it has become lasting, capable of eternity."[7] Rilke's insistence on the totality and completion of the art object, its eternal and lasting nature, thus demands a closure of this aperture.

In the opening description of Paris and Rouen, we note that Rilke's Rouen trip is almost capsized by "the glance of a woman" that "so affected" the poet that he "could see almost nothing afterward." Here, we must be reminded of that other great poet of the city, Charles Baudelaire, who in his poem "A une passante" is likewise struck by a woman's glance. In the midst of a bustling, noisy street scene, the poet crosses paths with a woman in mourning, but they are immediately separated by the crowd, causing the poet to regret not only the brevity of their encounter but, more especially, his inability to halt the passage of time. In other words, the poem evokes the temporal problem of modernity itself. As Elissa Marder has shown, Baudelaire's poem is thus not coincidentally marked by the language of photography.[8] Rilke's allusion to Baudelaire's poem is no accident here. Indeed, Rilke's own interest in Baudelaire is registered repeatedly both during his stay in Paris and in the pages of *The Notebooks of Malte Laurids Brigge*. Not only does Rilke draw on Baudelairean imagery in his own descriptions of the city—hospitals, death, masks, the elderly, the blind, the downtrodden—but further, the setting of the text as "poems in prose" shows more than a passing correspondence to Baudelaire's *Petits poèmes en prose,* which Baudelaire called a "portrayal of modern life" in his dedication of the work to Arsène Houssaye.[9] Like Baudelaire, Rilke struggles with not only the fact of writing poetry within the chaos, overstimulation, and fragmentation and under the peering eyes of the city but also the construction of a poetics of the metropolis itself.

Within this context, Rilke's allusion to photography brings the technological apparatus into direct association with a burgeoning metropolitan space. More fundamentally, however, Rilke's reference to the photographic plate articulates a conflict between the functional and epistemological effects of that technology and the author's understanding of poetic writing.[10] The "photographic" nature of his experience—that is, an experience marked by a profoundly problematic relationship to external reality and to the present as noisy, ceaseless temporal flow—registers an awareness of the profound changes initiated by modern life in the urban metropolis into the domains of human apprehension of the world, an understanding of one's position in it, and communication of that experience. In this sense, Rilke's allusion to the technological object can be used to reflect on the impact of that technology on his own work in a very different medium, namely, writing. In what follows, I address how Rilke refers to specific mechanical media as a way to consider the changing conditions of human experience at the beginning of the century and the possibilities of communicating that experience through literary writing. That Rilke rarely refers to actual photos or photographic techniques confirms only that he is not concerned with cataloging the new modern media. The descriptive passages from Rilke's prose or poetry do not function as linguistic transpositions or translations of photographic images. Rilke's vast influences from the realm of visual arts, especially Rodin and Paul Cézanne, are well known. Rather, what is at stake is a certain understanding of photography as emblematic of a critical relationship to time that may have devastating consequences for the integrity of the self, particularly with regard to memory, and of the work of art—a link that one of Siegfried Kracauer's early essays on photography makes clear. By looking specifically at Rilke's novel *The Notebooks of Malte Laurids Brigge* and selections from his *New Poems* (both works were started and finished in Paris), I consider how the emerging mediascape at the beginning of the century, particularly as associated with the metropolis, and the corresponding technological training of the sensorium are inscribed in the pages of his literary record.

In his compelling work on the photography of trauma, Ulrich Baer proposes an alternative to the traditional understanding of time as flowing, sequential, and continuous, and the photograph as an interruption or a frozen moment. Baer, following Vilém Flusser's lead, reintroduces us to a way of thinking about time and thus history as atomistic, explosive, a series of discontinuous bursts.[11] This way of looking at time privileges the event over its unfolding, the moment over the story, particularity over generality, and serves as a way to establish an ethics of viewing, or more precisely "witnessing," the photograph, especially photographs of trauma. In this regard, my discussion of Rilke and photography does not examine individual photographic images but instead focuses on the formulation of a photographic relation to the world in which neither the established model nor Baer's alternative is privileged. Critical to the idea of photography described by Kracauer, and evident in Rilke, is the notion of a nonsynchronization between personal, memorial time (the realm of art) and public, mechanical time (the world of commerce, of traffic—the city), and the attempt to reconcile the two, that is, to find a place for art in the world and for everyday life in art.[12] In formulating this argument, I offer the idea of *expansive* time as a concept for how the artwork, as opposed to the photograph, "keeps" time.

LEARNING TO SEE

The Notebooks of Malte Laurids Brigge, composed sporadically between 1904 and 1910, comprises seventy-one fragments that record a young Danish author's impressions during approximately one year in Paris.[13] Above all, however, they show a young writer struggling to employ the literary project to make sense of or master his experience of the city, and by extension his knowledge of himself. As he writes from the beginning, "I have taken action against fear. I sat up all night and wrote" (*Notebooks,* 16). The entries include highly visual, stochastic images of the city and its inhabitants; memories of his childhood and the history of his ancestors, which complement the fractured city images with a similar splintering of identity; and retellings of historical anecdotes and parables. Moving backward to the legends that make up European history, Malte seems to follow a trajectory similar to that of Rilke in his flight from the "photographic" experience of the city to the stained-glass images of the saints in Rouen's cathedral. This textual flight would seem a way to escape a certain problem of vision central to Malte's experience of the city and, more specifically, to the correspondence between that experience and the medium of the photograph. For this reason, my focus here is primarily on the images of the city and the childhood memories of part 1 instead of the legends of part 2. Each part presents very different models of vision: the first opens with the description of the Parisian street, as opposed to the tapestries that mark the start of the second. As the novel reveals, the experiential and poetic ideal to which Malte aspires is no longer recoverable but requires a change.

Most critical readings of the *Notebooks* imply a certain closure of the text, in which the crisis is overcome and a successful communicative modality is discovered that is appropriate to Malte's experience.[14] Through the so-called self-sufficiency and purity of vision and language, the experience of modernity is either transcended through the realization of Rilke's dream of another language or conquered in the return to stable narrative. These readings suggest that Malte can move from a state of alienation and confusion to an ideal poetic and autonomous space (in which he is no longer distressed by his metropolitan surroundings). However, we would do well to remember that despite the apparent success of the Prodigal Son (the concluding episode of the work), the *Notebooks* ends not with the realization of a project but with an enigmatic and ambiguous "noch nicht" (not yet). They certainly point to a crisis of writing and self-representation, but one that, I argue, is no longer strictly resolvable within the new urban and media-saturated arena, as the letter quoted in my epigraph already suggests.[15]

In that October letter Rilke sounds very much like the protagonist of his novel. Malte, a young man about his age, is also struggling with the visual repercussions of that city: "Have I said it before? I am learning to see. Yes, I am beginning. It's still going badly. But I intend to make the most of my time" (*Notebooks*, 6). Twenty-eight years old, he is the sole surviving member of an old aristocratic Danish family. He has been alone in Paris for three weeks. He identifies himself as a writer, although to date he has authored only a flawed monograph, a drama that was an inevitable failure because of its false premise, and a few immature verses (19). With his statement—"learning to see"—Malte explicitly positions himself as both an end and a beginning. Moreover, it is clear that this beginning has everything to do with a new visual model. But why must he learn and what is he learning? And how does this visual organization conflict with the traditional structures through which he might narrate his own story? For it is clear that this beginning is very much involved in the question of poetic writing. In a series of questions in which Malte exposes the limitations of his literary predecessors and outlines a project that he will pursue, one is struck not only by his insistence on the visual data to be recorded but also by his deemphasis of transcendent claims in favor of "countless singulars" (24). Thus he takes it upon himself to start with something new: "This young, insignificant foreigner, Brigge, will have to sit down in his room, five flights up, and keep writing, day and night. Yes, he will have to write; that is how it will end" (24–25). The nonstop process of Malte's writing mimics the endless recording of the photographic plate as Rilke describes it. In other words, poetry is not made to serve transcendent meaning by enabling the writer's art to escape the physical and temporal world. Rather, this kind of writing leads to an extreme crisis in self-knowledge, just as the open aperture of the photographic camera does. For in the ongoing and never-ending process of writing, a recording of data flows and sensory experience, there is no closure of the self and no unifying experience or perspective from which to organize or view the self within the city as complete. Seeking to escape the city (by removing himself to his room), Malte cannot help but record the minutiae of its sensorial effects.[16]

The fictional Malte is a young writer in Paris, just as Rilke was when he first came to the French city in late summer 1902 to write a monograph on Rodin, commissioned by Richard Muther, an art history professor at Breslau.[17] Many of the novel's fragments are taken directly from letters Rilke wrote to his wife, friends, and editor, describing his own reaction to the city, and from his descriptions of his actions and people he encountered there. For example, Rilke's anxiety is palpable in his letter to the painter Otto Modersohn, written about five months after his arrival in Paris: "Paris (we say it to each other daily) is a difficult, difficult, anxious city. And the beautiful things there are here do not quite compensate, even with their radiant eternity, for what one must suffer from the cruelty and confusion of the streets and the monstrosity of the gardens, people, and things. To my anguished feeling, Paris has something unspeakably dismaying. It has lost itself utterly, it is tearing like a star off its course toward some dreadful collision."[18] Here Rilke locates the source of his anxiety in the conflict between the "radiant eternity" of the beautiful things in the city and the onslaught of fleeting sense impressions and confusion of metropolitan life. This conflict rearticulates the distinction between his openness to the city as the photographic plate and his poetic and artistic ideal as removed from the temporal flow and "capable of eternity." For the star referred to in the final line is not a shooting star plunging into infinity on which one makes a wish, but one driven horribly off course. In his 1939 essay, "On Some Motifs in Baudelaire," Walter Benjamin uses the concept of the wish to indicate a fullness of experience, quoting Goethe on a wish made in youth that is granted in old age: "The further a wish reaches out in time, the greater the hopes for its fulfillment. But it is experience that accompanies one to the far reaches of time, that fills and divides time. Thus a wish fulfilled is the crowning of experience. In folk symbolism, distance in space can take the place of distance in time; that is why the shooting star, which plunges into the infinite distance of space, has become the symbol of a fulfilled wish."[19] Benjamin's description of the star suggests a notion of time as expansive, as opposed to linear—such that past, present, and future are not isolated points along a continuum but form an integral unity. Rilke's description of the city, however, is at odds with this notion of time, and the disruption in the fullness of experience is one way to account for his poetic crisis and his fear.

Malte's notebook entries begin with his immediate immersion into the city and the "cruelty and confusion of its streets" and are dominated by references to the overload of sights, smells, and sounds.[20] The first seven fragments introduce the prevailing themes of the text (and Rilke's letters from this period): death, illness, confusion, sensory assault. In the opening entry, the reader gains an initial sense of the effect of the photographic plate as described by Rilke himself in his 1913 letter. The sentences are concise, rendered without emotion, apparent reports of external images. There is, however, an insistence on the *I* that sees, which results in a paradox. For if there is, on the one hand, a selectivity to the images as if rendered by an active observer, there is simultaneously a helplessness before images that cannot be avoided. And the recordings are by no means comprehensive. Indeed, what Malte sees contradicts what can be found on his map of Paris. This opening passage strongly resembles one of the first letters Rilke wrote to Clara after he arrived in the city, in which he emphasizes the many hospitals, sickness, and death: "I have never felt that in any city and it is strange that I feel it in Paris of all places, where (as Holitscher wrote) the drive to live is stronger than elsewhere. Is this drive to live—life? No. Life is something quiet, broad, simple. The drive to live is hurry and pursuit. The drive to have life, at once, whole, in one hour. Of that Paris is so full and therefore so near to death. It is an alien, alien city."[21]

Coupled with these references to fear and disease is the sense of something moving too fast, like the star that has veered off course and is heading for a collision. Personal time and public time are out of joint. Even the relationship to death is posed in the inhuman time of mechanical processes and reveals the effects of technical modes of reproduction: "This excellent hotel [Hôtel-Dieú] is very ancient; already in the time of King Clovis people were dying here, in a few beds. Now there are 559 beds to die in. Like a factory, of course. With production so enormous, each individual death is not made very carefully; but that isn't important. It's the quantity that counts" (*Notebooks*, 8–9).

The city not only impacts the psyche but assaults the body. Malte is penetrated by the city's sensations and cannot shield himself from their impact and intrusion:

> To think that I can't give up the habit of sleeping with the window open. Electric trolleys speed clattering through my room. Cars drive over me. A door slams. Somewhere a windowpane shatters on the pavement; I can hear its large fragments laugh and its small one giggle. Then suddenly a dull, muffled noise from the other direction, inside the house. . . . And again the street. A girl screams, Ah tais-toi, je ne veux plus. The trolley races up excitedly, passes on over it, over everything. Someone calls out. People are running, catch up with each other. A dog barks. What a relief: a dog. Toward morning there is even a rooster crowing, and that is an infinite pleasure. Then suddenly I fall asleep. (4–5)

Whereas the preceding passage in the text emphasizes visual perception, this one stresses sound. Nevertheless, the effect on Malte is the same: he remains open to these sensations, and they cannot be shut off. Even inside his own room, Malte has no protection from the city. Indeed, in another early letter to his wife, Rilke complains that his rooms not only look directly into the windows of other inhabitants whose lives he is forced to witness but permit the others to look at him: "And when one only considers that these twelve windows that are before me when I sit at my desk function not only as frames but also, from the other perspective, as eyes that open directly into my life—then it is almost too much to bear."[22] Interior and exterior are no longer mutually exclusive terms. The sights and sounds invade the most private space and are notable for their violence: menacing vehicles, shattering glass, screams on the street. There is no causal or narrative connection among the elements assaulting his ears. Does the window pane break as a result of the door that has slammed? Is the crowd in the street running to or away from the girl's screams? In this aural confusion, only the dog's bark and the cock's crow provide relief, as they always do in the novel. These simple rhythms, the sounds of the country and the familial homestead, offer themselves up as antitheses to the horror of the city.

The opening fragments of the *Notebooks* reveal a highly sensitized reaction to a particularly urban environment, much like that described by the German philosopher and sociologist Georg Simmel in his 1903 essay, "The Metropolis and Mental Life." What we discover, however, is a certain failure on Malte's part to adopt the self-protective mechanisms that Simmel describes as necessary for the individual in the urban environment. And this has profound effects on Malte's writing. Simmel describes the modern city as a barrage of stimuli that transforms the physiological and psychological foundation of experience as a result of the increase in nervous stimulation and bodily peril. The urban dweller is exposed to a fundamentally different register of subjective experience, characterized by the physical and perceptual shocks of his or her environment. As a result, "the metropolitan type of man—which, of course, exists in a thousand individual variants—develops an organ protecting him against the threatening currents and discrepancies of his external environment which would uproot him."[23] As the individual becomes a "blasé," intellectualized creature, overly rational and indifferent to the distinctions between things, one's disinterested circulation in the city doubles the circulation of money and commodities as a function of which the qualitative, unique values of individuals are reduced to the purely quantitative level. Simmel's description of a "protective organ" is similar to the model of traumatic experience that Sigmund Freud delineates in *Beyond the Pleasure Principle,* in which he describes consciousness as a "crust" or "barrier" that protects the organism from the shocks of intense external stimulation that endanger the life of the organism. Paradoxically, then, consciousness wards off the external world that is the very condition of its possibility. Freud defines trauma as a breach between mind and memory, wherein "consciousness arises instead of a memory trace."[24]

We might think of Rilke's photographic plate as the poet's version of the "protective organ" described by Simmel or the crust or barrier of consciousness described by Freud. In this sense, the photographic plate is that on which the momentary shocks of perception are directly inscribed, though at the loss of their entering into narrative memory. What presents a crisis to the poet, however, is his profound awareness of this split. And it is this perceptual crisis that dominates the *Notebooks*. For the novel's title alerts us from the beginning that we are concerned here with a "recording." "Notebooks" is only a limited translation of the German word, *Aufzeichnungen,* which also signifies a drawing or a sketch, a chronicle in the historical sense, and something recorded or registered in the technical sense. Thus the same term is applied when referring to an image or sound recorded on film, on tape or disk, or in words. The medium employed in the novel is obviously verbal; however, it is implicitly informed by the effects of more technical media. It is a recording that seems to know of no filter, a problem that Rilke lamented in his own work in a letter to Lou Andreas-Salomé: "I am . . . clumsy about events that come and go, without the gift of selection, without the calmness for reception, a mirror turned this way and that, out of which all images fall . . . that is why it is so frightfully necessary for me to find the tool of my art, the hammer, my hammer, so that it may become master and may grow above all noises."[25] In other words, Rilke is searching for a poetic medium adequate to his art, a "tool" with which he might transmit a clear signal against the background of noise and temporal flux in which he is immersed. We might compare this act of selection and calmness with Rilke's description of Rodin's processes of work. From a series of sketches of innumerable, barely perceptible movements, from a multitude of angles and under various lighting conditions, Rodin amassed "the wealth of material from which he finally selected what was important and essential, to unite it in one perfect synthetic whole."[26] The resulting portrait or sculpture would not then represent the model in one moment in time, "embalming" time as André Bazin said of the photograph, but would secure the subject within an expanse of time.[27]

Rilke struggled with the form of the *Notebooks* in a letter written shortly before the novel was published: "I do not know how far one will be able to deduce a whole existence from the papers. What this imaginary young man inwardly underwent (through Paris and through his memories reanimated by Paris), led so far in all directions: more and more journals [*Aufzeichnungen*] could have been added; what now constitutes the book is by no means anything complete. It is only as if one found disordered papers in a drawer and just happened for the present to find no more and had to be content."[28] It is thus a recording for which a coherent model of organization, equilibrium, or proportion is ultimately never accomplished, although he described these attributes with great admiration in both Rodin's and Cézanne's work. The book Rilke describes is like the photographic plate that continues to inscribe images and yet can never be complete because the shutter never closes. Hence there can be no editing of the documents into a full and meaningful whole, for the task is never finished. Rather than a "whole existence," we read only a sketch, decontextualized fragments that cannot be reassembled into a unified identity. Malte will turn the scope of his recordings from his present circumstances in Paris to images from his childhood and even further back through European history in what we might view as an attempt to achieve transcendent unity, through which the "earthly happenings" might become transparent like the legends in the stained-glass window; however, this project will remain illusory.

Malte indeed recognizes that this conception of the poetic is an ideal to which he cannot return: "If my fear weren't so great, I would find some consolation in the thought that it's not impossible to see everything differently and still remain alive. But I am frightened, I am unspeakably frightened of this change. . . . I would so much like to remain among the meanings that have become dear to me" (*Notebooks,* 52). Significantly, the changes Malte alludes to are not restricted to his visual apprehension of the world; rather, this visual reorganization results in a problematic relationship to memory as the integration of life experience to which Malte will explicitly link the act of poetic writing:

> You ought to wait and gather sense and sweetness for a whole lifetime, and a long one if possible, and then, at the very end, you might perhaps be able to write ten good lines. For poems are not, as people think, simply emotions (one has emotions early enough)—they are experiences [*Erfahrungen*]. . . . For the memories [*Erinnerungen*] themselves are not important. Only when they have changed into our very blood, into glance and gesture, and are nameless, no longer to be distinguished from ourselves—only then can it happen that in some very rare hour the first word of a poem arises in their midst and goes forth from them. (20)

This passage recalls for us the transparent images of the stained glass, "the blood of its colors," thus creating an identity between that modality of representation and the idealized poetic act and further emphasizing the degree to which the metropolitan environment is characterized by an impoverishment of experience as described by Benjamin with reference to the star. And if the image of the wish on a shooting star gives rise to a belief that one's present moment in time is bound up with one's life in the future, then the reference to memory is the way to link present and past. Together, the memory and the wish make up the fullness of experience in personal, expansive time; however, it is precisely both of these concepts that Rilke's novel invalidates.

THE MEMORY IMAGE AND THE PHOTOGRAPHIC IMAGE

The assertion of Malte's failed relationship to memory may at first appear problematic to anyone who has read the novel. For isn't the text full of

Malte's *memories*? Indeed, the first half of the text is marked by multiple references to Malte's own childhood. However, his memories hardly constitute a coherent self:

> The fever dug into me and out of the depths it pulled experiences, images, facts, which I had known nothing about; I lay there, overloaded with myself, and waited for the moment when I would be told to pile all this back into myself, neatly and in the right order. I began, but it grew in my hands, it resisted, it was much too much. Then rage took hold of me, and I threw everything into myself pell-mell and squeezed it together; but I couldn't close myself back over it. And then I screamed, half open as I was, I screamed and screamed. (96)

The young Malte is "overloaded" yet "open." For to reject everything he has written to date and to fear that he will never be able to write again is for him deeply involved with a specific function of memory, or, in his case, its dysfunction, in integrating metropolitan experience. This is evidenced, for example, in his hallucinatory idealized counterpart of the image of that other poet whom he might have been allowed to become had he been permitted to spend his life in a country house closed off from modern life. "I would have lived there with my old Things, the family portraits, the books. I would have had an armchair and flowers and dogs and a strong walking-stick for the stony paths. And nothing else. Just a book bound in yellowish, ivory-colored leather with an old flowered design on the endpaper: on its pages, I would have written. I would have written a lot, for I would have had many thoughts, and memories of many people" (43). But the comprehensive pages of a life in the leather-bound book have become disordered; the stillness of this composed, interior world scattered by disquietude and frenzied activity; expansive time shattered into fleeting moments. This contrast is also evident in a passage from one of Rilke's letters that serves as a model for this scene. In a letter from Paris to his wife, dated October 4, 1907, Rilke describes looking through the shop window at an old antiquarian bookseller, content to sit in the stillness among his objects and his animals. Contrasted with the street scene from which perspective Rilke looks in, the shop not only offers an alternative temporality but separates itself from the frenzied commerce that so defines the modern city.[29]

In his essay, "Photography," first published in the *Frankfurter Zeitung* in 1927, Siegfried Kracauer attempted to clarify the condition of modern experience and knowledge through its radical identification with modern technology and the media that recorded and transmitted such knowledge.[30] In his analysis, photography is paradigmatic of a specific form of disjuncture that occurs between our integration of experience and our telling of life stories, and thus of the manner in which we understand not merely the world but ourselves. Further, photography and the distribution of photographic images play an important role in a shift to modern forms of consciousness. Kracauer formulates the terms of this shift or change through what he calls the memory image, as opposed to the photographic image. His articulation of this contrast—open to comparison with Benjamin's distinction between *Erfahrung* and *Erlebnis*, or experience and lived present—provides us with a terminology for defining the conflicting currents in the *Notebooks* as well as Rilke's letters of the period, particularly on integrating or organizing the subject and his relationship to time. In Kracauer's view, a conflict arises between the organizational structure of human understanding as informed by the memory image (which in Kracauer's essay is associated with writing and continuous narrative) and that informed by the photographic image (associated with visual or surface effects, recording fragments). Differences between the two modalities arise on the order of their relationship both to the referent and to time: "The photograph does not preserve the transparent aspects of an object but instead captures it as a spatial continuum from any one of a number of positions. The last memory image outlasts time because it is unforgettable; the photograph, which neither refers to nor encompasses such a memory image, must be essentially associated with the moment in time in which it came into existence" ("Photography," 54). If, for Kracauer, the memory image maintains its significance through its attachment to a truth-value—or what he will ultimately call a person's history or *monogram* (and what Malte refers to as that glance or gesture that is no longer to be distinguished from ourselves)—the photograph interrupts this unifying force. Thus in the *Notebooks*, for example, Malte's memories are not integrated into his conception of himself, and they cannot be organized into a complete self-portrait; rather, they remain fragments or shards in excess of a circumscribed self. That is, they function on the order of what Kracauer refers to as the photographic image. One is led to consider Rilke's project not (or at least not only) in terms of a possible recuperation of the condition of the poet at the fireside but in terms of a reevaluation of art's function by way of extraliterary modes of representation. In other words, how does one still write in the space of experiential crisis articulated and exemplified by the disjuncture between the memory image and the photographic image? In what follows I outline Kracauer's argument, particularly as it concerns how photographic techniques (re)form our understanding of the world and its communicability, to suggest how Rilke's own work can be read as a response.[31]

Kracauer begins his essay by contrasting two photographs—a contemporary photo of a "film diva" from an illustrated magazine and a photo of someone's grandmother taken some sixty years earlier (when she was the same age as the diva). Through these two photographs, Kracauer introduces the notion of a disjuncture or nonidentification between the photograph and the "original," which arises as a result of the order of temporal registration and the ensuing alterity in their orders of signification. For if the diva is easily recognizable because the time recorded is the present and "everyone has already seen the original on the screen" ("Photography," 47), the grandmother's likeness is no help in recognizing her because the ur-image of which the photograph is the copy does not correspond to the later generation's memory image of her: "Likeness has ceased to be of any help" (48). For the present, at least, the actuality of the diva's photographic image still corresponds with the memory image of the moviegoers who have just witnessed the "original" on the screen—an original that is, of course, only itself a reproduction of a body never present. The memory image of the grandmother, however, is the distillation of anecdotes and stories (namely, a narrative element) that one has always heard of her and, as such, is atemporal; she cannot be located within the temporality of the photographic image. Thus a rift opens up between the photographic image and the memory image.

For Kracauer, what one might call the organizing principle of memory is its personal significance, not in terms of its attachment to a particular time and place but in terms of the manner in which it constructs a cohesive and coherent network of reference. On the other hand, the organizing principle of photography is what is given as a spatial continuum at the moment that it came into existence. From the vantage point of photography, therefore, memory seems to be full of gaps, with no attention to dates and a seemingly arbitrary selection in which detail is filtered out. It is precisely this lack of contingency, however, that characterizes the memory image for Kracauer as a person's "actual *history*" removed from temporal and spatial constraints (51). Kracauer's contrast here recalls the cathedral's stained-glass windows. Reduced to a static, enduring image, the "last image" (51) of these historical figures communicates their history and essential truth. Whereas the memory image or legend dispenses with extraneous detail (that is to say, is not a mimetic process), not so the photographic plate, which remains open to the ongoing data stream and the external, visual trappings of the moment. A visual residue, as it were, is deposited over the photograph, obscuring the "transparency" of truth emanating from the memory image. By the standards of memory, photography "appears as a jumble that consists partly of garbage" (51), in a sense falsifying the memory image. As Susan Sontag concluded in her essay, "Melancholy Objects": "The contingency of photographs confirms that everything is perishable; the arbitrariness of photographic evidence indicates that reality is fundamentally unclassifiable."[32] Likewise, Rilke's text consists of disconnected images in which provisional patterns or orderings are immediately undone. Malte's Parisian images are extremely specific, but cannot be properly categorized. In this sense Malte's prose adheres to what one might call a photographic discourse—for a photograph always records more and less than the general pattern.

With the advent of photography and the distribution of images through mass media, reproducing the world in toto becomes accessible to the photographic apparatus. This leads, however, to a strange paradox, for if an age has "never before ... been so informed about itself, if being informed means having an image of objects that resembles them in a photographic sense," it is also true that no period has ever "known so little about itself," in that photographic images are a "strike against understanding" ("Photography," 58). The multiply reproduced image negates the very concept of original; thus "in the illustrated magazines, people see the very world that the illustrated magazines prevent them from perceiving" (58). That is, one no longer perceives the world as nonreproducible original; we experience an indifference to what things mean. No longer directed toward the memory image, any ordering of the photographic image is merely "provisional" (62); that is, it is always only temporary, not necessary, and in this sense will be comparable to fashion (55). One recalls Rilke's own description of the *Notebooks* as disordered pages in a drawer. Only provisionally ordered, the archive of which they are a component is never complete. In Kracauer's thesis, "this game shows that the valid organization of things remains unknown—an organization which would designate the position that the remains of the grandmother and the diva stored in the general inventory will some day have to occupy" (63). In Kracauer's description of what we might call an epistemology of photography, one notes not only the disintegration of the world into "a chaotic multiplicity of phenomena,"[33] but also the disintegration of the autonomous subject through the contingency of the photographic record.

Malte mentions actual photographs only one time in the *Notebooks*, when he is burning his father's papers after his death:

> I had begun by throwing the letters into the fire in bundles, just as I had found them; but they were tied together too firmly, and only charred at the edges. I had to exercise a good deal of self-control before I could loosen them. Most of them had a strong, convincing fragrance, which penetrated me as if it wanted to stir up memories in me as well. I didn't have any. Then some photographs, heavier than the rest, happened to slip out; these photographs took an unbelievably long time to burn. I don't know why, but suddenly I imagined that Ingeborg's picture might be among them. Each time I looked, though, I saw mature, splendid, obviously beautiful women, who suggested a different train of thought to me. For it turned out that I wasn't entirely without memories after all. (*Notebooks*, 160–61)

Odor, that key to the *mémoire involuntaire,* does nothing for Malte; only the photographs stand in for memories. But they do not evoke an understanding of his past; they do not correspond with who he is at present, as he sits in the room as an adult looking at them. Rather, he sees in them only eyes that had looked at him as a young boy, comparing him with his father. In other words, he catches sight of a glance—a fragmented image of an equally fragmented mode of seeing. The photographic medium for Rilke is always more than simply a glance captured: it is the reciprocal manner in which one is always likewise captured and shocked by a glance, as Rilke himself experienced in the "quiet lane in Rouen."[34]

Like Kracauer, Roland Barthes also construed photography and memory as mutually exclusive modalities: "Not only is the Photograph never, in essence, a memory (whose grammatical expression would be the perfect tense, where the tense of the Photograph is the aorist), but it actually blocks memory, quickly becomes a counter-memory." Curiously, Barthes immediately continues this thought in *Camera Lucida,* his dual meditation on the ontology of photography and his mother's death, with a reference to Rilke: "One day, some friends were talking about their childhood memories; they had any number; but I, who had just been looking at my old photographs, had none left. Surrounded by these photographs, I could no longer console myself with Rilke's line: 'Sweet as memory, the mimosas steep the bedroom': the Photograph does not 'steep' the bedroom: no odor, no music, nothing but the *exorbitant thing.*"[35] Although Rilke may once have idealized the conception of memory referred to by Barthes, it is clear in the *Notebooks* that Malte has no access to this modality of being. Indeed, we are perhaps already alerted to this difference from the beginning of the work, for Malte smells not the sweet odor of mimosas but iodoform, pommes frites, and fear (*Notebooks,* 4).

The aversion to the photograph is not only related to the epistemological considerations of framing, temporal and spatial disruption, and lack of depth; it is reinforced by the idea of being oneself captured as an image. That is, the photograph sets up a problem not merely of looking but of being looked at. We noted this earlier, for example, in Rilke's letter complaining about his neighbors' windows overlooking his own (a drawback that almost forced him to move). Through these frames, not only was he forced an alienated glimpse onto strange and fragmented lives to which he had no connection, but these frames functioned as eyes in whose glance he would be caught and thus alienated from himself. In a letter written many years after he had left Paris permanently, Rilke reiterated the extreme negative effect associated with mechanically reproduced images of himself: "Nothing has ever been more understandable to me than the gesture I once saw an Arabic woman in Kairouan (Tunisia) make when she threw both hands up in front of her face, realizing in horror that a photographic apparatus was pointed directly at her; this, precisely *this* horror is my involuntary response to being 'taken' [*abgenommen*]" photographically.[36] This horror of being "taken up" is the horror of the subject transformed into an object. In *Camera Lucida* Barthes comments on what the *Spectrum* (person or thing photographed) undergoes through photography. Given the related terms *spectacle* and *specter*, it is not only that the *Spectrum* is transformed into an image—the *I* becomes "Total Image" and, as such, an object—but in this process undergoes a version of death. Hence the instant of photography entails "that very subtle moment when . . . I am neither subject nor object but a subject who feels he is becoming an object: I then experience a micro-version of death (of parenthesis): I am truly becoming a specter."[37] This "death" entails a setting down of oneself beside oneself (a literal parenthesis): "The Photograph is the advent of myself as other."[38]

This scenario is dramatically enacted in the *Notebooks* in Malte's own revision of the mirror stage while at play as a young child. For if in Lacan's formulation, the infant's identity and unified body is gained as the result of a (mis)recognition of the specular image, Malte is obliterated by the image he sees in the mirror.[39] As a child, Malte spends an afternoon in the attic of his grandfather's house at Ulsgaard, trying on uniforms and costumes and admiring himself before a mirror "made up of irregular pieces of green glass" (*Notebooks*, 103). This episode is brought to a shocking conclusion, however, when he finds a closet with garments for masquerade, dons a mask, turban, and long cloak, and stands before the mirror "to find out what I actually was" (106). Flailing in front of his reflection, he knocks over a table, shattering porcelain objects and a perfume bottle. The shattering of glass functions as a catalyst for the "revenge" of the mirror: "It forced me, I don't know how, to look up, and dictated to me an image, no, a reality, a strange, incomprehensible, monstrous reality that permeated me against my will: for now it was the stronger one, and I was the mirror.... I lost all sense of myself, I simply ceased to exist.... I was unconscious and lay there like a piece of cloth among all those wrappings, yes, just like a piece of cloth" (107–8). Malte *is* nothing but an image seen and an image that sees. To "find out what [he] actually was," the subject reveals an essential alterity to itself, an alterity that takes on the structure of the photographic image.[40]

The broken perfume bottle is the key to an understanding of the passage. The perfume does not function as a metaphor for memory, the scent that permeates the nose to awaken, if only briefly, the rich fullness of a past event. Rather, in breaking, the bottle creates an image. The scattered shards reiterate what is already a fractured image in the mirror—and the liquid that oozes out of the bottle fixes a stain or silhouette on the floor, just as Malte's image is fixed on him ("taken" from him) by the mirror: "The most annoying sight of all was a perfume bottle that had broken into a thousand tiny fragments, from which the remnant of some ancient essence had spurted out, that now formed a stain with a very repulsive physiognomy on the light rug" (*Notebooks,* 106). The perfume has become a photographic fixer, just like the bath of chemicals that halt the development process in photography.[41] In this shock of the mirror image, in which he is rendered a thing, an object embedded in the world, a photograph—Malte undergoes a metaphorical death that his experience of the city of Paris as an adult endlessly forces him to repeat.

THE PHONOGRAPH STYLUS

The photograph is, of course, not the only medium of technical reproduction in the early twentieth-century mediascape. The *phonograph,* too, is a medium that registers emanations though not of light, but of sound. Both are techniques for recording and transmitting direct physical effects in time, and as such are modalities of information storage in marked contrast to the symbolic mediation of literature and the alternative temporality that poetry might offer. A literary work addressing these technologies would be one that described not only the differences among media but also its own limit as a medium of representation. In the essay "Ur-Geräusch" (Primal Sound) Rilke rethinks poetic language and literary representation through the modality of the phonograph.[42] The essay is constructed around a double memory. Composed in 1919, the author recollects a time fifteen years in the past when he was living in Paris (and composing drafts of the fragments that would eventually be collected in the *Notebooks*). The Parisian episode is likewise formulated around a recollection, this time a childhood memory from his school days. The link, or associative trail, bringing all three moments together is the groove formed by a phonograph needle—a groove that is both the recording and the retransmission of a sound. Although Rilke's essay initially reads like a hybrid gothic thriller, the piece ultimately insists on the continued relevance, if not the urgency, of the work of poetic art in a world in which new technologies offer only the illusory promise of sensory extension.

As a young student in a physics class, Rilke experimented with the construction of a crude phonograph consisting of a rotating cylinder covered with candle wax and the bristle of a hair brush attached to a paper diaphragm that was fixed at the end of a makeshift megaphone. When someone spoke or sang into the device, sound waves caused the diaphragm at the bottom of the megaphone to vibrate so that the attached bristle traced a groove into the wax of the revolving cylinder. When the bristle was then placed at the start of the tracing and the cylinder revolved again, the sound recorded just moments before was reproduced. The class of unruly young boys was silenced by the event, but Rilke recalls being fascinated not by the sound that the device emitted, but by the scrawls on the waxy cylinder itself: the *legible*, although not *readable*, encoding of speech. Some years later, while attending anatomy classes at the École des Beaux Arts in Paris, Rilke studied the human skeleton, focusing particularly on the skull, actually bringing one home to his garret. There, in the gloom, the shape of the coronal suture on top of the skull suddenly recalled to him the image of the curved lines on the wax cylinder of his childhood. Through this association, he was led to envision an even more fantastical experiment, in which the stylus of a phonograph would be dragged across this groove. What sound would be produced by an inscription that was not the graphical translation of a previous audio sequence, but a mark existing prior to and outside any particular moment of recording? Feelings of disbelief, shyness, fear, and awe all prevent Rilke from naming the tone that would enter the world, calling it only a "primal sound."

In *Gramophone, Film, Typewriter,* Kittler reprints Rilke's essay, stressing the poet's fascination for, and ultimate acquiescence to, the technology of the phonograph. In his reading, Rilke "celebrates the very opposite of his own medium." This so-called celebration consists of two related ideas: first, the notion of a "writing without a subject" and second, the recording or storage of "the white noise no writing can store."[43] From this perspective, the poet can only look on in awe at that which he is not able to accomplish with the pen. However, Kittler's reading does not take Rilke's entire essay into account. The essay is not, or not only, about this medium of mechanical reproduction, but about poetry itself. Rilke writes that he is initially fascinated with the skull because of the manner in which it surrounds and delimits that which has no boundaries: the imagination. This relationship between the material and the immaterial worlds is precisely what is stake in the idea of "playing" the coronal suture. In Rilke's formulation, which precedes Derrida's *Of Grammatology* by almost fifty years, the coronal suture is not the graphical translation of a sound (as Kittler would have it), but a *sound trace* that reverses the relationship between sound and writing. Writing is not derivative of sound, but its precondition.

From the description of the primitive phonograph and its echo in the coronal suture, Rilke turns to poetry, praising Arabic poetry especially because it partakes of all five senses equally, as opposed to the European tradition, which privileges sight, barely notices sound, and ignores the other three. And yet, according to Rilke, the perfect or complete (*vollendete*) poem requires that the world be grasped (*angegriffen*) with all five senses.[44] Our senses illuminate only a small portion of the possible field of experience; the task of the poet, Rilke argues, is its expansion. Rilke explicitly rejects the possibility that technology such as the microscope or the telescope can extend the field of the senses for us. These sensory extensions are not truly "experienced" (*erlebt*) because their apperception by the body is mediated. Only the artist extends the individual sense fields by way of the "five-fingered hand of his senses" whose "grasp" (*Griff*) is actively developed.[45] This extension can never be considered a permanent addition to the general field, however, but one that is experienced and reexperienced in the encounter with the work of art. Rather than cede the position of poetry in the modern mediascape, Rilke's musings on the technology of the phonograph lead him to an intense meditation on the materiality of language itself. In this formulation, verbal forms do not merely communicate meaning, but rather, the poetic act of writing and reading constitutes its own (primal) sensory experience in which the world is, at least provisionally, transformed and the "dark circles" of possible experience are made accessible.[46] Though potentially taking us beyond ourselves, the experience of art is simultaneously very much of the world and of the body—like the skull itself, the poem delimits that which is potentially without limit.

In later letters, Rilke posed similar experiments with sound, musing on the phonographic potential of the grain of a piece of wood or the path left by an insect.[47] With respect to the more practical reality of the technology of the phonograph, however, Rilke was profoundly ambivalent. In the second of two letters written to the critic Dieter Bassermann in the spring of 1926, Rilke argued that in evacuating the constraints of time and space, the phonograph necessarily forecloses certain aesthetic categories. Initially, Rilke writes of the "almost inconceivable advantage" of phonographic recordings of a poet reading his own work, whereby the auditor could establish a more genuine relationship with the poem under the acoustic guidance of the poet himself. However, such recordings are simultaneously undesirable and ultimately appalling, for they compromise the originality and power of the poem, or what Benjamin would have called its *aura*. Rilke therefore concludes: "But of course for *us* to whom certain revelations seem to get their most indescribable quality of greatness, melancholy, and humanity from their fabulous uniqueness, such a mechanical survival of the most mysterious and rich form of expression would be almost unbearable. It is still (besides being a need) also a strength and a pride of our soul to consort with the unique and irretrievably transitory."[48] By bringing the poem too close to the reader through countless repetitions of the poet's voice, the unique qualities that constitute the poet as a subject of individual feeling and expression are put into question. Indeed, two seemingly paradoxical ideas are at work across Rilke's writings on sound recording: the phonograph suggests the possibility both of an absolutely singular or unique language of the senses *and* of its endless reproducibility and repeatability. In his 1934 essay, "The Form of the Phonograph Record," Theodor Adorno maintains: "It is not in the play of the gramophone as a surrogate for music but rather in the phonograph record as a thing that its potential significance—and also its aesthetic significance—resides."[49] For through the curves inscribed by the phonograph record, music which had previously only been conveyed through systems of notation now "turns itself into writing. Decisively, because this writing can be recognized as true language to the extent that it relinquishes its being as mere signs: inseparably committed to the sound that inhabits this and no other acoustic groove."[50] The voice recording of the poet on the phonograph record ultimately blunts the voice, foreclosing the possibility of the unique encounter. An astute observer of media, Rilke ultimately insists on the critical role of the poet in the modern technological world. Although individual media technologies may appear to extend our senses, there are in fact troubling ways in which they further fragment experience by widening the chasms between the individual senses, thus ultimately, taking us furthest from ourselves and our individual, embodied experience of the world.

THE SHUTTER CLOSES

In "On Some Motifs in Baudelaire" Benjamin considers the example of the French poet to explore the consequences of the modern period, not only for the urban dweller, but more specifically, for the urban dweller who is also a writer. Benjamin thus investigates both the question of change in the structure of human experience, as occasioned by the technological and demographic terrain of the city, and the question of where this change is registered in the act of literary production itself. An important aspect of the experience of modernity is radical discontinuity and the shock that radical discontinuity engenders, and this experiential structure is incompatible with traditional modes of storytelling and lyric poetry, which rely on a continuity of experience in the subject both in time and in space and the possibility of sharing that experience with others. In other words, the traditional modes rely on memory. In "On Some Motifs in Baudelaire" Benjamin registers the loss of the structure of experience and the disruption of memory as such, much as Kracauer does in "Photography." For the two mutually exclusive structures elaborated in Benjamin's essay—*Erfahrung* and *Erlebnis*—are much like Kracauer's elaboration of the memory image and the photographic image both in terms of their definition and in terms of their effect (and are likewise similar to Freud's distinction of a memory trace and consciousness). Benjamin's essay addresses, of course, a nineteenth-century poet; however, the terms he defines here can aid our reading of Rilke (to whom Benjamin dedicated only one short essay to rebut an unflattering obituary of the poet), for Rilke's *Notebooks* register the loss of the intelligible fullness of experience through the recording mechanism of the text itself. The prose fragments are in stark contrast to Rilke's previous lyric output—a genre that, as Benjamin noted with reference to Baudelaire, may no longer be "in rapport with the experience of its readers."[51] The fragments are experiments that address the possibility of organizing experience through other media.

All of the constituent components that Benjamin cites as contributing to a shift in modern consciousness—namely, the proliferation of information, the loss of communicable experience, the anxiety and restlessness of the city, the attitude toward death, and the function of memory—are alluded to in Rilke's novel. Further, we know from Rilke's letters that he was acutely aware of how the mass media presented certain problems to the poet, as exemplified in this passage from a letter to Ellen Key, dated April 3, 1903: "Of *that* particularly [journalism] I have a nameless horror! I feel too clearly the apparent kinship between literature and journalism, of which one is an art and so looks to eternity, and the other a trade in the midst of the times: more in the times than any other. And I am so far away from the times, from all their wishes and all their successes; I *cannot* participate in them. I have nothing *in* them, not even a home."[52] Following Freud, modern media are presented as literally *unheimlich*. The atemporality or eternality of art is precisely what is at stake and what seems to be in dispute during Malte's sojourn in Paris. Rather than the transcendent moment of poetic creation, Malte stumbles through a series of lived-through present tenses. The writing project thus requires an alternative model of poetic creation.

In the *Notebooks*, Malte fondly recalls a former neighbor who sought to combat the horror of time passing with the atemporality of poetry. When he was living in the Russian city of Petersburg, Malte lived next door to a man who lay in bed all day "and recited long poems, poems by Pushkin and Nekrasov, in the singsong tone that children use when they are asked to recite a poem" (169). And although Malte is led to all sorts of wild imaginings about "this fellow with his poems," an accidental visitor solves the mystery through "a simple, unambiguous story, which put an end to the swarming maggots of my conjectures" (169–70). For it seems that the neighbor, Mr. Kusmitch, had fallen into the singular mistake of taking a metaphor literally. After calculating his life expectancy, Kusmitch finds himself "rich" in years, particularly after converting the relatively large fifty-year note into ever smaller, though for that reason more prolific, denominations: years to days to hours, minutes, and, finally, seconds. As he soon finds, however, a second is more quickly spent than a year, and although he tries to save time whenever possible, by rushing to work or skipping breakfast, he finds that by the end of the week his savings are depleted. It occurs to him, then, to demand the return of his time, to convert his small change back into "four bills of ten and one of five, and the rest he could keep and go to hell with" (172). But his devilish banker never returns, and he is left alone with the "great embarrassment" of time (173). His personal banker is, of course, his doppelgänger—he sees himself as a cinematic image, just as his own life is passing by with the fleeting nature of a filmstrip.

And his excessive awareness of his eventual temporal bankruptcy is soon paralleled by the physical consciousness of time's passing:

> He suddenly felt a breath on his face; it moved past his ears; it was on his hands now. He opened his eyes wide. The window was definitely closed. And as he sat there in the dark room, with his eyes wide open, he began to realize that what he was feeling now was *real* time, as it passed by. He recognized, with absolute clarity, all these tiny seconds, all equally tepid, each one exactly like the others, but fast, but fast. . . . He jumped up, but the surprises were not yet over. Beneath his feet too there was something moving; not just one motion, but several, which strangely shook in and against one another. He stiffened with terror: could that be the earth? Of course it was. The earth did, after all, move. He had heard about that in school; but it was passed over rather quickly, and later on was completely hushed up; it was considered not a proper subject for discussion. (173–74)

Kusmitch's only relief is to lie down and recite poetry: "When you recited a poem slowly, with a regular emphasis on the rhyme words, then something more or less stable existed, which you could keep a steady gaze on, inwardly of course" (175). And he has only the highest estimation for those who can continue to walk outside despite the earth's motion. Malte writes that this story was "extraordinarily reassuring" to him (175); however, it is not clear that he is reassured that poetry would provide the much-needed antidote to his own hypersensory condition. It is significant that Kusmitch's solution of reciting poetry does not allude to an idealized poetic content that would effect his own transcendence from the material and fleeting world; rather, it is merely the measured cadence of poetic meter that appears to mark the possibility of another temporal dimension. Kusmitch signifies for Malte the beginning of the way out of his poetic crisis, revealing how his conception of the lyric could perhaps be reformulated so as to combine the contradictory elements of the fleetingness of time passing with the eternality of art—in other words, where the lyric could accommodate both the immediacy of the photographic image and the truth content of the last memory image.

Some of the poems in Rilke's *New Poems* suggest a way out of this impasse, and I will conclude this chapter by looking at two of them. These poems, which are oriented to the world of external reality, reveal the effects of what one might call a photographic sensibility on the production of poetic language itself. Most of the poems present the effects of an object (in my examples, a caged animal and a daguerreotype) on the poet's consciousness, rather than expressing a purely emotional response (e.g., to his father's death). The poems aspire to be both wholly products of the poet's imagination and wholly free of the poet's individual subjectivity. Thus despite the vivid outlines of many of the objects described, these works are also intensely personal and exceed the temporal constraints of the short succession of moments described. They are most emphatically *not* photographs.

The depiction of the relation between the self and the city within a visual framework is announced with the first of Rilke's *New Poems,* composed for the most part concurrently with the accumulated fragments of the *Notebooks.* "The Panther," the earliest of Rilke's *New Poems,* was composed in 1902, shortly after the poet first arrived in Paris.

> Sein Blick ist vom Vorübergehn der Stäbe
> so müd geworden, daß er nichts mehr hält.
> Ihm ist, als ob es tausend Stäbe gäbe
> und hinter tausend Stäben keine Welt.
>
> Der weiche Gang geschmeidig starker Schritte,
> der sich im allerkleinsten Kreise dreht,
> ist wie ein Tanz von Kraft um eine Mitte,
> in der betäubt ein großer Wille steht.
>
> Nur manchmal schiebt der Vorhang der Pupille
> sich lautlos auf—. Dann geht ein Bild hinein,
> geht durch der Glieder angespannte Stille—
> und hört im Herzen auf zu sein.
>
> [His gaze has from the passing of the bars
> grown so tired, that it holds nothing anymore.
> It seems to him there are a thousand bars
> and behind a thousand bars no world.
>
> The supple pace of powerful soft strides,
> turning in the very smallest circle,
> is like a dance of strength around a center
> in which a great will stands numbed.

Only sometimes the curtain of the pupils
soundlessly slides up—. Then an image enters,
glides through the limbs' taut stillness,
dives into the heart—and dies.]⁵³

Although the poem's central figure is a caged panther in the Jardin des Plantes—the botanical garden and zoo in central Paris⁵⁴—as Lawrence Ryan has noted in his commentary on the work, "the main theme of the poem" is neither the animal itself nor what the figure of the animal might symbolize to Rilke, but rather "has to do with the act of seeing."⁵⁵ Like many of the poems in *New Poems*, "The Panther" plays out on multiple levels of seeing and being seen. Positioned at the beginning of Rilke's sojourn to Paris and his own apprenticeship, we can understand the panther's modality of sight as analogous to that which informs Malte's visual reorganization in the *Notebooks*. The opening and closing of the pupil's shutter is none other than that of the camera. However, we note a critical distinction between the apparatus Rilke described in the letter of October 1913—the "photographic plate that has been exposed too long"—and the camera that is the panther's eye. For by the final stanza of the poem, the ceaseless flow of images is interrupted and the aperture closes.

In the opening stanza of the poem, we become aware of a reversal of movement. The panther does not pace the perimeter of the cage; rather, it is the bars of the cage that move past him. In the endless procession of the thousand bars, the panther cannot hold on to anything visually. The failure here of a certain visual model is implied in the notion of the bond. The lack of this function recalls Rilke's own complaint to Lou Andréas-Salomé quoted earlier: "I am . . . a mirror turned this way and that out of which all images fall."⁵⁶ This problem of bonding the image is one of fixing it, like the fluid leaking out of the bottle in the attic that fixed a "profile" on the floor. However, in the photographic camera, in order for an image to be fixed the shutter must close again—the flow of visual perception must be interrupted. This is to say that in the ongoing flow of fragmented images and chaotic stimulus (the world outside the cage as the larger metropolis itself) the present as such cannot be apprehended in its passing.

If from the perspective of the first stanza, the bars of the cage themselves appear to be in motion, in the second stanza, the panther itself moves in the smallest of circles, defining the boundaries and parameters of its own world. This is the world of the imagination, a world cut off from or at least metaphorically isolated from the blur and ceaseless flow of the external (that is, material) world. The tempo is changed, and the steps of the panther define an alternative rhythm in keeping with the individual will. Here the subject is ahistorical and disembodied, ignoring the world from which it is set apart. The poet proposes an alternative world of inner strength and creative possibility, in which all interaction with "real" time and space is renounced.

The final stanza offers a stark contrast to the fluidity of the two preceding stanzas. Dashes visually interrupt the lines that likewise describe an interruption in which the shock defense or the screen of consciousness is broken with the rapidity of a camera shutter's opening and closing. The image entering the panther's body suggests the possibility of being present to a moment but only through a particular modality of sight. For the passing moment is not incorporated in the experiential or narrative context of what one might once have called the panther's inner world; rather, the image moment dies immediately with its passing, and is experienced only as an interruption. This is to say that the "end" of the image is what allows it to be properly recorded. Experience of these present and fleeting moments can only happen after the fact of their passing into death, that is, a past on which the present is, paradoxically, fixed. With the poem, "The Panther," Rilke simultaneously presents movement and the recording that interrupts that movement, that is, both the fleeting nature of the present and our problematic encounter with it as always past. These images, which are only apprehended "from time to time," are the snapshots of that vast city, both undermining and advancing its poetic representation within a more fluid and unstable array of aesthetic categories.

Read within the larger media context and not just as part of Rilke's poetic oeuvre, the visual reorganization of the world of "The Panther" brings together many of the motifs of the *Notebooks* in highly condensed form, and serves as a means by which Rilke expresses the paradox or crisis of modernity through the language of photography. With this move he indicates the extent to which this technological medium impacts, not only one's perception and understanding of the world, but further, the manner in which poetic language can register this shift. As Rilke's allusion in the final stanza reveals, the changing mode of signification brought about by a medium like photography radically affects the discourse as well as the subject of representation. Malte informs us in one of the first fragments of the *Notebooks*, "I am learning to see"—the apprenticeship in the visual domain has indeed profound effects on the production of the literary record.

Turning our attention to another poem in the collection, Kracauer's description of the grandmother's photograph in his essay "Photography" bears an uncanny resemblance to parts of Rilke's "Jugend-Bildnis meines Vaters" (Portrait of My Father as a Young Man), a poem composed not long after his father's death in 1906.[57]

> Im Auge Traum. Die Stirn wie in Berührung
> mit etwas Fernem. Um den Mund enorm
> viel Jugend, eingelächelte Verführung,
> und vor der vollen schmückenden Verschnürung
> der schlanken adeligen Uniform
> der Säbelkorb und beide Hände—, die
> abwarten, ruhig, zu nichts hingedrängt.
> Und nun fast nicht mehr sichtbar: als ob sie
> zuerst, die Fernes greifenden, verschwänden.
> Und alles andre mit sich selbst verhängt
> und ausgelöscht als ob wirs nicht verständen
> und tief aus seiner eignen Tiefe trüb—.
>
> Du schnell vergehendes Daguerreotyp
> in meinen langsamer vergehenden Händen.
>
> [In the eyes dream. The brow as if in touch
> with something far away. About the lips
> immense youth, unsmiling seductiveness,
> and across the full ornamental braids
> of the slim aristocratic uniform
> the saber's basket-hilt and both the hands—
> waiting, calmly, urged toward nothing.
> And now scarcely visible: as if they would be
> first, grasping the distant, to disappear.
> And all the rest self-shrouded
> and erased as if we didn't understand
> and by something deep in its own depths dimmed—.
>
> O you swiftly fading daguerreotype
> in my more slowly fading hands.][58]

The first twelve lines enact the effect Kracauer describes: the image in the daguerreotype reveals no "truth" of the subject pictured but merely its surface.

The description of the image itself moves quickly from evoking an ambiguous expression in the figure's facial features only to devolve almost immediately to the details of a uniform, the fashion behind which the man himself disappears (*verschwänden*). Indeed, the image is identified as that of the poet's father only in the title, functioning like a caption that must tell us what we are reading/looking at. And in the final couplet the reader learns of the particular medium of this visual image, the daguerreotype. Like the grandmother's photograph described by Kracauer, the photographic image of the poet's father is not coextensive with the poet's memory image of him. Rather, he is reduced to, or voided by, the "snowy" details of the recording of a specific moment of the past. He is no longer locatable behind the visual residue.

The poem that Rilke has written, however, is itself not a photographic image, nor is it simply a translation of a photograph into another medium.[59] For the poem includes more than just the daguerreotype of the father—the last line opens up to include the poet within the frame, through his hands that hold the image. The poem is not merely about a photograph but, more important, about a poet *looking* at a photograph. The poetic medium thus contains and simultaneously differentiates itself from the photographic medium. And it is, in a sense, this differentiation that becomes necessary for the poet to continue writing lyric poetry. The poem articulates different levels of seeing: what the figure pictured sees or did see ("In the eyes dream"), what one sees in the photo (the detail of the uniform), and the sight of oneself looking at the picture ("in my more slowly fading hands"). It is therefore not a reproduction of a photograph but a rendering of the encounter with a photograph and the manner in which that image denies a possession of it that would transcend its materiality and timeliness. For Rilke's final lines reveal how the temporal dimension of the photograph and the poem are not synchronized—swiftness is opposed to slowness. The daguerreotype is incomplete as an object, provoking misunderstanding, as opposed to the poem's balance, permanence, and intentionality. Although the poet does not attempt to reproduce a subjective "memory image" of his father, the detail and residue of external reality create a space in which generational difference, human relations, and loss can be expressed. In that sense, the poem doubles the object described, not by reproducing a particular photographic image but by representing or reanimating an encounter with that object.

Concluding his essay on Baudelaire, Benjamin affirmed the poet's success at presenting the elusive quality of life under modern conditions—in his poems, "the nature of something lived through (*Erlebnis*)" is "given the weight of an experience (*Erfahrung*)."⁶⁰ The experience of the city both undermines and advances poetic representation with a more fluid and unstable array of aesthetic categories. As I have shown here, one way to think through this problem in Rilke's work is through conflicting concepts of time and attendant crises of memory and self-identification. To create a work of art that will not be "jolted"⁶¹ by the circumstances of the world is to create art that neither masters nor is outside the flow of time but is deeply imbricated in time's passing, creating experiences of what I have called here *expansive* time. As a final image, we might think back to Rilke's Parisian star tearing off its course and the alternative he offers in his reflections on art in a letter on Cézanne:

> Ah, we count the years and introduce divisions here and there and stop and begin anew and waver between these options. But everything that we encounter is so very much of one piece, and so intimately related to everything else, and has given birth to itself, grows, and is then raised so much to come into its own, that we basically just need *to be there*, if only unassumingly, if only authentically, the way the earth is there in its affirmation of the seasons, light and dark and wholly in space, longing to be supported by nothing but that web of influences and forces *where the stars feel secure* [my italics].⁶²

Although Rilke states in this same letter that his character Malte has not been up to this task, he will place himself in a lineage from Baudelaire to Cézanne in which the work of art is both possible and necessary in the age of its technical reproducibility.

three

Kinetic Writing and Kino-Books

The seeing objective-eye of the recording apparatus pounces on anything and everything, examines it long and hard, preserving it inside itself and conserving on the filmstrip what has been seen, so that whenever we wish, we can examine it again. I think it is only through film that we have now learned to see. The joy of seeing is awakened. We no longer want to connect sober letters into words whose spelling and interpretation tax the mind, but rather enjoy the image-text in an easy and fleeting manner. . . . The public shelves the dull book; the newspaper is hastily thumbed through, and in the evening, the craving for images is satisfied by the cinema.

"Neuland für Kinematographentheater"
(1910)

It is impossible to exaggerate the amount of written material devoted to cinema in the first decades of the twentieth century.[1] The subjects of these essays, articles, parodies, critiques, and reviews depended, of course, on the professional and ideological interests (to say nothing of the artistic ambitions) of their authors and their intended readers. One finds technical pieces for projectionists, marketing strategies for proprietors of movie houses, tips for camera operators, thinly disguised promotional materials funded by the studios, and polemics praising or condemning the new medium. The first German publication to devote a special section to film was *Der Artist*, the trade publication for the variety and circus arts. That the first forays into a discourse on film are to be found here gives evidence of the link between the early history of film and these entertainments. Tom Gunning has characterized the period of filmmaking before 1906 as a *cinema of attractions,* privileging spectacle and sensation over narrative continuity, and strongly influenced by the vaudeville acts, traveling circuses, and variety shows during which they were first shown to the public.[2] Likewise the publications in which early texts on film appeared underscore the degree to which film was considered a component of these traveling entertainments before the construction of permanent movie houses. Coincidental with the evolution of longer playing films and the beginning of a properly narrative cinema, the first publication devoted exclusively to the "arts of projection," *Kinematograph: Organ für die gesamte Projektionskunst,* appeared in 1907. This new film journal was brought out by the publisher of *Der Artist,* and its editor-in-chief previously held the same title at the earlier publication. Other prominent early film journals included *Licht-bild Bühne* (first published in 1908); *Bild und Film* (1912–1915), the most influential publication of the Kino-Reform movement, a watchdog group dedicated to maintaining high bourgeois values in the new medium; and *Film-Kurier* (1919–44), the first German film daily and the largest film publication in Europe by the 1930s. In 1919 alone, seventeen new publications devoted to film were introduced in Germany, according to the bibliography collected by Erwin Ackerknecht. By 1930, approximately 160 film publications (including three daily newspapers) either were or had been in publication (some with a very limited run) in the German-speaking world.[3] To this, one must add the mounting number of film reviews and feature articles in the feuilleton pages of the city dailies beginning around 1913.

The literary authors whose diverse writings on film have been loosely labeled the *Kino-Debatte* comprised a substantial subgroup of contributors to these publications. The primary areas addressed by these authors include descriptions of film's industrial mode of production; depictions of the conditions of mass reception and the effects of film on the viewing public; and, most important, questions concerning film's aesthetic classification and its relationship to the traditional arts. In the decade or so after 1907, one notes an explicit shift from a comparative mode (film and theater, film and literature) to a more proper ontology of film as a distinct aesthetic category. In other words, an initial discourse on film that borrowed from the dominant aesthetic criteria of established art forms develops into a theorization of film from its own proper material and aesthetic standard. Béla Balázs's *Der sichtbare Mensch* (1924) can, to some extent, be seen as the culmination of this process.

The anonymous contribution to the *Licht-bild Bühne* in 1910 with which this chapter opens heralds the new discursive territory—the "new land" (*Neuland*) of its title—that was beginning to be tentatively mapped out. Maintaining that "it is only through film that we have now learned to see," the author reiterates Rilke/Malte's own famous phrase, "I am learning to see," though with less dramatic consequences. Both phrases indicate that the organization of sense perception itself is changed with the introduction of mechanical media and imply that these new modes of perception are not wholly compatible with the medium of print. If Rilke, however, recognizes the mediated nature of all experience and ultimately privileges poetry's role in the expansion of sensorial possibility, the celebrator of film asserts the primacy of the cinematic image because of its stimulating effect and ultimately its (paradoxical) immediacy. Impacting the viewer like a drug, film becomes an addiction that must be satisfied on a nightly basis, and the public streams in as if "hypnotized."[4] Although film is described as a substitute for the book, the terminology nevertheless becomes confused: film is an "image-text" (*bildliche Lektüre*),[5] and one "revels" in the "reading" of cinema (den Kino . . . wo man in Lektüre schwelgt).[6] The radical distinction of film and literature simultaneously occasions a linguistic confusion suggesting that a set of differentiated terms was not yet available by which to theorize film from its own proper medial perspective.

Early essays on film include consideration of its scientific and technical features, its moral and educative function, and its status as mass entertainment. However, with the introduction of the *Autorenfilm* and the movement of high-profile figures from the established (and respected) arts into the cinema, filmic narratives became more complex, leading to more critical comparisons with traditional theater and literature, along with the inevitable question: Is this art? The year 1913 marks a watershed in the literature-film debate in part because of many crossover events that lent fuel to the discussion. *Der Andere* (The Other), directed by Max Mack, premiered in January 1913. The film, an adaptation of the successful play of the same name by Paul Lindau, who assisted with the screenplay, portrays a schizophrenic district attorney who discovers that he has been living a double life as a criminal. The film starred none other than Albert Bassermann, one of the most popular German stage actors of the time, despite frequent calls for boycotts of the cinema by members of the theatrical community.[7] Because of Bassermann's role in the film, the entire community of theater critics went to the movies, some for the first time, and the majority blasted his performance as "degrading."[8] Bassermann's appearance in the film was all the more unexpected because he was reportedly so camera-shy that he would not even permit himself to be photographed. In his review of the film for the *Berliner Börsen-Courier* (January 22, 1913), Emil Faktor, that newspaper's regular theater critic, noted this very point: "In truth, the reason we came was because Bassermann was playing. Primarily, out of malicious glee [*Schadenfreude*]: we wanted to see how after years of opposition to being photographed, he would now glide by in effigy for hours; and second, it goes without saying, because we were curious."⁹ It is perhaps no coincidence that the actor who never wanted to be photographed, that is, to have his image mechanically reproduced, appeared first in a film whose story line required him to appear not once but twice in the film, as both district attorney and criminal. The film thus presents the conditions of its own technical production. In his review, Faktor admits his own bewilderment by the new medium, conceding that he has no experience with film and thus no means of judging the work or of critiquing an actor who does not speak. The reviewer is thus led to a strange conflation of the senses, concluding that one must "listen with your eyes."¹⁰ Not yet versed in a film-specific discourse, the theater critic had to borrow from an art form with which he was familiar.

Another 1913 film notable for the participation of figures from the so-called established arts was Stellan Rye's *Der Student von Prag* (The Student of Prague), starring Paul Wegener. The popular author Hans Heinz Ewers wrote the screenplay. *Der Student von Prag* is generally acknowledged as the first *Autorenfilm*, a term used to refer to any dramatic film either adapted from an original literary work or produced from an original screenplay commissioned from an established literary author. Ewers would go on to become one of the most successful screenwriters of his time. Like *Der Andere*, this film doubles its lead character. After making an impulsive deal with an unscrupulous magician, the student, an expert fencer, sees his image walk out of the mirror and is pursued by this double for the rest of the film. The relationship between the cinematic double, or *doppelgänger*, and the romantic literary tradition was already noted in a review of the film's premiere:

> It was a real première. A lot of tuxedoes. The poet sat in a private box, occasionally visible with very pretty ladies. A monocle gave its master the necessary bearing. Goethe, Chamisso, ETA Hoffmann, Alfred de Musset, and Oscar Wilde were also present. They were not averse to the fact that Dr. H. H. Ewers, the legendary celebrator of black masses, had achieved a technical masterpiece that was greeted by an enthusiastic audience. They succumbed to the unique magic of Prague's golden city. Later in the bar they could not forget the unbelievably slender, beautiful, frisky legs of Lyda Samonova.¹¹

The review is typical of a type of discourse surrounding early film that sought to legitimate it, or in some cases to satirize it, through its appropriation of the signifiers of high culture. In this case, not only was the film premiere staged like a theatrical premiere, with attendees issued invitations and attending in formal dress, but the screenplay author himself appears as a double of his literary predecessors, complete with monocle. The final sentence, however, serves as a corrective to the film's aesthetic aspirations. Although a "technical masterpiece," the film does not evoke intellectual contemplation, but erotic stimulation from the spectacle of the leading actress's legs.

Other literary adaptations premiering in 1913 include the Danish studio Nordisk's production of Arthur Schnitzler's play *Liebelei,* for which Schnitzler also wrote the screenplay, and the Swedish production of Hugo von Hofmannsthal's *Das fremde Mädchen: Mimisches Traumspiel in 3 Akten,* directed by Mauritz Stiller. Also in this year, the noted actress Eleonora Duse played her first and only film role in *Ashen,* an adaptation of the Nobel Prize winner Grazia Deledda's novel *Cenere* (Ashes). Finally, *Atlantis,* directed by August Blom, premiered, adapted from the novel by Gerhart Hauptmann, who also wrote the first drafts of the screenplay. Repeatedly, film reviewers demonstrated their ambivalence on the subject of cinematic adaptations of literary works. In his review of *Atlantis* for *Der Tag,* Julius Hart argued that film, limited to the presentation of the external world and its material effects, could never adequately represent mental states, psychological motives, or the mystical connections between events as the novel does.[12] Despite the dismay of the critics, further evidence of the *Autorenfilm* craze is noted in the establishment of production companies with names like Autorenfilm Co. GmbH, Literarischer Lichtspiel-Verlag GmbH, and Literaria-Film GmbH. Although the increase in importance of literary adaptations for German cinema around this time is clear, Helmut Diederichs rightly cautions us that "the Autorenfilm contributed more to film theory than it did to the actual practice of cinema" because these so-called art films were not popular with the masses and were hardly representative of the vast majority of films produced at the time.[13] They did not necessarily engage the general filmgoing public, but were exercises for artists in already established media drawn to the possibilities of the new one. They project new possibilities for multiple media in the shifting mediascape, and they opened the floodgates for the lengthy tradition of film criticism that continues to this day

In this watershed year, 1913, Hermann Häfker, an early film critic and advocate of cinema reform, remarked on the fundamental change inaugurated by the new technologies of the early twentieth century by referring explicitly to the distinction between earlier forms of recording and the new media: "We have reached the point where those sensory impressions generated by 'waves' of a physical nature can be fixed and reproduced, which is to say that these waves—the optical and the acoustic—are captured in their own materiality and 'write themselves.'"[14] Something new had emerged into legibility, even if it could not be read in any book. This emergence, however, raised the urgent question: With the end of the monopoly of print, how is print reconceptualized when the acoustic and optical realms "cease not to write themselves"?[15] Literary writing redefines itself in congruence with this other form of representation, this other mode of narrative. The boundaries between different media are not permeable, however, but are defined by technological thresholds—or what Robert Musil, in his review of Balázs's *Der sichtbare Mensch*, called "contact areas" (*Berührungsflächen*) and "demarcation areas" (*Abgrenzungsflächen*).[16] For many authors these incompatible data channels contribute to a more general anxiety surrounding the split between word and image as vehicles for representation, and the so-called image-text becomes a highly unstable site for thinking through the question of art. These distinct channels—print, image, sound—draw attention to differences in communicative media that are in excess of their mutual translatability. As a result, the discourse on literature and the new media at the beginning of the century is in no small part an interrogation of what makes any medium unique and differentiable from other media.

Early film criticism in Germany, particularly that advanced by members of the literary community, was therefore concerned not only with film but also with the changes in the literary medium within a mediascape in which aesthetic reception was increasingly programmed by mechanical forms of recording and representation. The subject of these writings on film is the status of writing itself—a writing that must be more properly theorized through its own medium-specific standard. Under the pretext of examining and analyzing the medium of film, these authors necessarily produced the first attempts at establishing literary criticism as a subset of a more general media theory. My intent here is to challenge the established argument that members of the literary community were merely trying to delineate the boundaries of their own art form in order to view film negatively as a lesser art. I do not wish to reargue the point that early film was merely subject to an aestheticization based on the principles of writing, for this is only one early stage of the discourse. Rather I am interested in examining how the notion of writing itself was changed by how one began to think about film. If in the first years after its introduction, film was frequently compared to increasingly complex existing cultural categories such as the pantomime and then later the theater and the novel, one notes a transition where film itself becomes the starting point from which the traditional arts are reconsidered by the destabilization of aesthetic categories. This shift could only come about with the emergence of alternate technologies for the recording of experience. In the expanding media environment at the beginning of the twentieth century, the repercussions of the so-called boundary conflicts noted by the writers of the period lead to a reciprocity among media. Early film criticism, then, is an attempt to understand both film and literature as media.

This is not to say, and it would be a mistake to conclude, however, as Kittler does, that literary works of the period were wholly subordinated to the determinations of some kind of technological imperative. Just as film is not wholly subordinate to writing, writing is not wholly subordinate to film. As we saw in the previous chapter, Rilke does not ultimately privilege photography or phonographic recording, seek to imitate these other media, or abandon writing, but insists even more fervently on the unique experiential effects of poetry. His insight was to recognize that this experience is neither wholly removed from nor completely accounted for by the world of commerce, technology, and modernity. By the early decade of the twentieth century, the photographic images that had preoccupied Rilke were now moving, and it is the response of the author to the possibility of the moving image that I take up here, especially through screenplays (real and imagined), essays, and film reviews produced by literary authors of the period. Tellingly they show a distinct preoccupation with a limited number of themes: the coordination of acts of reading, writing, and going to the movies. Through these diverse scenarios, we gain a sense of how the authors viewed not only the new and unfamiliar medium of film but more important, their own medium of print.

IN THE *LADENKINO*

In early 1913, a group of young German and Austrian writers visited the city of Dessau, southwest of Berlin, and went to the movies. On the program in the tiny theater was a film adapted from a popular novel, *Das Abenteuer der Lady Glane* (Lady Glane's Adventure). The film was short and poorly produced, but what dismayed this audience the most was the miserable piano accompaniment and the presence of a narrator who delivered a running commentary throughout in a loud Saxon accent, while using a pointer to indicate particular scenes and persons of interest on the screen. The *Ladenkino* or, literally, storefront movie theaters (also referred to as *Schlauchkino,* tunnel-theaters, because of their shape, or *Flohkisten,* flea-boxes, for obvious reasons) like the one frequented by the poets were the first permanent movie theaters in Germany, to use the word "theater" rather loosely, and were the first real competition to the traveling or touring movies screened at impromptu sites (*Wanderkino*). In his history of German film, Friedrich Zglinicki provides a short description of these locales: "These first permanent cinemas were beyond shabby. An empty shop, a few rows of chairs set up, a flickering screen, garish advertising posters—and the *Kinntop* [a contraction of *Kinematographie*] was ready. Mother sat at the cash register, Father collected the tickets and kept the peace, and Son played piano or worked the gramophone."[17] Although these movie theaters were a far cry from the grand film houses that would soon be built, they are important to the history of film because they are a critical component in the evolution of how movies were distributed, projected, and seen. In 1910, there were 456 movie houses in twenty-nine states across Germany; by 1913, this number had increased to 2,371, with 316 movie houses in metropolitan Berlin alone (and 206 in "Alt"-Berlin).[18] The narrator or *Erklärer* (literally, the one who makes clear or explains) that the group in Dessau encountered was not unusual, although *Erklärer* had begun to go out of fashion before 1913 with the increasing use of intertitles. Indeed, in the early years of cinema the *Erklärer* played a vital role translating the "language" of cinema to a public that often could not make sense of the images before them. The narrator would, for example, instruct the audience that a certain amount of time had elapsed between two successive scenes, for this was not always readily apparent to inexperienced filmgoers. The manipulation of time and space that the film medium introduced visually contrasted sharply with one's experience of these same parameters in the world beyond the screen. The *Erklärer* also helped the audience to distinguish among various characters on the screen, a difficult task before the employment of titles and credits. If the film had a particularly weak or opaque plot, the *Erklärer* would liven it up for the audience and often saved a miserable show from disaster. In short, the *Erklärer*'s task was to translate the two-dimensional film into a three-dimensional, multisensory world for an audience that was still learning how to receive technical and moving images.

The rather unsatisfactory experience of the group in Dessau led to prolonged discussions on the current state of cinema, which was seen as adhering too closely to established dramaturgical and literary traditions (and failing miserably in the attempt, thus necessitating the use of the *Erklärer*) rather than employing the new, though as yet unformulated possibilities of the technology specific to moving images. The writers in this group—including Kurt Pinthus, Walter Hasenclever, Else Lasker-Schüler, Max Brod, Albert Ehrenstein, and Richard Bermann, all young authors of the expressionist avant-garde—resolved to publish their own collection of screenplays to serve as a model for the new medium. *Das Kinobuch*, edited by Pinthus and published by the Kurt Wolff Verlag in 1913, is a collection of sixteen original screenplays and was the first publication of its kind in German for the general public. The publisher's advertisement for the book reveals an obvious tension in the paradoxical project of publishing a book of screenplays intended to showcase uniquely cinematic effects: "Half joke, half serious attempt to provide the cinema with new content and scenarios, the *Kinobuch* offers a gallery of films created by writers specifically for the cinema without the use of previously published material. . . . Each author has made an effort to see cinematically and to invent some short literary form for his or her film-idea. The *Kinobuch* is an ever-changing film theater that you can carry in your pocket and enjoy at any time."[19] The plan was to incorporate the authors' expectations of or presuppositions about cinematic perception into a written text—or, to write the effects of film into text. Unfortunately for the group, the book was barely noticed by the critics. As Herbert Tannenbaum noted in his review, it is "an experiment that certainly doesn't hurt, but certainly doesn't help either."[20] That is, it did not help realize the broader goal of developing an alternative way of filmmaking that would adhere to the technical specificity of, and establish new aesthetic categories for, film.[21] One should not be surprised, then, that none of the screenplays ever made the leap from page to screen, for these were indeed experiments in incorporating cinematic effects into text, and ultimately, in demonstrating the incompatibility of media. In other words, the implicit goal of these young authors was not to stop writing and flock to the film studios, but to show how film was distinct from and not reducible to a mere visual translation of literature. This book, which purported to serve as some sort of model for the future direction of film, clearly had a dual agenda.

Pinthus—better known as the editor of *Menschheitsdämmerung*, an anthology of expressionist poetry—wrote the introduction to the *Kinobuch*. In it he elaborates his ideas for the future direction of film. He goes to great lengths to stipulate the need for a distinct boundary between film and the more traditional arts (theater and literature), maintaining that film will remain a poor imitation of the traditional arts as long as filmmakers aspire to nothing more than translating theatrical and literary effects into the purely visual realm of moving pictures. This was a frequent argument employed at the time not only by supporters of the new technology but also by its detractors. In stating what film was *not* in relation to the traditional arts, critics of film could deny that film had any artistic merit. However, Pinthus uses this rhetorical strategy to different effect—he asserts that film is neither a substitute nor a surrogate for literature and theater but something of an entirely different order. For Pinthus, the visual qualities specific to film should be the foremost criteria in the creation of films, as opposed to diegetic models borrowed from literature. The specifically cinematic attributes he outlined include the lack of spatial constraints; the presentation of movement, both within a shot and in the succession of shots; and the use of film tricks. Pinthus reveals here his particular interest in the degree to which space and time can be manipulated through the visual image to create a form of expression not available in other media. He therefore decries the prevailing trend in cinematic adaptation of literary works, claiming that this will be the downfall of the medium. In order to formulate the essence of the screenplay, one must "recall the almost forgotten original essence of cinema."[22] That is one should integrate the purely visual and spectacular modes of the earliest films—Gunning's *cinema of attractions*—with film narrative, as opposed to merely subordinating them to the plot.

Many of the ideas Pinthus advances in his introduction to the *Kinobuch* reiterate claims he made in his review of the 1913 premiere of the Italian film *Quo vadis?* adapted from the popular novel by the Polish Nobel Prize winner Henryk Sienkiewicz published in 1896. The novel and subsequent film depict the end of the Roman Empire under Nero and the advent of the Christian era. Pinthus's review, "Quo vadis—Kino?"[23] which appeared in the *Leipziger Tageblatt* on April 25, 1913, was one of the first film reviews to be published in a daily, large-circulation newspaper.[24] Pinthus opened with a description of the formal invitation he received to the premiere, which like the premiere of *The Student of Prague,* included a request for formal dress: the film premiere modeled itself on the grand premieres put on by established theatrical stages throughout the city. In Pinthus's view, the staging of the premiere was only the latest in a series of ill-conceived ways in which film sought to imitate the theater without acknowledging its fundamental difference from theater. And this is a point that is repeatedly criticized by Pinthus. On the one hand, Pinthus's review of the film is positive, praising the director for having selected precisely those images from the novel that could not have been presented on the stage, such as the burning of Rome and the death of the Christians in the arena. On the other hand, he finds the narrative overly convoluted and the plot unable to keep pace with these stimulating visual events. Pinthus laments that no one would be able to understand the narrative at all were it not for the intertitles, thereby providing evidence for the heart of his argument that films are not appropriate vehicles for novels. Thus in this review Pinthus delineates medial boundaries. Drawing his analogy from the subject matter of the film itself—Quo vadis: *Kino*?—Pinthus considers film doomed if it fails to exploit the technology through which it is produced.

Pinthus voices here a concern that other writers of the period likewise sought to articulate, namely, the distinctions among literature, drama, and film. Herbert Ihering, a prominent film critic who wrote for the *Berliner Börsen-Courier* from 1920 to 1932, echoed Pinthus's position in the following statement:

> A German film can be bad for a variety of reasons. It either fails to be a film or indulges in high-flown experiments. It either imitates literature or looks like a picture postcard. Its use of the material is either crude or sentimental. But when it is bad, then it is primarily because it is not film in the first place. . . . The German film is often bad because it wants to be something other than film. The American, because it wants too much to be film. The German, because it neglects the cinematic elements (the composition of movement). The American, because it exaggerates the cinematic elements.[25]

In his essay, "Kinokunst" (Film Art) of 1913, the poet Oskar Kanehl espouses a similar view by calling film a "third way" that must be considered distinct from both literature and drama.[26] Although for Kanehl, film has not yet developed to its full potential, he argues that it should nonetheless be considered "art," and he disparages both filmmakers who try to imitate poetry, drama, and the novel and critics who make ill-conceived comparisons with these other art forms. At its best, film permits expressive possibilities that were by necessity falsely channeled through inappropriate media before and can only now find true expression. Indeed, in Kanehl's opinion any author who permits his or her novel to be adapted for film does not simply devalue the work but casts its original merit into doubt. Carlo Mierendorff's 1920 essay, "Hätte ich das Kino" (If I Only Had the Cinema), employs a highly stylized prose to take an ironic stance on the same question. As the title indicates, the writer, a political journalist, voices his regret at not having cinematic effects at his disposal as an author. However, the prose itself attempts to adopt what the writer identifies as these very effects, matching linguistic formulations as much as possible to their cinematic ones: the brevity and speed of film is reformulated through the use of extremely short phrases and one-word sentences; the fragmentation of film translates as abrupt leaps of thought and changes of direction in the prose; and the visual nature of the moving image finds its counterpart in the essay's numerous vivid descriptions. What is clear from the title of the article, however, is that this can only be a provisional experiment, for the two media are in fact not interchangeable.

The blending of media in early film is perhaps not so surprising, for as Pinthus noted, "The movie public is largely a public that reads novels."[27] Its audiences were therefore already programmed for a particular mode of reception. Because the characters in a film are not inhibited by space or time, Pinthus concedes that the film is more closely aligned with the novel than with the theatrical arts. His statement already anticipates, however, Bertolt Brecht's later formulation of the reverse side of the dictum: "The man who writes the stories is a filmgoer too. The mechanization of literary production cannot be thrown into reverse. Once instruments are used, even the novelist who makes no use of them is led to wish that he could do what the instruments can: to include what they show (or could show) as part of that reality which constitutes his subject-matter; and above all, to assume the attitude of somebody using an instrument."[28]

Thus the *Kinobuch* (whether we take it seriously or as a joke as its editor and publisher suggested), whose contributors attempted "to find some literary form that is somehow appropriate to film" and who "made an effort to see cinematically," indeed this book whose stated goal was to show how film could be freed from the influence of literature was, at the same time, very much concerned with the current state of writing.[29] For of what would a textual recording of a film consist? In an article that appeared in the *Schaubühne* in September 1913, Richard Bermann, who contributed two screenplays to the *Kinobuch* addressed its neglect by the critics: "The most basic literary decorum prohibits me from writing on the subject of this book. Nevertheless, the book is so important or could be so important, that literary decorum, even the most basic, can shut its hypocritical mouth."[30] In its contributors' eyes, the book had the potential not only to impact the film medium but also the literary medium, and to change fundamental aesthetic assumptions about literature. Thus not only is a definition or theory of film at stake, but concurrently, a definition or theory of literature. For in this competition among media, the battle lines were being drawn, and in these early creative works, we can obtain a glimpse of how this conflict was thought through. This interrogation of film by the members of the literary community is not only concerned with the possibilities (both positive and negative) of cinematic representation, but functions as a theoretical space in which to articulate the manner in which this new medium demands that the author rethink the possibilities of the book (the old medium). What emerges from these early twentieth-century writings on film is a picture of the author who must rethink the status and position of writing itself, as it becomes increasingly apparent that writing cannot be distinguished from its own particular means of recording and transmitting information. Writing is just one medium in competition with a host of other media. In this sense, the title, *Kinobuch*, is fitting: it conflates two media even as it attempts to distinguish them. It records creatively the parameters of the literature-film debate, or as Pinthus concluded in his introduction to the collection: "Perhaps this unreal world (a world realizable in cinema) mirrors more of our real earthly world than we might think."[31]

Especially because of this insistence on the specificity of media, when reading through the screenplays in the *Kinobuch*, one is struck by what is perhaps a very simple question. If their stated purpose (from Pinthus's introduction) is to serve as some sort of model for the potentialities of film, then why do so many of them construct their scenarios around scenes of writing or reading? Pinthus states explicitly in his introduction that the prohibition from words is a critical component of the essential nature of film. And Pinthus is by no means alone in this regard. One finds repeated reference to the absence of words in these early films both as a liability and a benefit, and I will return to this question. So why do these screenplays portray scenes in which the word would constitute such an important component? One could assume that these authors *cum* amateur screenplay-writers followed the cardinal rule of "write what you know." Or on a more metaphoric level, perhaps, the scenarios could be read as a dramatization of the distinction between film and literature, for the writers that appear are, for the most part, overwhelmed by the films in which they appear. What these story lines reveal foremost, however, is the recognition of the position or status of the literary author who is situated in a world in which aesthetic reception is increasingly programmed by mechanical forms of recording and representation such as film, as Brecht maintained. What we notice most often in these and other brief scenarios that will be explored in this chapter is the breakdown of the writer's artistic production, whether through the staging of failed texts, the replacement of texts by other media, or, most dramatically, the author's refusal to write. These contributions in which the activities of writing or reading are thematized give evidence to how technology infiltrated the scene of writing. Cinema is not merely a metaphor but indicates the degree to which writing cannot be conceived apart from the broader mediascape. The confrontation with new media reflects literature's understanding of itself.

THE MECHANICAL POET: *KINOBUCH* (1)

The first screenplay in the collection, "Leier und Schreibmaschine" (Lyre and Typewriter), is by Richard Bermann, an Austrian novelist and travel writer.[32] As the title indicates, this screenplay presents the conflict not only between literature and film but also between the anachronistic image of the classical Orphean poet and more modern means of producing print.[33] What we discover is that literature is not only in conflict with another medium but, moreover, must adapt to its own technical reproducibility. The film scenario adopts the strategy of the film within the film (as many in the *Kinobuch* do, and further evidence of its reflective mode) and opens with the image of a female stenographer and her boyfriend returning home from the movies while she relates to him the storyline of another movie, which, as she states, "proves how important we typists are—we who transcribe your poems, and sometimes even motivate them."[34] The interior film then opens with the image of a poet who alternates between sitting at his desk chewing on his pen, struggling to formulate lines that he will recite into the mirror, and throwing himself on the sofa in utter exhaustion and desperation. Quite literally, of course, he cannot find the words. While bemoaning his trouble in the local artists' cafe, he spies and falls in love with a young woman whom he follows home, and learns that she is a typist named, appropriately enough, Minnie Tipp *(tippen* is German for *to type)*. Ms. Tipp must refuse his advances, however, because he has not given her anything to type. Alone again in his garret and unable to produce a single line, the poet is visited by Cupid, who appears and fills his sterile inkwell with a magic fluid. Now the poet's pen writes as if by itself, and soon the whole room is full of manuscripts, which he promptly brings to the typist. In the love duet that follows, he dictates while her fingers dance over the keys and, after some panic on how he will pay her bill, which she has also dutifully typed up, they live happily ever after. As the interior film closes, the boyfriend of the external frame can only comment that the film reveals the "spiritual danger" (*geistigen Gefahren*) of the typewriter. Because how could poems produced so quickly be any good? What was good was the chewing on the pen and the poet's sighs.[35]

If the couple of the outer frame function as doubles of their own cinematic counterparts, what we find is that the boyfriend still adheres to an earlier discursive network that valorizes the experience of intellectual contemplation as manifested in the pose of a poet who presumes himself beyond any specific medium and in direct contact with the Spirit. It is no coincidence, however, that *Dichtung* (poetry) and *Diktat* (dictation) share the same etymological root, for as Kittler has shown, in the discourse network of 1900, the *Dichter* (poet) is the one who dictates, not the one who has transparent access to the absolute signifier/-ied.[36] Once separated from the poet's hand, the typewritten manuscripts reveal the scandalous materiality of the Word, utterly disconnected from the so-called Spirit or soul that motivated it. With his pronouncement, the boyfriend not only summarizes the ambivalence of many authors of the period toward mechanical type as opposed to handwriting but also restates the terms of the debate on the use of machines that appear repeatedly in the literature-film debate of the period. As a mechanical process, film is unable to communicate the depths of the artist's soul. If the film medium is never distinct from the technology through which it is produced and transmitted, the invention of the typewriter makes clear that this is also the case with writing. As the only medium for the transmission of a temporal data stream, the fact that writing is a medium could be overlooked during the nineteenth century; however, the technological specificity of the typewriter cannot be ignored. If handwriting links the hand, the eye, and the letter in a continual translation of the poet's inner world, the typewriter's introduction of standardized print and spacing produced through a machine separates that same hand and eye and letter. In the earliest typewriters, the typist could not see what had been written until three or four lines after the fact, thereby verifying in its technical positivity Benjamin's assertion (via Valéry) that we are no longer familiar with earlier conceptions of art and the artist as a result of the dislocation of the soul, the eye, and the hand.[37] Once the hand no longer plays an integral role in the act of production, the aesthetic classification of the object produced is open to question and fundamental assertions concerning the art object must be reformulated. That Malte's hand appears so prominently in Rilke's *Notebooks,* emphasizing the young poet's uncanny relation to his own hand, should thus not surprise us.

The contrasting positions taken up by Paul Ernst, a novelist and dramatist in the classical tradition, and Alfred Polgar, a political reporter and theater critic who also wrote on cultural trends, illuminate the manner in which the increasing prevalence of technology, particularly film technology, began to undermine traditional theories of representation. In his 1913 article, "Möglichkeit einer Kinokunst" (Likelihood of a Movie Art), Ernst sees little with which to answer affirmatively the query implied in his title. His argument concurs with that of the boyfriend in Bermann's screenplay. The crux of Ernst's thesis is a critique of the machine-made essence of film:

> It is simply thus, that art is primarily a function of the soul, and the soul simply cannot be found in the actual. When Albrecht Dürer paints a lawn with scientific precision, then we have a work of art because the little aquarelle has come from his mind and his heart; when cinema presents us with a meadow stirred by the wind, then this is no work of art, even though for the unschooled observer the film presentation is certainly more impressive than the inconspicuous little picture. . . . In cinema, the attempt is made to produce art, man's highest achievement, through machines. It is obvious that this attempt must fail; however, that the attempt can be made is one of the worst indications of the degeneracy of our age.[38]

The argument against film is similar to arguments against the typewriter as a poet's tool because of its inherent technicality. In other words, film can never become art because it bypasses the human. Ernst's antitechnological sentiment is directly contradicted, however, by Alfred Polgar, whose 1911 article, "Das Drama im Kinematographen" (Drama in Film), also takes up the example of filming a meadow in nature:

> The meadow in the movie theater smells better than the one on the stage because cinema shows a real, actual meadow. I have complete confidence in the aroma of this meadow which is suggested to my nose by the imagination of my undisturbed fantasy. But it also smells better than the natural, living meadow which can never exhale such a dear and pure aroma as my blooming meadow which is and is not. . . . Only in dreams and in the movies is there reality without slag. In both cases, the laws of nature are repealed, gravity denied, existence is without limitations.[39]

In Ernst's example, the essence of art, as indicated through the example of the Dürer aquarelle, is that the representation of nature, even the most scientifically precise, is a function of the unique hand and mind of the individual who created it. The observer of the art object thus has a unique spiritual connection with the art object. This is the *auratic* element of art described by Walter Benjamin. However, in Polgar's formulation, the "purity" of the object of representation is not a function of the mind or soul of the artist but is rather a material characteristic of the medium of film, which from the general flow of information selects and filters a data stream without noise, or in his preferred analogy, "slag" (the waste element of a metal separated from its ore). For Ernst purity and truth is a product of the mind, whereas for Polgar, technology has taken over this function, a function that, as he clearly states, is also a product of the dream state. The comparison between film and dreams is a common one during the period and a topic to which I will return shortly.

A critical point implied in these two quotations is the state of mind of the viewer of the film. In the essays of the period, one notes the frequent analysis of the various perceptual faculties involved in the reception of literature and other traditional arts as opposed to film. It is in this context, for example, that one finds discussions of the metaphysical depth of literature. Reading is described as an intellectual process, not a physical act, that requires profound contemplation with a minimum of excitability or nervousness (*Reiz*). Conversely, film is criticized as a medium in which a strong element of excitability is induced by the continuous flow of images passing by at speeds too high to permit poetic contemplation. However, with this technological effect, film is also more closely aligned with the exploding sensory and information overload of the concurrent burgeoning growth of the metropolis itself, as we will see in the following chapter. *Geist* or spirit/mind and *Schaulust* or the desire for spectacle are declared incompatible. With film, everything is present to the eye (if only for fleeting moments during which one is in a state of constant distraction), whereas literature assumes the fantastical or hallucinatory effect of the Word. In his response to a questionnaire distributed and printed in 1913 by the *Börsenblatt für den Deutschen Buchhandel* entitled "Kino und Buchhandel" (Film and the Book Market), the Nobel Prize winner Paul Heyse responded: "The adaptation of literary works strikes me as harmful because the word, and thereby its spiritual meaning, is eliminated through its reduction to mere mimicry, and the public's proclivity to look at images is fueled."[40] The intellectual depth and latency of the book is elevated over the perceived immediacy of mechanically reproduced images through film. Heyse's conception of the "word" categorically denies its medial status, arguing rather that it grants transparent access to spiritual meaning. Film, on the other hand, is discussed only in terms of its medial characteristics. What Heyse represses here, however, is the manner in which the medial effects of film reveal precisely the limitations of other media, including the printed word. In his response to a questionnaire distributed by the *Frankfurter Zeitung* in 1912 that asked respondents to address the value or unimportance of film, Walther Rathenau responded quite bluntly: "Art has nothing to do with entertainment. Art enriches the soul, entertainment blinds the soul to its own poverty."[41] Other writers (including Hofmannsthal and Döblin, as we will see) declared that this so-called spiritual or transcendental character of language had long since vanished and that film should be accepted as an aesthetic category through which we, as modern subjects, are increasingly trained to view and comprehend so-called reality.

During the second decade of the century, the critique of technology is employed both to denounce an antihumanism inherent in the technical medium and to criticize a kind of overstimulation of the masses in lieu of traditional notions of contemplative reserve before the art object. These two arguments are combined into a third line of attack that draws a distinction between the linguistic and visual media based on the value of language. This is the point implied, for example, in Paul Heyse's response just quoted, as well as in Oskar Kanehl's "Kinokunst," cited earlier, when he writes: "No art form is as indebted to the *word* as the literary novel, and despite the wildest hopes for its *technical* perfection, the silent, mimed film-novel will always remain a physically effective, stimulating, agitating, and ultimately artistically deficient creature."[42] Although the Word is repeatedly invoked as the essential difference between film and literature or theater (it will take Lukács to point out that the difference is of an entirely other order),[43] this spiritual conduit of meaning was, in the words of Egon Friedell, an early film critic, "gradually losing its reputation." For as he states, "I don't think we are as inclined to grant the word such absolute hegemony these days. Rather, one should perhaps say that words these days are already somehow overdetermined and thereby strangely indifferentiable."[44] And in remarks on his career as a screenplaywriter, the author Hans-Heinz Ewers, best known for his screenplay for *The Student of Prague*, wrote that he was happy to be free of words in the film medium: "That was precisely the thing that excited me: at last the chance to do without 'words,' these 'words' that were until now everything for the poet and without which he himself was unthinkable. These 'words'—which after all were only a vague, and never a fully exhaustive, surrogate for the *deepest feeling!*"⁴⁵ In these latter depictions, the radical shift in human experience and modes of perception occasioned by the increased mechanization of public and private life results in a shift in consciousness such that the subject of poetic contemplation is no longer available for address. We see this as well in the expressionist model of turning away from rationality as a legitimate model of organization.

The earlier autonomy of literature as a medium of representation is menaced by a proliferation of information in print and visual media that fractures or shatters any unified consciousness that would stand in poetic contemplation. As Walter Benjamin instructs us in "The Storyteller," the seeming immediacy, verifiability, and plausibility of information undermines the authority of narrative experience as a subjective and communicative event. Richard Bermann's screenplay, "Lyre and Typewriter," can be read as a sort of interface between the author and technology, in which the author recognizes the impact of the larger technological environment, the mediascape, on forms of consciousness and attempts new ways at recasting communication techniques. In "The Work of Art in the Age of Mechanical Reproduction," Benjamin writes of the very *necessity* of this work: "Man's need to expose himself to shock effects is his adjustment to the dangers threatening him. The film corresponds to profound changes in the apperceptive apparatus—changes that are experienced on an individual scale by the man on the street in big-city traffic, on a historical scale by every present day citizen."⁴⁶ The experimental genre serves to challenge the threshold of traditional narrative from within literature itself in order to address and accommodate this shifting social dynamic.

THE LANGUAGE OF DREAMS AND FILM: HOFMANNSTHAL

Hugo von Hofmannsthal combined both sides of the technological debate surrounding the film medium in his 1921 article, "Der Ersatz für Träume" (The Substitute for Dreams).⁴⁷ We recall that Alfred Polgar concluded his remarks on the technological efficiencies of film with the statement: "Only in dreams and in the movies is there reality without slag." Hofmannsthal uses this comparison to suggest that for the modern urbanite, movies actually take the place of dreams not least because both are experienced in an environment free of words. For Hofmannsthal (reiterating Egon Friedell's criticism of language), words have become an untrustworthy medium of communication, or a medium with too much baggage (Polgar's "slag") attached. Borrowing extensively from Freud's description of the unconscious and his *Interpretation of Dreams* (1900), Hofmannsthal argued that the images of film are a direct presentation of the unfulfilled childhood wishes and desires of the public.

"Der Ersatz für Träume" is constructed around the following statement: "What people want from cinema, said my friend, with whom I happened upon this topic, what the workers want from cinema is a substitute for dreams. They want to fill their fantasy with images, powerful images, in which the essence of life is concentrated; images that both stem from the inner world of the audience and cut them to the quick."[48] In other words, they experience the images as both emanating from within them and impacting them externally through perception. Or rather, not everyone responds to film in this manner, but more specifically the citizens of big cities and industrial areas, for these people have been negatively impacted by an existence ruled by the assembly line and the number. The facades of their houses cannot be differentiated, the environments in which they work and pay taxes are always the same, and their work on machines consists of repetitive motions of pushing and pulling or twisting, so that in the end, the people themselves are transformed into machines ("ein Werkzeug unter Werkzeugen") and are stripped of any sense of individuality.[49] This lost selfhood is only subsequently recaptured by the sensual impact of film images. That these images are silent only contributes to their positive reception because of the growing suspicion on the part of moviegoing audiences that language itself has always already been co-opted by the power structures by which they are ruled and thereby only contributes to the perpetuation of their mechanical and mechanized existence. That the entire apparatus of moviemaking—from production and marketing, to distribution and reception—is inextricable from the apparatus of power will take a later generation of media critics to recognize. In the friend's description, the experience of film brings us most back to ourselves, not because the moving pictures present something new, but because they remind us of that which is most our own, namely, our dreams.

This formulation is consistent with Freud's theory of regression in dreams outlined in the seventh and final part of *The Interpretation of Dreams*.[50] Briefly, Freud describes here how the dream state reverses the temporal sequence of the waking state. When awake, the mental apparatus receives sensory input, and our memory of these perceptions is retained in mnemic systems that are linked through association and facilitating paths. These unconscious memories only enter consciousness through the screen of the preconscious. In the dream state, however, the unconscious functions as the motive force, and rather than being transmitted from the sensory end to the motor end (the temporal direction of the waking state), the excitation moves in a backward direction toward the sensory end of the apparatus. Freud calls this activity "regression" and defines it as occurring "when in a dream an idea is turned back into the sensory image from which it was originally derived."[51] In Hofmannsthal's essay, this regression becomes a reciprocal movement between the unconscious and the film screen. For as he states, the images that the eyes see flashing across the film screen correspond with the "underground vegetation" or roots of our innermost, though inexpressible, thoughts.[52] In this view, film images eschew normative communication (language) and provoke more immediate responses of feeling and affect, allowing the viewer to enter into a more authentic, less intellectualized relationship with the world. With his essay, Hofmannsthal makes the first attempt at connecting the dream-work and cinematography, and substantiates the claim made already by Hugo Münsterberg in 1916, that "every dream becomes real" in film.[53] Although Freud never mentions the word "film" in his *Interpretation of Dreams*, he tells us that "the secret of dreams was revealed" to him in a dream he had in 1895—the year in which cinematography made its debut.[54]

Hofmannsthal's essay both contributes to the discussion concerning the relationship between scientific understandings of psychical processes and information technologies and furthers his study of the so-called language crisis. Reading "Der Ersatz für Träume" side-by-side with the more widely read "Chandos Letter" of 1902 creates the impression that Hofmannsthal may have considered film not just a substitute for dreams but for poetry as well. The "Chandos Letter" makes clear that it is not just the masses of factory workers who consider the word with some skepticism (as his "friend" in the film essay maintains). As he informs the English philosopher Francis Bacon, Chandos, a man of letters, decides to abstain from writing altogether because he can no longer decipher any meaning from the words he sees on the page or construct new linguistic formulations that would adequately express his relationship to the world around him.

Chandos's writing crisis is described in terms very similar to those articulated by Malte/Rilke in the *Notebooks*, although with very different consequences. Like Rilke, Hofmannsthal uses a double or an alter ego of himself to describe the crisis experienced by someone with an overwhelming alienation from the act of writing. Hofmannsthal eloquently forwards the letter of Lord Philip Chandos (son of the Earl of Bath and another aristocrat at the end of his lineage) to Bacon explaining why he must give up writing forever. Forwarded, because Hofmannsthal signs his short work with Chandos's name (much as Rilke signs his own short prose sketches with Malte's name); and yes, eloquent, although paradoxically so, for as Chandos states: "I have lost the ability to think or to speak of anything coherently" [über irgend etwas zusammenhängend zu denken oder zu sprechen].[55] Chandos does not lack recourse to words, but an organizing principle or valid normative formula through which the fragmentary nature of his sights, thoughts, and subsequent writings might hold together. One might have suspected as much from one of the last works he had proposed to write (but could, of course, never finish), an *Apophthegmata* in which he would present

> the most memorable sayings which . . . I had managed to collect during my travels. With these I meant to combine the brilliant maxims and reflections from classical and Italian works, and anything else of intellectual adornment that appealed to me in books, in manuscripts or conversations; the arrangement, moreover, of particularly beautiful festivals and pageants, strange crimes and cases of madness, descriptions of the greatest and most characteristic architectural monuments in the Netherlands, in France and Italy; and many other things. The whole work was to have been entitled *Nosce te ipsum*.[56]

To know thyself ("Nosce te ipsum") appears an impossible enterprise, requiring the limitless recording of the textual, visual, and pathological archive.

Ultimately, it is Chandos's experience with a particular visual technology that forever severs his relationship to the Word and leads to his disavowal of writing. Upon looking through a microscope, he views a piece of his own skin at an "uncanny closeness" so that his "little finger look[ed] like a field full of holes and furrows."[57] Just as abstract signifiers can no longer comprehend the individual event or the so-called signified, his own body loses its comprehensive unity—the parts seen under the microscope no longer add up and are no longer connected (*zusammenhängend*): "For me everything disintegrated into parts, those parts again into parts; no longer would anything let itself be encompassed by one idea. Single words floated round me; they congealed into eyes which stared at me and into which I was forced to stare back—whirlpools which gave me vertigo and, reeling incessantly, led into the void."[58] If the injunction to "know thyself" can only be achieved by a limitless recording—a recording that would leave nothing out and in which the signal is indistinguishable from the noise, or in which everything is present but no essential meaning can be distilled—then surely this poses a problem for language, ever since Saussure's object of study was the atemporal network or system of *langue* (that is the rules for the possibility of combination) and not the temporal and embodied event of utterance or *parole*.[59] In other words, his desire for self-knowledge calls for a solution for which language is not adequate. A different modality of communication is thus required for Chandos, "a medium more immediate, more liquid, more glowing than words."[60] A medium, one notes, that is defined through its speed, quality of simultaneity, and visual characteristics.

Chandos and Malte both remark on the change they have undergone: Chandos no longer recognizes himself as the author of his earlier works, and Malte asserts that he must stop writing letters because he is changing, and "if I'm changing, I am no longer who I was; and if I am something else, it's obvious that I have no acquaintances."[61] Chandos stops writing as a result of this crisis, Malte starts.[62] The two cases presented through these texts appear quite similar, including the depiction of a storied lineage that has come to its end. Is the poet the last of his line or the first of the new?[63] For Malte (as for Rilke), this crisis does not result in a turning away from language and writing but rather a new understanding of it; Rilke does not stop writing poetry with the *Notebooks* but turns to a new mode of lyric expression as evidenced by the *New Poems*. Tellingly, Chandos retires to his family's rural estates, whereas Malte goes to Paris. If the loss of a sense of self, the fragmentation of his identity, and his inability to "connect" things is no less problematic for Malte than it is for Chandos, at least in the sensory overload of the city of Paris, Malte is surrounded by the visual effects that Chandos could only describe as chimeras of his mind.

Two points of conjuncture are extremely telling in regard to a comparison of Hofmannsthal's "Chandos Letter" and his "Substitute for Dreams." The first concerns the relationship to words that prompts Chandos's language crisis and his disavowal of writing: "At first I grew by degrees incapable of discussing a loftier or more general subject in terms of which everyone, fluently and without hesitation, is wont to avail himself. I experienced an inexplicable distaste for so much as uttering the words *spirit, soul,* or *body*.... The abstract terms of which the tongue must avail itself as a matter of course in order to voice a judgment—these terms crumbled in my mouth like mouldy fungi.... All this seemed as indemonstrable, as mendacious and hollow as could be."[64] Just like the audience in the movie theater who no longer trusts words, sensing the manner in which they are inextricable from a power structure and a worldview that they do not share, Chandos finds that he must abstain from linguistic formulations that to him are at best merely hypocritical and at worst utterly devoid of meaning. Furthermore, there is a direct link between the two texts in terms of the images that they describe. In the film essay the effects of the images moving on the screen serve as an alternate experience to the oppression of language; in the Chandos letter, these same images from nature are employed to replace the experiential void brought on by the loss of writing. Both texts describe a turning away from language in favor of visual images, but more telling perhaps, there is a conspicuous overlap between the actual images both texts valorize. In the film essay, Hofmannsthal details the images that moviegoers reencounter from their dreams: "a dark corner, a breath of wind, the face of an animal . . . the dark space behind the cellar stairs, an old barrel in the courtyard half-full with rainwater, a crate full of lumber."[65] The images that Hofmannsthal described almost twenty years earlier in the "Chandos Letter" likewise emphasize objects from nature along with simple implements and built structures: "A pitcher, a harrow abandoned in a field, a dog in the sun, a neglected cemetery, a cripple, a peasant's hut—all these can become the vessel of my revelation"; and, "on another evening, [I found] beneath a nut-tree a half-filled pitcher which a gardener boy had left there, and the pitcher and the water in it, darkened by the shadow of the tree, and a beetle swimming on the surface from shore to shore."[66] Both sets of images release in their viewers a fuller connection with the world around them, freeing them from the restrictive and negative constraints of language.

Hofmannsthal is himself known for having renounced lyric poetry around 1900, despite his early success in this genre. Although this decision could hardly be directly attributed to the introduction of new media, it is clear that the so-called language crisis of this period is not divorced from questions introduced in the context of the broader mediascape: How are spatial and temporal coordinates redefined? How is the social construction of reality impacted by alternate forms of its recording and presentation? How are aesthetic criteria shifted? Rarely remarked in the scholarship, abundant evidence exists of Hofmannsthal's interest in film in addition to the film essay.[67] Hofmannsthal's first film, *Das fremde Mädchen*, directed by Mauritz Stiller and starring Grete Wiesenthal, premiered on September 5, 1913. Tellingly, the subtitle of the film identifies it as a "dream-play" (*Traumspiel*). Initially, *Das fremde Mädchen* was a pantomime, written in 1911, and no substantial changes were made between the stage and film productions. Because the film adheres so closely to the staged action of the pantomime, no visual instructions such as cuts or camera setups distinguish it as particularly cinematic. However, as a pantomime the film does demonstrate Hofmannsthal's interest in the kinetic arts and the possibility of using movement to communicate in a medium other than the verbal. Hofmannsthal's second foray into film was with the screenplay *Daniel Defoe,* which evolves as a series of images culled from various stages of the author's life. The treatment for the film includes instructions for linking scenes that bear no immediate relationship to each other and function as an early example of montage. In 1923, Hofmannsthal wrote a screenplay for *Der Rosenkavalier,* which was eventually directed by Robert Wiene (who had directed *The Cabinet of Dr. Caligari* a few years earlier), although Wiene apparently ignored most of Hofmannsthal's suggested treatment. *Der Rosenkavalier* premiered on January 10, 1926, in the Dresden Staatsoper with Richard Strauss himself conducting. That same year, Hofmannsthal wrote a screenplay for *Lucidor,* based on a short story he had written in 1910; the film was never produced. Finally, in an interview in December 1928, Hofmannsthal mentioned plans for another film (for which no screenplay exists) that was to have starred Lillian Gish with Max Reinhardt directing. If film was not an absolute substitute for literature, it is clear that Hofmannsthal was interested in the possibilities opened up by the new medium in its (apparent) immediacy, its freedom from overdetermined verbal forms, and its duplication of the viewer's own mental processes.

THE DOPPELGÄNGER: *KINOBUCH* (2)

Max Brod's contribution to the *Kinobuch,* "Ein Tag aus dem Leben Kühnebecks, des jungen Idealisten" (One Day in the Life of Kühnebeck, the Young Idealist), dramatizes the conflict between literature and film on various levels: internalized representation through the intellect as opposed to externalized visual presentation; deliberate contemplation as opposed to unrelenting speed; stasis as opposed to motion.[68] It also reinforces another distinction between the two orders of fiction on the temporal level. For if in print, verbal narrative always represents a past event as past, in film the past event is experienced as present. Here, the medium-specific threshold is organized around the shift from a representational to a presentational mode. As a result, in the viewer's reception of cinema the distinction between fiction and reality on the perceptual level becomes increasingly difficult to define, catching early film viewers in a crisis of knowing.

In the introduction to his screenplay, Brod proposes a film titled "Dichter bei seiner Arbeit" (Poet at Work), in which the poet's eyes would glaze over while sitting at his desk and the surroundings of his study begin to fade away and transform themselves into the images of his latest work, "Versöhnung zwischen Vater und Sohn" (Reconciliation Between Father and Son). The physical effects of optical recording and transmission substitute for the symbolic mediation of the linguistic realm. In this introduction, Brod picked up on an idea he had already proposed in "Kinematographentheater," an essay published that same year in which he describes a visit to the cinema and outlines scenarios he would like to see produced.[69] One scenario likewise presents a poet alone in his room who flies into a desperate rage, despairing over the difficulties of his supposedly sagacious, though concurrently, reticent medium. In the *Kinobuch,* Brod observes that the technology of film can achieve new artistic effects that once could only have been "imagined" on the stage or in the pages of the novel through the use of "all-powerful words" (*allmächtige Worte*—an attribute more commonly phrased with reference to the Divine).[70] Film exteriorizes the interior effects of the reading experience itself; both of these poets function as doubles for Brod himself. In effect, the introduction to his *Kinobuch* screenplay must be understood as the outer frame to the subsequent film scenario itself. And this "reconciliation" between generations signals nothing less than the shift to the medial conditions of 1900, and the differentiated means for the processing, storage, and transmission of data. Likewise, the reconciliation "Kühnebeck" portrays is between two media that are in constant play throughout. In Brod's screenplay, the confrontation of writers and readers with film reflects a certain understanding of literature itself.

Young Kühnebeck is a schoolboy addicted to reading, or at least addicted to a particular genre of reading: Karl May is one of his favorites.[71] We also learn that Kühnebeck is particularly susceptible to flights of fancy, hallucinating everything that he sees or reads into the fabric of the ongoing film of his imagination. Brod sets up the slippery distinction between reality and film fantasy early in the screenplay through the use of calculated film tricks and editing devices, similar to the one described in the poet's room in his introduction. For example, an organ-grinder in the courtyard of the family's home metamorphosizes into an entire orchestra with the organ-grinder as conductor. When the boy throws himself around the conductor's neck in appreciation of his music, the conductor is immediately changed back and does not disguise his chagrin. Perhaps uncertain of his audience's ability to distinguish between the two, Brod conscientiously thinks to provide appropriate intertitles, demarcating "Fantasy" and "Reality." This device reaches its climax, however, not while the boy is observing the world, but while he is reading a thriller about a foreign stranger terrorizing the inhabitants of a house and the hero who saves them. As Kühnebeck reads in the attic, he begins to hallucinate himself into the story as a master crime-stopper likewise protecting his family downstairs from an intruder who threatens them. It seems this is not pure fantasy after all, however, for there really *is* a stranger in the attic with him who has followed the family home intending to rob them. As the sequence of shots alternates between the book, Kühnebeck's fantasy, and the scene being played out in the attic, it becomes increasingly difficult to distinguish between fantasy and reality or to differentiate among the complicated narrative and visual frames embedded in the film. Kühnebeck becomes a double of his own character, reproducing himself into an ever more complex set of Chinese boxes. Which is the *reality* and which the *representation*? Although for Kühnebeck, one cannot rightly say that this question even comes into play, for he is in a sense already programmed to see reality as film. Through this device, Brod simultaneously reveals to the film viewer that in the space of cinematic reception, one can never be entirely sure whether one is inside or outside the frame. Indeed, as Brod's introduction or prologue to "Kühnebeck" shows, even the act of writing the screenplay has been co-opted into the cinematic narrative. Brod masterfully depicts an essential component of cinema: the manner in which it reorganizes processes of perception, reorienting space and time in the modern mediascape.

In an interview, Samuel Weber has commented on this same effect:

> With film, too, there is a separation of the theatre from the "outside world," but the proximity of its representations to our everyday process of perceiving is such that we can no longer be confident about distinguishing what is fiction, what is supposition, what is construction and what is "objective reality." Thus, film doubles the reality of everyday perception, our visual and auditory perceptions, while at the same time revealing them to be full of suppositions and even projections. This cinematic duplication of reality thus tends to render the latter uncanny: both all too familiar and all too strange.[72]

Weber borrows his term, of course, from Freud who outlined his thoughts on this subject in "Das Unheimliche" (1919), drawing on a wealth of etymological investigations, literary examples, and anecdotal observations. At its most benign, the experience of the uncanny is a result of unlikely coincidence: for example, we might be thinking of a person and then suddenly run into them around the next corner. Or we might be reading a book and suddenly find ourselves confronted with a situation that we thought to be only a product of our fantasy of the text. Our perceptual world doubles our mental world, effacing the distinction between reality and the imagination, and provoking a kind of intellectual uncertainty because we are not certain whether we are in the realm of the fantastic or the real. The frequency of the motif of the double or the *doppelgänger* has often been theorized as an important component of early German cinema; however, this is not merely a theme or motif of a particular film narrative, but presents to its viewers one of the essential elements of film, namely, its mechanical doubling of our own processes of perception. Brod's screenplay highlights this effect by doubling the manner in which we perceive the various fictional levels of his film, rendering any absolute distinction ultimately uncertain. In this sense we cannot, or can no longer, say that the cinematic image serves merely as a visual translation of the content of the printed text the writer produces and the hero reads, but rather that it introduces an experiential realm of an entirely different order.

A more striking example of this uncanny effect was recorded in 1910 during a visit of the German Kaiser to Vienna. In a magazine article, Berthold Viertel, a dramatist and theater critic and later a Hollywood film director, described a bizarre event when after participating in the official duties attendant on the reception of a head of state, the Kaiser and his wife went to the movies only to find themselves, quite literally, the stars of the show.[73] There on the screen, the lifelike images of the monarchs appeared to speak and wave and laugh, while their audience in the film applauded. And the audience in the movie theater watching the film applauded as well. While the monarchs in the picture showed their gratitude, their doubles in the theater did likewise. Viertel declares himself aghast at "this horrible doubling of representation," and that primarily because it is the Kaiser, or the so-called chosen one, who is doubled. Should one, as he asks, be allowed to reproduce Grace so frivolously? For in this doubling effect of film, where is reality locatable? The moment of horror reaches its apex when suddenly a tear occurs in the film and the movie theater goes dark. Viertel asks: Did the tear also go through reality? As the audience sits in the suddenly blackened and silent room, can they be assured of their own existence? There in the picture, one Kaiser performs his highest duty, and below in the audience, the other one sits simply as a spectator who is humanly amused by the portrait of his own dignity. Or is this amusement only a further fulfillment of his duty? And the people who watch, twice present and for that reason twice as happy, cheering for their own good cheer, greeting their own naive selves in the mirror—couldn't one receive a shock, as if having seen one's own ghost?

The reaction of the novelist Gerhard Hauptmann upon seeing his own image on screen is another example of this cinematic uncanniness. He related the experience to a friend in a letter: "Saw a talking-film of myself. I was filled with loathing. Vanity. I saw a man I hardly knew. His voice was strange to me, and thus new. It didn't appeal to me. An air of illicit eccentricity clung to him. A twittering arrogance. He moved his mouth as if he didn't have any teeth. He had a large mass shoved back between his right jaws. . . . Was that me? That one of my texts?"[74] It is not merely that one is shocked, and perhaps disgusted, by the sight of one's own double, the appearance of the mechanized double gives evidence to a perceptual experience that literature might aspire to but never attain. For it is surely no accident that Hauptmann does not only misrecognize his own body but also, like Malte and Chandos before him, his own texts and himself as the one who could have produced them. The data stream available for linguistic selection is of a radically different order than that afforded in the visual realm—a condition that Brod's poet understood well. Kittler has argued that this distinction results in a zero-sum game to the detriment of literature: "Literature no longer even attempts to compete with the miracles of the entertainment industry. It hands its enchanted mirror over to machines."[75] However, as the authors we have looked at here demonstrate repeatedly, film does not simply pick up where literature leaves off. Indeed, an awareness slowly creeps into these reflections on media that the sense of immediacy and authentic visual pleasure that film supposedly introduced was itself the product of an increasingly finely tuned apparatus. Writers like Rilke or Hauptmann do not reject sound recordings or moving pictures of themselves simply out of vanity, but because the recording mechanism reifies the experience of the literary encounter. Frequently posited as a generational transition, new media do not replace but redefine traditional art forms.

Other authors of the period were well aware of this so-called changing of the guard. For example, the author, journalist, and art critic, Adolf Behne comments on the diminishing relevance of literature in the economy of the modern mediascape in his 1926 essay, "Die Stellung des Publikums zur modernen deutschen Literatur" (The Public Attitude Toward Modern German Literature), awarded first place in an essay contest co-sponsored by a leading cultural journal and a bookstore: "The book is nothing more than a means of transport, just a form of communication. As soon as we have a more intensive form or a better means of transport, the old one is doomed. Book culture seems comparable to me to bayonet culture in the age of lewisite [a chemical-warfare agent]."[76] For Behne, the primary distinction between literature and film is not the usual verbal/visual dichotomy, but results from the unique spatial and temporal characteristics of each medium: "Film is the simple, proper, and legitimate continuation of the book—Edison is the new Gutenberg. Those little booklets we had as schoolchildren whose pages became the moving images of a primitive film when we flipped through them become significant as an important transition. Once the sequence of pages in a book were used not just spatially but temporally, there was film."[77] In other words, as soon as the textual marks in the book were no longer used as meaningful signifiers providing access to some spiritual unknown but were to be read as purely physical effects transmitted in time, one had already begun to undermine the traditional presuppositions of poetic language. Brod's screenplay, which dramatizes how the act of reading is commuted to the act of filming, enacts the transition that Behne described.[78] Indeed the poet of the introductory frame has already made this shift from one medium to the other, for in the moment that his visual hallucination begins, he stops writing. And the letters on the page before him can no longer be linguistically interpreted, but serve only as material effects in the expanding visual scene.

THE PHANTOM: MANN

Thomas Mann does not write about film and its doubles or *doppelgängers*, but refers to a no less uncanny figure, the phantom, thereby making explicit the unique temporal condition of film in which nothing ever dies. Mann's essay, "Über den Film" (On the Film), was first published in *Schünemanns Monatshefte* in August 1928.[79] Although his argument is grounded in the firm belief that film is not art (he draws the reader's attention to his use of the term "phenomenon" [*Lebenserscheinung*] as opposed to "art" [*Kunst*]), this author of high German letters nonetheless insisted on his love of film. In the opening lines of the essay, he declares his passion for movies, claiming that he does "not tire of the joys of spectacle."[80] As his short catalog of films reveals, however, Mann is not a fan of film narrative, per se, only its purely visual elements: the *cinema of attractions*. And he criticizes those who approach film armed with aesthetic criteria drawn from the established arts. Because film does not adhere to these criteria, its critics can only express their distaste for the new medium. According to Mann, film lacks the representational distance and intellectual contemplation that art affords (*aura*): film is "not art, it is life, it is actuality."[81] Mann illustrates his claim that film is not art with the observation that one cries so often at the movies: "Say what you like, the atmosphere of art is *cool*; it is a world of spiritual valuations, of transmuted values, a world of style, of handwriting, of the most personal design, an objective world, a world of the intellect ('For it comes from the intellect,' says Goethe)—meaningful, refined, chaste and serene, its agitations are strictly second hand [*Mitteilbarkeit*], one is at court, one keeps oneself in control."[82] Here Mann anticipates Marshall McLuhan's famous distinction between hot and cold media.[83] In Mann's view, the mediated quality or distance of the "cool" art object can never be the case in film, which transfers its agitation directly onto the spectator. Despite this shortcoming, however, Mann suggests that the novelist might nonetheless learn from the film's presentation of mnemonic techniques, its psychological suggestion, and its precision of details.

Surprisingly, after dismissing the artistic possibilities of film, Mann concludes his essay with some thoughts on the filming of his own novels, including his dissatisfaction with the adaptation of *Buddenbrooks* (directed in 1923 by Gerhard Lamprecht) and his endorsement of the potential possibilities of a cinematic adaptation of *The Magic Mountain,* particularly the "Snow" sequence during which Hans Castorp dreams of exotic Mediterranean sites. The scene that Mann refers to is indeed a flight of literary fancy: a hallucination that Castorp experiences when he becomes lost in a snowstorm and briefly loses consciousness. In this sequence, Castorp initially experiences the sights and sounds of a gentle landscape and people by the sea, and Mann employs powerful visual descriptions to evoke the many turns in the dream which culminates in a barbaric sacrificial ritual inside a temple. However, as evocative as this scene may be, the tenor of which is quite different from the bulk of the novel, Mann's novel actually presents a much more evocative cinematic moment shortly before its conclusion during a séance held one evening by some of the inhabitants of the sanitarium. This séance scene could be considered a mini-screenplay embedded in the novel that reflects directly on the powerful (and sometimes terrifying) effects of film, and that repeats elements from a scene described much earlier in the novel when a party of residents from the sanitarium takes a trip to the movies.[84]

Early in the novel, we read of a visit to the movie theater in the small town in the Alps, during which "all sorts of life, chopped up in hurried, diverting scraps that leapt into fidgety action, lingered, and twitched out of sight in alarm, to the accompaniment of trivial music, which offered present rhythms to match vanishing phantoms from the past."[85] The abrupt termination of the film, however, leads to a strange feeling of discomfort in the audience:

> When the last flickering frame of one reel had twitched out of sight and the lights went up in the hall and the audience's field of dreams stood before them like an empty blackboard, there was not even the possibility of applause. There was no one there to clap for, to thank, no artistic achievement to reward with a curtain call. The actors who had been cast in the play they had just seen had long since been scattered to the winds; they had watched only phantoms, whose deeds had been reduced to a million photographs brought into focus for the briefest of moments so that, as often as one liked, they could then be given back to the element of time as a series of blinking flashes. Once the illusion was over, there was something repulsive about the crowd's nerveless silence. Hands lay impotent before the void. People rubbed their eyes, stared straight ahead, felt embarrassed by the brightness and demanded the return of the dark, so that they could again watch things, whose time had passed, come to pass again, tricked out with music and transplanted into new time.[86]

In the sudden absence of the illusion before them with its curious blend of dream and reality, the audience is left unsettled in their experience of time and acutely reminded of their own mortality.

In his essay on film, Mann referred to the images as "living shadows. They speak not, they are not, they merely *were*—and were precisely as you see them—and that is narrative," or more precisely, "narrative in pictures."[87] However, the experience for the filmgoer is not that of reliving the past as past, rather the past is again made present and the dead live. For those people in the movie theater who live so close to death themselves, it is perhaps a comforting thought: an afterlife in the world. Through these moving pictures, the inevitability and unidirectionality of time's arrow is freed. These phantoms may be released from temporal and spatial constraints, but this release has nothing to do with transcendence.

This technological condition of film is dramatically reenacted in the séance scene, which marks the beginning of the novel's conclusion and Castorp's eventual departure from the sanitarium and reentry into the temporal flow of worldly affairs. A young Danish girl arrives at the sanitarium who possesses the uncanny arts of telekinesis and spiritual somnambulism, channeling a spirit she names "Holger." In an earlier appearance, Holger had announced that he can call anyone back from the dead, and Castorp attends the séance with the intention of asking for his cousin Joachim, whom he had originally accompanied to the sanitarium and who had died some months earlier. Mann describes the setting in which the séance takes place in terms vaguely reminiscent of the *Ladenkino*, the small, cramped rooms in which films were first screened. The room is darkened, save for some reddish light from a lamp covered with a shawl, and the participants all take up chairs in order to view the proceedings. Elly, the medium, appears dressed in a white gown, glowing like an early vision of a film star, and the proceedings are accompanied by lighthearted music playing from a gramophone in the corner. Several hours pass by during which Elly/Holger goes through a lengthy pantomime of dramatic exertions, and the company urge the dead spirit to appear. At one point an intermission is even called and the lights are raised again, so that the participants can stretch their legs and smoke a cigarette. Finally Joachim's ghost materializes:

> The record had come to an end, the last chords of brass had died away. But no one turned off the machine. The needle moved to the middle of the disk and scratched idly in the silence. Now Hans Castorp lifted his head, and without having to search, his eyes looked in the right direction. There was one more person than before in the room. There, off to the side of the semicircle, in the background, where the red light was swallowed up in night that the eye could barely pierce, between the doctor's wide desk and the folding screen, there on the patient's chair turned toward the room, where Elly had sat during the pause—there sat Joachim. It was Joachim with the shadowy hollow cheeks and warrior's beard from his final days, with lips arched proud and full. He sat leaning back, one leg crossed over the other.[88]

Joachim's image appears to emanate from the light source, and the scraping sound of the gramophone needle serves almost as a reminder of the sound of the film reels turning, which so many filmgoers of the period have described in their anecdotal observations. The group assembled in the room is frozen before the image, this phantom from their past that lingers again in their midst. The sight of Joachim eventually becomes unbearable to Castorp; after asking the phantom for forgiveness, he immediately crosses the room and turns on the light, leaving the others stunned. In this reenactment of the processes of cinematic reception, the reaction to the image is markedly different from that experienced by the filmgoers in the novel's earlier scene. In the former, they want to continue to see the past images made present again, but here, in the face of a dead man, Castorp is left with the sensation of having broken a temporal law. Stories of his past deeds can be told and memories of him shared. Castorp even writes about his dead cousin. But the image itself is taboo, as if his ghost had been disturbed by being called into the present.

This experience serves as the primary catalyst that finally impels Castorp to make plans for his own departure after so many years, and to reenter the temporal stream. For the entire novel to this point has, in a sense, been outside time. As the narrator comments during an interruption of the plot early in the novel: "It is always the same day—it just keeps repeating itself. Although since it is always the same day, it is surely not correct to speak of 'repetition.' One should speak of monotony, of an abiding now of eternalness."[89] The sensational, visceral experience of the film/phantom image shocks its viewer from the serene and intellectual contemplation that had been the nature of Castorp's experience to this point. This "cool" atmosphere, as Mann maintained, likewise defines a suddenly outmoded theory of art, including the novel we have been reading to this point. Castorp leaves the mountain to, as it were, take up again the role of the living. As Geoffrey Winthrop-Young has argued, "Mann conceptualizes new media technologies by showing how they work, which fantasies they fulfill, what they will lead to, and how they are changing our bodies and minds—and all the while depicting them with a living (as opposed to deadly) accuracy few writers can match."[90] In the brief foreword to the novel, the narrator informs the reader that this is an old story "covered with the patina of history," taking place "on the far side of a rift that has cut deeply through our lives and consciousness" and therefore must be told in a way "much older than its years."[91] The rift that he refers to is the so-called Great War, the same war that Castorp leaves the mountain to join. But this rift, to some extent, must also be thought of as that brought on by technological, and not just military, incursions into the aesthetic realm. This is to say that the expanding mediascape of the early twentieth century—one that is remarked on in a variety of ways in Mann's novel through his references to x-rays, phonographs, photographs and other media technologies—does not simply introduce new modes of rendering time and space, but these very temporal and spatial disturbances have lasting effects on the human subjects who encounter them, forcing a reconsideration not only of one's mortality but of the very nature of experience itself. With Döblin's work, as we will see in the next chapter, the author will not merely catalog these media technologies in a formal style "much older than its years" but will demonstrate their effects in the composition of the prose itself.

POETICS OF THE CAMERA: *KINOBUCH* (3)

In his own contribution to the *Kinobuch*, "Die verrückte Lokomotive" (The Crazy Train), Kurt Pinthus explicitly links the film medium with other technological innovations of the period.[92] Pinthus even uses his main characters—Erna, a lovely newlywed and engineer, and her new husband Peter, a poet—to symbolize, in his words, "the union of old-fashioned poetry and modern technology."[93] Indeed, a ballet performed at their wedding reception is choreographed around this very theme. The screenplay is divided into four acts that draw from three different narrative genres: melodramatic love story, fantasy sequences of a train voyage, and desert island comedy. The first act employs cross-cutting to dramatize two simultaneous love stories: the one portrays the luxurious environs and idyllic romance of the practical engineer and the poet, culminating in their marriage; the second shows the squalid quarters of a locomotive engineer and his unfaithful wife, and reaches its climax when he discovers her affair with a popular comedian from a variety show (a nod to the film's roots). The second act is set on the train itself and consists of crosscuts of the interior of the lovers' carriage, the locomotive engineer at the train's controls, and the scenery passing by outside the windows of the moving train. In his rage, the engineer opens the throttle and sends the train racing over the European landscape. Eventually the train leaves the tracks, flying through the air like an airplane and gliding under water like a submarine. It is not until the heroine, Erna, throws the engineer from the train and takes control of it herself that the train finally comes to an abrupt stop in a tropical forest on a primitive desert island. In the final third of the film, the stranded passengers engage in a variety of slapstick adventures until they are eventually rescued by a passing ocean liner.

The fascination of film with the railroad is usually dated to one of the Lumière brothers' first short films, *L'Arrivée d'un train*. In this film short, which consists of one continuous take recorded from the platform of a train station, we see a train coming in from the top right of the screen and pulling into the station, before stopping in a cloud of steam. In this early phase of filmmaking, the camera takes the position of a recording eye from one constant position, registering the movement of the object recorded. The audience sees an image of the train from the point of view of the camera. Although the film did not yet incorporate editing techniques in which different shots are assembled into a complex visual scene, its effect was nonetheless formidable on a public seeing moving pictures for the first time. Walter Hasenclever, an expressionist dramatist and himself a contributor to the *Kinobuch,* recalls seeing this film (or at least one like it) in 1900 at the age of ten: "Silently, a train came ever nearer from a great distance, and suddenly appeared to drive right into us. I cried out loudly."[94] Within a few years, another popular genre involving the train was the so-called travel film, which employed a camera mounted on the front of a locomotive or held out the window of a moving train to record the passing scenery. Here, the movement captured is of an entirely different order than in the Lumières' film because the camera itself moves (as opposed to the object in front of the camera) and the simulation of movement is transferred to the audience watching the film. Biograph's "The Georgetown Loop" of 1901 is a prime example of this genre, presenting vertigo-inducing drops outside a window, recorded as the train moved through a narrow mountain pass. These two different types of film photography exemplify two types of movement that the film camera permitted, and that Pinthus highlighted in his attempt at writing a theory of film in the introduction to the collection. Film both records the movement of objects within the frame and presents movement through the succession of individual shots. According to Pinthus, it is only by combining these two effects that one begins to exploit the full possibilities of the film medium.

The central portion of Pinthus's film, the wild train ride, best demonstrates how he sought to achieve these effects. In his directions for the film, he notes that as the train roars by, the passengers inside "see the world flying by as if it were chopped up into individual pieces."[95] In other words, the view outside the moving train was to reproduce the experience of the spectators themselves in the movie theater, in which the images likewise "fly by." In this way, Pinthus directly presents the perceptual possibilities introduced by the new film medium and demonstrates again to the audience how film reorganizes their relationship to space and time. Pinthus is adamant that film should follow a different logic than either literature or theater, one in which "the weight and causality of things fall away."[96] He uses his screenplay to explore what Egon Friedell described in similar terms: "Cinema is sketch-like, abrupt, full of gaps, fragmentary. For modern tastes, that is an eminent artistic advantage. The realization of the beauty of the fragment is beginning to make headway in all of the arts, for in the end, all art is nothing but a skillful and occasionally brilliant elision and linkage."[97]

Pinthus's instructions for the editing of his film show that he was far ahead of the mainstream of German filmmaking. Barry Salt has compared early films from Europe and America to discover why it was that in 1912 Germans watched more American films than German films or even films from any other country.[98] He answers this question through a statistical analysis in which he calculated the average shot length (ASL) of a selection of Danish, French, German, Italian, Swedish, and American films, based on the ratio of the total measure in feet of the reel to the number of total different shots in the film. The lower the ASL, the faster the plot would generally move and the more stimulating the visual effects on the audience because of the larger number of cuts. Salt's results clearly show that the move to faster cutting was led by the Americans, whereas German films had among the highest ASL in Europe. The German films are notable for their continued use of very long scenes and extremely slow cutting, leading Salt to conclude that the reason German audiences preferred American films was that "American films were in general more exciting, gripping, and entertaining."[99] Pinthus's screenplay is, therefore, remarkable for the rapidity of cuts between scenes. For example, the screenplay calls for numerous rapid scene changes or cuts between shots of various compartments in the train and shots outside the windows, and the speed of these cuts increases as the train careens ever more out of control. In this section of the film, Pinthus demonstrates his understanding of the fundamental mechanics of the film medium, and its ability to produce stimulating effects based not only on movement within a shot, but perhaps more important the movement produced as a result of the succession of different shots.

Pinthus's use of a self-reflexive mechanism—the mechanical reproduction of the mechanics of movement—also draws attention to the politics surrounding the discourse on technology, for the true heroine of the film is indeed the female engineer. As Sabine Hake concludes from her analysis of other examples of early German films of this type, "Those in control of the new technologies overcome all adversities and emerge victoriously in the end. By contrast, those opposing technological progress for moral or political reasons are subject to mockery."[100] Erna demonstrates her control not only of the train but of the visual tricks of the new medium itself. While she and her husband-poet are on the train, speeding along on their honeymoon, she throws his precious manuscript out of the window and the pages change into colorful birds that fly away.

In his analysis of the discourse on film during the first decades of the century, Helmut Diederichs notes the split between two different conceptions of film.[101] Diederichs calls the first the "theater-aesthetic" phase, during which the camera is, for the most part, limited to the process of reproducing actions occurring in front of the lens. The artistic qualities of the film were thus dependent on the scene in front of the camera and the capabilities of the actor. The second phase is, in Diederichs's view, the first properly film-specific aesthetic phase, where one uses the apparatus of the camera itself as an art instrument, frequently changing its position for the production of different effects. Through these editing techniques, the film upends traditional temporal and spatial relationships. It is this second phase that eventually leads to the more fully developed theories of cutting and montage, as found in the works of Sergei Eisenstein and Béla Balázs. For Diederichs, this second phase begins in Germany with the German release of Eisenstein's *Battleship Potemkin* in 1926. However, Pinthus's text of 1913 and the writings of the actor and director, Paul Wegener, of the same period, clearly indicate that these ideas on film-specific theories of the medium can and should be dated much earlier.

Paul Wegener, the director, actor, and screenplay writer best known for his films *The Student of Prague* (1913), *The Golem* (1914 and 1920), and *Rübezahls Hochzeit* (1916), was once called by his friend, the author Frank Thiess, a child of the electric light, belonging to a generation that would choose an arc-light over the sun because it can be turned on and off at will.[102] Wegener was highly critical of films that did not take advantage of the technological possibilities of the medium, and he saw his own role as a filmmaker to develop ideas that did exactly that. In a lecture delivered in 1916, titled "Neue Kinoziele" (New Cinematic Goals) and later published as "Von den künstlerischen Möglichkeiten des Wandelbildes" (On the Artistic Possibilities of the Moving Image), Wegener argued that film needed to break with earlier art forms and to develop new modes of representation. In a prescient synopsis of Marshall McLuhan's later statements on the "rear-view mirror" effect by which we "march backwards into the future," Wegener argued that all new techniques attach themselves to forms that are already established, and for this reason, a new idea often takes time to find its proper mode of expression.[103] Wegener cites as examples the first steamships, which resembled enormous schooners, only with tall smokestacks amidships instead of masts; the first train wagons, which resembled stagecoaches; the first automobiles, which resembled carriages; and of course, the first films, which drew on pantomime, stage plays, and illustrated novels.[104] Not surprisingly, Wegener was highly critical of film adaptations of literary works: "The true poet of the film must be the *camera*. The possibility of photographing that which is large as small or small as large, of superimposing or blending photographs; the ability to constantly change the point of view of the spectator; the countless tricks through splitting the image, mirroring, and so forth; in short, the *technique* of film is crucial to the choice of its content."[105] As Walter Benjamin would also take care to explain in "The Work of Art in the Age of Mechanical Reproduction," the film cannot be distinguished from the technologies by which it is produced. This is not merely to say that the images that the filmmaker records must be visually stimulating, but that the diegetic mechanisms of the narrative itself must conform to the technological capacities of the medium. At one level, Wegener expresses the not uncommon idea that film introduces an alternate means of recording and transmitting information: "Film is first and foremost a *visual* business. The film-poet [*Filmdichter*] must begin with the image, think in images, and select subjects that can be expressed in images."[106] More important for Wegener, however, film radically alters the manner in which information itself is organized and perceived.

In his 1924 work, *Der sichtbare Mensch*, Béla Balázs formalized these concepts into a general theory of film, addressing his writing to three distinct groups: the keepers of aesthetic tradition and art history, film directors and other friends of the discipline, and the filmgoing public.[107] In his opening remarks, Balázs is concerned foremost with the need for a theory of film. As Pinthus had already argued over ten years earlier, Balázs refutes the standard claims by members of the art establishment that film is not art because of its industrial and commercial roots, maintaining that such claims employ obsolete aesthetic categories by which to judge film (and citing by way of analogy the critique that an airplane is a bad automobile because it does not handle well on the road). Indeed, it is just such a film theory that will broaden the appreciation of film beyond its financial success, by making the unconscious knowledge of the experienced film director and the experience of the spectator explicit. Comparable to a new sense organ, each new art form introduces a new relationship between humans and the world, and film is just such a new art form, reintroducing the body as a vehicle for nonverbal expression: "Humanity is already in the process of relearning the long since forgotten language of expressions and gestures. Not the substitution for words as in sign language, but rather the visual correspondence of the unmediated, embodied soul. *Man becomes visible again.*"[108] This loss of the true mother tongue ("die eigentliche Muttersprache der Menschheit") is largely the product of print culture, "a dematerialized, abstract, overintellectualized culture that has reduced the body to a mere biological organ."[109] As a result, a successful screenplay can never be the result of a purely literary fantasy, as is evident in Balázs's detailed notes, in which he delineates the unique properties of film.

In his lengthy review of Balázs's book, the Austrian author Robert Musil opens with a lengthy excerpt of Balázs's defense of and call for film theory, arguing that the film theorist simultaneously creates an unexpected paradigm for literary criticism.[110] Musil ultimately rejects, however, the idea that literature must necessarily remain a formal product of the symbolic, that is to say, the intellectualized and abstract, domain. All art, Musil argues, is to some extent an abstraction in that it constitutes a splitting off from life, a disturbance of reality, by way of which the reader, the viewer, or the spectator is presented with a new relationship to the world. This essential characteristic of art is, at least in Musil's view, especially relevant in the early twentieth century. Reiterating arguments that Georg Simmel had made in his essay "The Metropolis and Mental Life," Musil criticizes the dehumanizing effects of a money economy that reduces all humans and objects to quantifiable norms through a strictly positivist, causal logic. Paradoxically, film—the art form perhaps most indebted to and reflective of modernization—may offer the way out of this mechanized and totalized worldview by presenting the fleeting traces of a wordless experience that frees humanity from what we call "understanding." In the symbolic categories of its objects, in fleeting images, and in the reliance on expression and gesture, film reverses the overintellectualization that modernization has forced on mental and sensorial operations.

Despite this opening up or glimpse that film theory may provide, however, Musil argues (against Balázs) that the experience of film is, at its core, not so radically different from the experience of print. Although an element of incommensurability always exists between expressive possibilities (one can never fully translate a picture into words or a poem into prose), Musil rejects the notion that the symbolic nature of verbal art, or what Balázs called the dematerialization of literature, in itself precludes the desired aesthetic experience of challenging the overrationalized processes of modernization. To be sure, the encounter with the literary work is informed by the reading experience itself, just as new knowledge gained is always to some extent filtered through that which is already known. However, every new experience both exceeds *and* reinforces given or known formulas. Therefore, the task of the work of art is to continually reformulate and renew the picture of the world and its internal relations—through each specific instantiation (*Erlebnis*) the artwork bursts asunder the formulas of experience (*Erfahrung*). Although other successful art forms, music especially but also film, are constructed according to this logic, literature performs this task most explicitly by working with the material of formulation itself. Although film and literature are autonomous categories, both can serve to unmask normative values and present an alternative relationship to the world. In similar fashion, Musil welcomes Balázs's film theory because it likewise unmasks a bankrupt literary theory, opening the possibility of reformulating and renewing literary writing itself.

Film came to public attention through the traveling carnivals, sideshows, circuses, and variety shows—surely an unbridgeable distance from the high reaches of the arts, literature, and theater. However, as films moved into permanent movie houses, and as figures from the established arts began increasingly to work in the film industry, the opinions surrounding the new technology started to change. No longer could the literary artist ignore this other and competing medium of communication, for not only were the readers of books flocking to the theaters, but so too were the writers of these books. The authors of the *Kinobuch* were some of the first to theorize the limit or boundary of the two media. They were the first to attempt to produce a formal theory of film narrative based on mechanical and visual principles that would distinguish film from poor imitations of other established media. Finally, they were among the first to realize the implications of the artistic revolution inaugurated by the new technology. Although Thomas Mann went on record as a lover of film, he would never consider it an art form because it was not classifiable within the reigning aesthetic paradigm. What he did address, however obliquely, was the idea that artistic categories and notions of the aesthetic would themselves change as a result of the alternate modes of recording and transmission, of representation more generally, brought about by the new medium of film. It is in this light that we must understand Yvan Goll's prediction in 1920: "The basis for all future art is the cinema. No one will be able to manage without the new movement because we are all rotating at a different speed than ever before."[111]

four

Crisis of the Novel: Döblin's Media Aesthetic

> The word-film is rolling. The movie camera will never be able to present literature, but literature must learn from the movies. And it has already learned. Now is not the time for plots that drag on, a stagecoach pace, and painstaking psychological detail.... The arrival of an express train is exciting, but the paperbacks that you buy for one Mark are boring.... Döblin's work matches the tempo of our lives.
>
> JOSEPH ADLER, "EIN BUCH VON DÖBLIN,"
> DER STURM, JULY 1913

The word-film is rolling. In his review of Alfred Döblin's first collection of short stories, *Die Ermordung einer Butterblume und andere Erzählungen* (The Murder of a Buttercup and Other Stories, 1913), Joseph Adler brings three seemingly disparate elements together: literature, film, and transportation systems. Adler does not advocate the increasing trend of adapting literary works for cinema; he negates this possibility from the start. Instead, Adler recommends that literature adopt the high-speed movement of cinematic images, which for their part are associated with the movement of an express train, suggesting that the excitement provoked by the two technologies is of a similar order. Increasingly trained to perceive the world through these two media, cinema and the railroad, modern consciousness experiences a disconnect with a literary medium that, plodding along like a stagecoach, only exacerbates temporal and experiential confusion. Adler voices here the shift in temporal and spatial awareness introduced by these forms of mechanized movement that Wolfgang Schivelbusch has so clearly elucidated in his study of the effects of nineteenth-century industrial transportation on human activities, including the sphere of speculative and philosophical consciousness.[1] For example, Schivelbusch quotes Heinrich Heine, the nineteenth-century poet and journalist: "What changes must now occur, in our way of looking at things, in our notions! Even the elementary concepts of time and space have begun to vacillate. Space is killed by the railways, and we are left with time alone."[2] The novels Adler continues to find in the bookstores, however, are out of sync with this tempo and with these accelerated forms of sensory apprehension, and for this reason he is grateful to have found a suitable vehicle in Döblin's film-like prose. But why does Adler write of the text in terms that suggest a media hybrid? The word-film is rolling.

Döblin's story "Die Ermordung einer Butterblume," first published in the cultural journal, *Der Sturm*, in September 1910, relates the escapades of Herr Michael Fischer, who while walking through the woods one day, swings his walking stick at a patch of buttercups, neatly decapitating one. He instantly regrets the act. Tormented by grief and guilt over the death of Ellen (the name he later gives the flower), Herr Fischer transplants another flower from the woods to a pot that he keeps in his bedroom, thereby absolving himself of his previous crime by keeping a wildflower alive that would surely have had a much shorter lifespan if left alone in nature. He is, however, suddenly and conclusively released from further penance when the housekeeper accidentally knocks the pot over and throws the weed and the pottery shards into the trash. It is not immediately evident why Adler compares this short fable to film, and W. G. Sebald will later read this story as an early sign of the demonization of nature and of the increasing violence that will occupy Döblin's work.[3] The story is certainly brief and moves at a quick pace, as Adler noted, primarily because of its very short sentences and rapid changes in perspective. The story is also striking for its abundance of visual detail depicted from a variety of constantly changing angles and positions. For example, after committing the "murder," Herr Fischer experiences a flashback of the event. Döblin uses the flashback to introduce temporal variation and play into his prose, reenacting the scene in slow motion: the walking stick slowly makes contact with the flower, the blossom is lofted into the air, and the buttercup leisurely (but irrevocably) returns to earth some distance from its stalk. The next sentence immediately shifts to a close-up of the now decapitated stem, where white liquid begins to ooze from the gash left by the murder weapon. The reader never discovers why Herr Fischer reacts so strongly to his spontaneous act; the protagonist does not undergo any transformation by the end of the story and there is no part of the story that describes what motivates him psychically. An event is simply presented to the reader. But this is not to say that this is a naturalistic description. The measured pace of the memory sequence and the immediate "cut" to a detailed image of the stem demonstrate deliberate temporal and spatial manipulations that in their now near ubiquity are almost rendered invisible to a contemporary reader.

It was perhaps Döblin himself who led Adler to dub the text a film of words, for just two months earlier, Döblin had published his own media manifesto in the same journal. The manifesto, "An Romanautoren und ihre Kritiker" (To Novelists and Their Critics), also known as the "Berliner Programm," details the author's own brand of "Döblinismus"[4] as a literary writing that indeed takes account of the introduction of new media by recommending that literary writing adopt a "cinema-style" (*Kinostil*):

> The "wealth of visions" must pass by with the utmost conciseness and precision. Coax from language the limits of expressiveness and animatedness. There is no room in the novel for casual storytelling; one does not narrate, one builds. The storyteller has a rustic's [*bäurische*] familiarity. Brevity, economy of words is necessary; original phrases. Make extensive use of periods, which permit the quick comprehension of simultaneous and successive events. Rapid developments, mixed together in catchwords; in general, one must attempt to achieve the highest degree of exactness through suggestive turns of phrase. The whole thing must come across as present, not as something merely spoken of.[5]

Döblin notes here three critical elements of his cinema-style that are likewise present in "Die Ermordung einer Butterblume": the highly visual nature of exact depictions; the brevity of phrases and sentences that flow in rapid succession; and the actuality of events depicted as immediately present before the reader in an attempt to circumvent the symbolic mediation of the linguistic register. In other words, Döblin focuses on precisely those elements which distinguish film from literature: visuality, speed, and the recording and transmission of material effects. For if in Goethe's nineteenth century, Faust (and by extension the reader) could still call forth a "wealth of visions" (*Fülle der Gesichte*) with a chain of phrases and incantations, Döblin's audience needed only to look at the film screen to encounter spirits, evil or otherwise.[6]

Because the technical conditions for representation had changed so radically by the twentieth century, Döblin asserts that the author who continues to work within a nonmechanical medium must follow suit: "Some things are steadfast over time. We can still enjoy Homer—art keeps. But work methods change over the centuries, just like the surface of the Earth. The artist can no longer run to Cervantes without being consumed by moths. The world has grown deeper and wider; the ancient Pegasus, outflanked by technology, was dumbfounded and turned into a stubborn mule. I assert that any good speculator, banker, or soldier is a better poet than the majority of today's authors."[7] A speculator, banker, or soldier: all professions, of course, that rely on the speed and accuracy of information in real time. But what of a neurologist like Döblin, with a busy practice in the working-class neighborhood on the east side of Berlin? Unlike the grounded Pegasus, the doctor-author Döblin would not be outpaced by technology, but would incorporate it into his literary texts. He accomplishes this not merely by referring to technological novelties and new media throughout his writings (although he does this too), but by engaging alternative recording media within the formal style of his prose. Döblin's statements regarding literary technique differ significantly from Rilke's position on the relationship between poetry and new media as we saw earlier. Whereas Rilke struggled with the crisis in poetic language initiated in part by metropolitan life and mechanical modes of recording, Döblin shows how other media are fundamental to the development of a new literary language. Both authors are deeply aware of the mediation of experience, but if Rilke insists that sensory experience is constituted by the materiality of writing and the encounter with poetry, Döblin will emphasize the ways in which we hear, see, and move through the world, whether on the radio, in the movies, or on the elevated trains. Döblin's project is thus to show how literature might not just describe but reenact the experiential effects of moving pictures and sound recordings.

In late September 1929, the Prussian Academy of Art and the Reichsrundfunkgesellschaft cosponsored a conference in the city of Kassel under the title "Poetry and Radio." Döblin delivered the opening address in his capacity as a member of the Academy's "Section for Poetic Art" (Sektion für Dichtkunst).[8] Döblin began by examining the formal characteristics of both radio and literature in order to assess their compatibility. Specifically, he asked whether it was possible to transpose literature into the medium of radio. That is, can one move literature from the printed page to the broadcast booth? His short answer was no. He insisted that radio is not merely a new technical means of transmission but also, at least as far as literature is concerned, "a transforming medium."[9] Döblin described radio as fundamentally an acoustic instrument capable of transmitting sounds, words, and tones to an indeterminate number of people simultaneously. Literature, on the other hand, he characterized as follows: "The majority of our literature is governed by press-type, and—we want to underscore this—the organ through which this literature crowds into our head is the eyes. . . . Literature is constructed through language, which in itself, is still an acoustic element. If since the invention of the printing press literature has progressively become a mute region, this is not necessarily a benefit. Indeed, it is most definitely a drawback for literature and for language. Simply put, typography or press-type has transformed literature and all of us in an unnatural manner into mutes."[10] For this reason Döblin concludes, "Our contemporary novel has been bred from the design of the book."[11] Traditional literary genres such as the epic, the novel, drama, and poetry are therefore not immediately suitable for radio because they are inseparable from their specific means of production and reception. For example, the drama consists of both acoustic and visual elements; poetry is informed not only by the meanings and sounds of words but how they have been arranged on the page. Verbal texts are not transparent and transcendent carriers of meaning but are tied to the technology of the letter.

Two points in Döblin's lecture are particularly illuminating for my argument. First, Döblin emphatically stresses the idea that media differ in how they select, combine, and transmit data and in how data are received from each. Literature, radio, and film are thus not interchangeable. They operate according to different standards, both in terms of their production and their reception. Döblin's call for a cinema-style should therefore not be confused with an imitation of film per se. Rather what Döblin in effect lays out are the technological thresholds that distinguish one medium from the other. The expanding variety of media that make up the mediascape at the beginning of the century are only partially connected. Furthermore, in positing radio as a new medium that is both separate and distinct from a printed text, Döblin is able to distinguish what a printed text *cannot* do. Without speaking, the reader of the book encounters the text in isolation. And this very recognition of literature as silent—not simply the muteness of the text, but also its dematerialization—is the result of something else having started "speaking." Literature, radio, and film are therefore not merely different, but competing media. The emergence of mechanical media for the distribution and reproduction of visual and acoustic effects results in radical shifts in the production, recording, and transmission of knowledge in general. These alternate media effectively break writing's monopoly and reveal writing precisely as a particular medium and not the universal medium it was once considered to be (which is to say, not a medium at all).

Once technical media are able to fix nonlinguistic data flows, alternate information systems and networks are revealed. In its encounter with other media, the technology of the text and literary discourse is thereby altered.

The issues that Döblin raised in his lectures and essays published shortly after the turn of the century and throughout the 1920s concerning the conflictual relationship between literature and other media, especially how literature could record the effects of new media through a reorganization of models of literary language, are put into practice in his novel *Berlin Alexanderplatz: The Story of Franz Biberkopf* (1929). In what follows, I explore the degree to which Döblin's perception of twentieth-century literature, and more specifically the novel, is a response to the status of literature in its relatively new position as a competitor with other, mechanical media, mainly radio and film. Seen in this context, Döblin's *Berlin Alexanderplatz* investigates how the novel, or the medium of print more generally, could register the emergence of these new media. New formal strategies enable an expansion of the possibilities of recording in the medium of print both the alternate modes of perception that these other media have opened up and the consequent shift in the experience of reality.[12] In this manner Döblin's novel neither rejects nor offers an alternative to new media, but accepts them and uses the larger mediascape to record modern metropolitan experience.

LITERATURE OF ATTRACTIONS

Döblin's publisher refused to accept the original, abbreviated title submitted for the novel—*Berlin Alexanderplatz*—on the grounds that it named only a train station, thereby prompting the addition of the subtitle: *The Story of Franz Biberkopf*.[13] But why was this addition necessary? Why not use the name of a train station? As Döblin had already noted in "Der Geist des Naturalistischen Zeitalters" (The Spirit of the Naturalistic Age), published five years before *Berlin Alexanderplatz*: "It is, of course, utter nonsense these days to worship one of Phidias's columns and then to refer to the subway as a mere transport system."[14] In the collision, or at least uneasy alliance, between these two names, we note the confrontation of two different models or strategies of writing. If the text itself—with its stochastic collection of advertisements, newspaper articles, government documents, stock market figures, weather reports, scientific descriptions of the human anatomy, and more, interwoven with the thread of a story line tracing Biberkopf's actions over one year in Berlin—if this novel does not fit the traditional model of a linear, cohesive narrative, then at least the title will (and from the publisher's point of view, the book will have a better chance of selling, if people think they know what they are getting). Almost every emerging technology from the end of the nineteenth and the beginning of the twentieth centuries is accounted for in Döblin's massive novel. On the one hand, we read the naturalistic portrayal of one man's life in the exploding metropolis of Berlin. The banal plot of "The Story of Franz Biberkopf" is easily summarized. As the novel opens, Biberkopf has just left prison after a four-year incarceration for killing his fiancée. Over many hundreds of pages, this exhaustive and exhausting novel follows this man who has vowed to go straight, but who inevitably winds up again a petty criminal and a pimp, is run over by a car, loses the one "golden heart" in his life to a brutal murder committed by a psychopath, is committed to an insane asylum under false charges of having committed the murder himself, and finally comes to walk the streets again presumably a changed man. However, *Berlin Alexanderplatz* is not merely this story and this narrative, for its operating principle is one of information overload that exceeds the frame of a traditional narrative. By including countless passages that list streetcar routes, menus, advertising posters, the stock of a store, and the like, and juxtaposing a multiplicity of happenings and events, the novel exceeds the boundaries of traditional narrative and stands in marked contrast to the wholeness and harmony that function as the dominant normative criteria of narrative closure.

Perhaps the only thing that all readers of Döblin's *Berlin Alexanderplatz* appear to agree on is its unshakable position in the pantheon of German modernist texts and its preeminent status as a city novel.[15] At times it has been considered two separate and distinct works interleaved and placed in a single binding. As a result, the long tradition of criticism of this novel revolves around the question of the split title: Is this a novel about a location in the city, the Alexanderplatz in Berlin, or is this a novel about an individual person, Franz Biberkopf? And if the novel is primarily to be read as Biberkopf's story, then is this a traditional "novel of development" (*Entwicklungsroman*) or something else? One line of criticism ignores, for the most part, the "Berlin" half of the novel in favor of interpretations of the story of Franz Biberkopf. In these readings, Döblin has been interpreted as rejecting organized class conflict, presenting reactionary and counter-revolutionary arguments, foreshadowing the National Socialist takeover, and even, advocating a Christian worldview.[16] More commonly, however, the novel has been read as a dramatization of the conflict between the individual and the city.[17] This reading of man against metropolis easily slides, however, into a reinterpretation of the Biberkopf tale as an updated, urbanized *Bildungsroman*, nonetheless allied with traditional humanistic discourse.[18] Even when multiple levels of textual construction are acknowledged, the assumption of a model of human progress recoups the narrative chaos into a unified and contained work. We remember that we noted a similar move in the long line of readers of Rilke's work. The third line of criticism takes seriously the notion of a *Großstadtliteratur*, citing Döblin's novel as paradigmatic of the evolution of the city-novel from nineteenth-century descriptions of the city from a position of distance and objectivity (the city as backdrop for the protagonist's story) to a narrative form that parallels the presentation of the city itself (the city as protagonist).[19] Not simply shown a city, the reader experiences the text much as one would experience a city with its multitude of sensory stimulations, and the conflict between the individual and the city is reformulated as a discursive conflict. It is in this latter body of writing on Döblin's novel that his formal strategies are taken up most directly, particularly the "montage-text" through which the city is presented.[20] Indeed, *montage* is a term that seems to appear in almost every reading of *Berlin Alexanderplatz* after Walter Benjamin declared in 1930 that montage was its stylistic principle.[21] I have indulged in this overview not only because of the large amount of bookshelf space already devoted to Döblin but because these three disparate approaches all share a common assumption: literature and media (in this case, the city) are mutually exclusive realms, and it is this dichotomy that needs to be reassessed.

In "Krisis des Romans" (Crisis of the Novel), Benjamin favorably compared Döblin, whom he called an "epic writer," to traditional novelists. He begins the essay with an analogy: the novelist (Benjamin's counterexample for Döblin's work is André Gide's *Les faux-monnayeurs*) journeys out alone on the sea, whereas the epic writer stays on the shore and collects whatever the tide washes up. As a result, the work of a novelist like Gide is "pure interior, knows no exterior, and is therefore the opposite pole of a purely epic style, which is storytelling. Gide's ideal novel is—and this is where he shows himself in stark contrast to Döblin—the pure writerly-novel."[22] *Les faux-monnayeurs* is the epitome of a self-reflexive writing with its fictional character's journal about a novel he is writing (likewise titled *Les faux-monnayeurs*), accompanied by Gide's own journal entries during the composition of the novel. Gide's novel is an extended meditation on its own means of novelistic production. Döblin's novel will, in a sense, be no less self-reflexive; however, it raises the question: What happens when the novel does not merely present itself as a novel, but as a transportation system, or as a film, or as a newspaper, a telegram, or a radio program? In other words, what happens when the novel records the mechanical penetration of reality, and how the urban public knows and perceives the world? According to Benjamin, Döblin "explodes" the framework of the novel:

> The stylistic principle of this book is montage. Petit-bourgeois printed matter, scandals, misfortunes, the sensations of '28, folk songs, advertisements rain down in this text. Montage explodes the "novel," explodes its construction as well as its style, and opens new, very epic possibilities. Formally, above all. The material of montage is by no means arbitrary. True montage depends on the document. In its fanatical battle against the work of art, Dada used montage to turn everyday life into an ally. They were the first, even if with some uncertainty, to proclaim the autonomy of the authentic. In its best moments, film offers to habituate us to it. Here, montage is for the first time used to the advantage of the epic. Through the various Bible verses, statistics, and hit songs, Döblin confers authority on the epic proceedings. They correspond to the formulaic epithets of the ancient epic.[23]

Benjamin's phrase "explodes the 'novel'" (sprengt den "Roman") immediately associates Döblin's novel with cinema by recalling earlier essays in which Benjamin described film in precisely the same terms: "Having discovered the dynamite of tenths of a second, film exploded [*sprengt*] this old world of incarceration, leading us into adventurous journeys among the scattered ruins."[24] Among the similarly scattered ruins of the traditional novel, Döblin leads his readers on an adventurous journey that is wholly exteriorized to produce psychic effects in the reader that mimic the experiences of walking through the metropolis and watching a movie. Just as film does, Döblin's novel trains the sensorium of its readers to parry the shocks of the metropolis.[25] For as Benjamin is quick to assert, the montage cells of Döblin's novel are by no means arbitrary (nor could they be and still appropriately be termed montage); they collect and record the multiplicity of events assaulting the urban sensorium. Benjamin is the first (and perhaps only) critic to articulate why this allusion to an extraliterary medium was not merely a stylistic whim or a one-off trick, but a *necessary* condition for a work presenting the twentieth-century metropolis.

As a text, Döblin's work has less affinity with the novel than it does with the arresting posters and continually updated notices that blanketed the city of Berlin. Norbert Bolz provides us with a provocative description of this newspaper city: "The textual environments of this poster world are constantly changing and confer on the physiognomy of the city the character of a newspaper page proof."[26] In the mid-1920s, over four thousand titles, including daily newspapers, tabloids, weeklies, journals, and illustrated magazines, were published on a regular basis in Germany. Berlin alone had forty-five morning papers, two midday papers, and fourteen evening papers.[27] And the pages of Döblin's original manuscript of *Berlin Alexanderplatz* imitate this pasted-up look: paragraphs and headlines of newspapers were literally cut out of the dailies and pasted in between the lines of his own handwritten text like a dadaist collage.[28] To some extent, however, the typeset text of the book copy is the more provocative, for in the handwritten manuscript one can easily discriminate between the lines Döblin wrote himself (i.e., the fictional narrative) and the texts that he collected and recorded throughout the work (i.e., the authentic documents of the city). With the visual distinction erased, the source of every line is in dispute, and as a result all are potentially material artifacts and not the product of a unified and isolated authorial imagination. As Döblin himself admitted: "It has happened to me, as I was writing this or that historical book, that I could barely stop myself from copying entire documents, indeed sometimes I collapsed amongst the files in awe and said to myself: I cannot do it any better."[29]

Döblin's response to Benjamin's review, "Krise des Romans?" (Crisis of the Novel?), makes clear that the author's use of a cinema-style or literary montage is a necessary counterstrategy to the crisis provoked by the incompatibility between the nineteenth-century novel and modern life:

> A small number of authors are particularly sensitive; they have their specialties, like a marked enthusiasm for nature or a predilection for technology, a predilection for the social, a predilection for the spiritual. They hoard information and impressions from the outside world, and bring them into the novel. This kind of novel has indeed a different face from the commercial novel. But it has remained the same old novel. The gentlemen are stuck. They have something to say, but pour it into the old mold. They are afflicted: they don't even like the old mold for the most part, but what to do?[30]

This so-called crisis produces questions like: Is the novel still a novel? Is it still possible to write novels in our time? However, this theme and its attendant questions are premised on the illusion that the novel, or indeed writing, is unaffected by the evolution of other media that represent the world in a radically different way. With the invention of mechanical, that is, non-print media, one can begin to record unwritable data flows of sounds and images, thereby revealing the spaces or the gaps in which writing is silent. If all experience is mediated, then new channels alter the perception of reality. This is to say, and one must be explicit here, that Döblin does not draw on cinematic (and other technical) motifs simply to imitate a growing popular medium of expression, but rather to effect a much-needed change in the character of print as a medium. For this reason, the filmic qualities of Döblin's text have everything to do with the status of writing and very little to do with the creation of a film per se. In formulating this complex idea, one must take seriously the critical disaster of the film adaptation of *Berlin Alexanderplatz* that Döblin produced shortly after the appearance of the novel (a point to which I will return at the conclusion of this chapter). A radio play based on the novel was likewise disappointing.[31] Döblin was very much concerned with the role of new media in changing literary aesthetics and promoting new modes of textual representation; he remained, however, a "producer of writing" (*Schriftsteller*).

Berlin Alexanderplatz has been compared to film since the earliest reviews of the novel: "Everything arranges itself into a sparkling, flickering film strip, into the word-film *Berlin Alexanderplatz*"; "It is truly a film that flows by"; and "Döblin's technique comes from the cinema."[32] In these descriptions, film functions as an analogy or a metaphor that proves useful in describing the formal qualities of a text for which no literary terminology quite seems to apply. This idea of a word-film reaches something of a high point with Ekkehard Kaemmerling's study comparing specific passages of the novel with specific cinematic techniques such as close-up, slow motion, and montage.[33] What Kaemmerling fails to discuss, however, is why Döblin, who twice had published critical pieces *against* film, may have been so influenced by film technology for reasons other than its general pervasiveness in the cultural milieu at the time. While many critics are quick to refer to film or to terminology drawn from film theory with regard to Döblin, very little if any account is taken of how this adoption of alternative media strategies reflects profound changes in the theorization and production of the literary text. It is not necessary (or even possible) to consider Döblin's novel, or even his theory of the novel, as an attempt to translate the text into film or even radio—and this despite (or rather, as evidenced by) the radio play and film of *Berlin Alexanderplatz* that Döblin was involved in within two years of the novel's publication. Indeed like so many readings that analyze the formal solutions the text advances, critics have failed to address Döblin's arguments that representation of the modern metropolis cannot be accomplished through traditional narrative means. The temporal and spatial disturbances brought on by the experience of urban life are increasingly conceived in terms of radically different categories of representation introduced by nonprint media.[34] For this reason, in so much of the writing of the period, we find a conflation of modernity, film, and the city.

In "The Work of Art in the Age of Mechanical Reproduction," Walter Benjamin claimed: "During long periods of history, the mode of human sense perception changes with humanity's entire mode of existence. The manner in which human sense perception is organized, the medium in which it is accomplished, is determined not only by nature but by historical circumstances as well."[35] As human existence was increasingly mechanized at the turn of the century as a result of industrialization, rapid transit, and the growth of cities, as well as the proliferation of newspapers, sound recordings, and film, fundamental questions concerning human identity, subjectivity, and memory were posed as we saw earlier in our analysis of Rilke, and uncertainty was introduced on the distinction between so-called objective and constructed reality as we saw in the screenplays from the *Kinobuch*. As Hermann Kienzl, a composer and music critic, wrote in 1910: "The psychology of the cinematic triumph is metropolitan psychology. Not only because the metropolis constitutes the natural focal point for all radiations of social life, but especially because the metropolitan soul—that always hurried soul, curious and unanchored, tumbling from fleeting impression to fleeting impression—is also the soul of cinematography."[36] Döblin likewise was interested in the relationship between modern technology and human experience: "Physiologically, other organs and areas of the brain are employed in the new epoch. The exhausted, old parts are recovering. Muscles, eyes, ears, and their nervous-psychic projections move into the foreground. One wants to move, see, hear. Previously, one poured out one's energies only occasionally in times of war; now there is technology: that is a constant state of war, a permanent conquest of the world which is indeed without limits."[37] The human subject continuously engages technology in an attempt to comprehend the world, but this is not the only battle being waged. The various media at one's disposal to comprehend that reality also come into conflict.

Early twentieth-century technologies are often evoked as paradigmatic of modernity because of their presentation of speed, motion, and simultaneity, and the privileging of visual perception. As Kienzl wrote, the "metropolitan soul" is the "soul of cinematography," at least since the unique properties of cinema were, by the 1920s, definitively associated with montage and cutting, or what Kienzl described as "tumbling from fleeting impression to fleeting impression." But to what extent is the metropolitan soul the soul of literature? In a short review of James Joyce's novel *Ulysses*, Döblin identified the crisis of the contemporary novel in his contemporaries' inability to keep pace with the reorganization of human sense perception:

> One has to know that art forms are systematically related to a particular manner of thinking and a general existential milieu. That is why forms are constantly superseded. . . . Cinema has penetrated the sphere of literature; newspapers have matured and are the most important and most broadly disseminated forms of print, everyone's daily bread. The experience of people today is governed by the street, the scenes changing by the second, the signboards, automobile traffic. . . . The predilection for fabulation and its constructions come across as naive. This is the core of the so-called crisis of today's novel. The mentality of the authors has not adapted itself to the age.[38]

Döblin's rejection of "fabulation" is consistent with a later statement in the article "Literatur und Rundfunk" (Literature and Radio), in which he similarly criticizes literature that has been "written for its inner meaning."[39] The sense impressions of the street, with its changing scenes, merchant signs, crowds, and traffic profoundly alter the relationship of the individual both to one's environment and to the apparatus of one's own consciousness, to the extent that it may no longer even be possible to speak of the "inner" self as unified and harmonious and the text can no longer function as a continuous exterior translation of the non-material imagination. According to Döblin, any attempts are naive or childish and only further reduce the relevance of literature. This is why new strategies must be devised. In this media war, the novel itself undergoes a change, and Joyce's realization of this situation explains Döblin's positive response to his work: "[*Ulysses*] attempts in its own way to answer the question: How can one still write literature?"[40] Döblin recognizes and affirms that the author produces texts and the public reads them in a mechanical age quite different from his predecessors. Therefore, the medium of the novel must likewise change in order to incorporate that reality shift and the temporal and spatial confusion of these new perceptual modes. In these essays, Döblin declares the "material link between technical standards, changes in apperception, and media theory."[41]

In his work on the early relationship between film and literature in Germany, Anton Kaes outlines three major phases of development, corresponding approximately to the first three decades of film technology.[42] In the first phase, inaugurated with the first public screenings of moving pictures, film was considered a technical curiosity. Most literary figures hardly concerned themselves with the new medium, and writing on film was for the most part either directed toward a technical audience or addressed its novelty. With the emergence of permanent theaters and the improvement of recording and projection techniques, however, the second decade in film history is marked by the growing competitive relationship between the cinema, on the one side, and mainstream literature and theater on the other, a conflict that was explored in detail in the previous chapter. During this period, traditional theater owners experienced a marked decline in ticket sales and therefore considered cinema a threat to their livelihood. On the other hand, film adaptations of literary classics became increasingly popular during this period as did screenplay collaborations among literary authors, and in 1912, the Verein deutscher Schriftsteller (Association of German Writers) openly acknowledged the interaction of literary art and the film industry.[43] Paradoxically, however, the so-called literary ambitions of film incited increasing criticism of film as inferior to the traditional arts. The 1920s finally ushered in a third phase in which the nonliterary origins of film were increasingly recognized. It is in this last phase that we find an increasing body of work in which filmmakers and film enthusiasts attempt to formulate an ontology specific to the cinematic medium (although as was noted previously, Pinthus's theory of film predates this period by some ten years). Prominent names here include, although are not limited to, Rudolf Arnheim, Béla Balázs, Siegfried Kracauer, and Sergei Eisenstein. With this emphasis on the unique possibilities of the film medium, some members of the intellectual elite reject the characterization of film as parasitic and inferior to established art forms.

I want to review briefly some of this film discourse, especially Eisenstein's work, in order to readdress Döblin's so-called literary imitation of film, for it seems to me that many of the critics who speak of cinematic devices (such as montage) in the novel fail to elaborate on the use of the terminology within the emerging film theory of the period. With respect to Döblin, "montage" is usually employed to refer very broadly to the juxtaposition of various scenes and a general sense of linguistic chaos. This is perhaps because most readings of *Berlin Alexanderplatz* restrict themselves to the novel, with only passing reference to Döblin's advocacy of a *Kinostil*. However, from Döblin's essays, as we have seen, one can indeed specify how this term, montage, should more appropriately be used in conjunction with the novel. *Berlin Alexanderplatz* was not Döblin's first attempt at a cinema-style, and he authored two screenplays before (and six after) the publication of the novel.[44] This novel is not some instantiation of a "film-novel" (whatever that might be), but part of a larger and more far-reaching project involving the repositioning of literature within the larger mediascape. It is imperative that one examine closely Döblin's earlier texts, particularly his essays that both directly and indirectly address the question of new media, in order to understand how these ideas are worked out and refined in *Berlin Alexanderplatz*. First, however, I want to turn to Eisenstein's description of montage, for it is through a similar reconceptualization of the construction of the work that Döblin radically alters traditional notions of representation and representability.

As my brief description and synopsis of *Berlin Alexanderplatz* and Benjamin's own description of the novel make clear, Döblin eschewed the use of traditional narrative when writing his novel. Döblin's literary cinema-style is essentially a rejection of the relentless forward progression of plot in favor of montage (a word he never used explicitly): "The novel has nothing to do with plot.... The epic writer is not concerned with simplifying or with beating or trimming the text into shape for the sake of plot. The novel layers, piles up, turns over, pushes; in today's drama, reduced to mere plot, the motto is 'Onward!' The slogan of the novel is never 'forward.'"[45] Döblin's characterization of his novelistic style is remarkably similar to Eisenstein's concept of a "montage of attractions," which he developed in order to create a new mode of artistic (specifically, theatrical) presentation outside naturalistic and mimetic representation. According to Eisenstein, the montage of attractions "liberates film from the plot-based script and for the first time takes account of film material, both thematically and formally, in the construction."[46] Rather than being absorbed into illusory depictions, the spectator is subject to the sensual and psychological impacts of events occurring before one's eyes.

> An attraction ... is in our understanding any demonstrable fact (an action, an object, a phenomenon, a conscious combination, and so on) that is known and proven to exercise a definite effect on the attention and emotions of the audience and that, combined with others, possesses the characteristic of concentrating the audience's emotions in

any direction dictated by the production's purpose. For this point of view a film cannot be a simple presentation or demonstration of events: rather it must be a tendentious selection of, and comparison between, events, free from narrowly plot-related plans and moulding the audience in accordance with its purpose.[47]

The attraction is thus wholly directed to the reaction of the audience; it is an event, not a theme. Although the attraction may evoke a psychological reaction, it does not present a psychological problem as an end in and of itself.

Eisenstein insists on the critical distinction between a conception of montage as what drives the plot forward and montage as an event producing conflict. It is only in the second sense that "montage" distinguishes film as a medium. Indeed, it is the "nerve of film."[48] Whereas "cinema," for Eisenstein, refers to the film studio, the production costs, the movie stars, and the movie's plot, "cinematography" is distinguished first and foremost by montage.[49] At the most general level, montage refers to the juxtaposition or the superimposition (Eisenstein's preferred term) of separate shots to present a single image, movement, or idea. Eisenstein was clear to distinguish himself on this point from his contemporary Vsevolod Pudovkin by specifying how montage functions. For Eisenstein, it is false to consider montage a way to describe an event and as achieved simply by assembling single shots one after another like building-blocks; nor is montage the mere linkage of individual pieces in the progressive unfolding of an idea. Rather for Eisenstein, montage is always marked by collision and conflict between elements, and this within a single shot (a montage cell) or between successive shots:

> What then characterises montage and, consequently, its embryo, the shot? Collision. Conflict between two neighbouring fragments. Conflict. Collision.
>
> Before me lies a crumpled yellowing sheet of paper.
>
> On it there is a mysterious note:
>
> "Series—P[udovkin]" and "Collision—E[isenstein]."
>
> We have already got into a habit: at regular intervals he comes to see me late at night and, behind closed doors, we wrangle over matters of principle.
>
> So it is in this instance. A graduate of the Kuleshov school, he zealously defends the concepts of montage as a *series* of fragments. In a chain. "Bricks." Bricks that *expound* an idea serially.

> I opposed him with my view of montage as a *collision*, my view that the collision of two factors gives rise to an idea.
>
> In my view a *series* is merely one possible *particular* case.[50]

For Eisenstein, montage is a way of representing that which cannot be represented (i.e., something that cannot be graphically depicted). He demonstrates this with examples of Japanese ideograms, in which two or more individual hieroglyphs are combined to represent something that cannot itself be rendered graphically: water and an eye to signify "to weep"; a dog and a mouth to signify "to bark." In their juxtaposition the symbols produce a concept (or in the case of film, a psychic effect) that is of another order than a simple addition of the two individual components.

In Eisenstein's use of montage, cinematic signifiers are no longer bound to the narration of stories and the creation of a closed diegetic universe. The specific stylistic devices and formal qualities of this cinema are instead exhibitionistic; they stimulate shock and surprise directly. This cinema "expends little energy creating characters with psychic motivations. . . . Energy moves outward towards an acknowledged spectator rather than inward towards character-based situations essential to classical narrative."[51] Döblin describes the effect of his techniques of literary montage in very similar terms: "This outpouring before our eyes has the added benefit that it uniformly and simultaneously leads the author and audience from surprise to surprise and without constraint from thrill to thrill. It has the benefit that every situation effortlessly gives birth to the next."[52] Döblin's "Der Bau des epischen Werks" (The Construction of the Epic Work), from which the statement is taken, was published four months before *Berlin Alexanderplatz* and can be read as a metacommentary on the novel's form and a barometer of his artistic concerns at the time. Döblin speaks about the text by referring to its visual and presentational characteristics, qualities not usually associated with print. In this essay and others of the period, he attempts to formulate a theory of how language, and more specifically its use in the novel, could produce the same effects on the reader as the technical medium with which it is compared. The novel includes a brief preface that is punctuated by references to conflict and collision: "Three times this thing crashes against our man, disturbing his scheme of life. It rushes at him with cheating and fraud. . . . Finally it torpedoes him with huge and monstrous savagery."[53] This introduction, in a sense, programs the reader on how the novel is to be read: a montage of collisions, shocks, and cuts.

Döblin's writings on film date from a short article titled "Das Theater der kleinen Leute" (Ordinary People's Theater), published in December 1910, in *Das Theater*.[54] In it Döblin makes it clear that his appreciation for specific technical aspects of new media like film should not be mistaken for unequivocal praise, for he takes a rather dim view of cinema, or at least the film industry as an institution, although not without humor: cinema, he proposes, might provide at least the cure for alcoholism and cirrhosis of the liver. Ironically, even while denigrating cinema, the essay already exhibits some of the qualities of the *Kinostil* Döblin will later advocate in the "Berliner Programm": visual detail, fleeting physical descriptions, and verbs of quick motion. Indeed, the centerpiece of the essay functions almost as a film within a film as the description of individual members of the audience abruptly shifts to the film screen and back again.[55] "Inside in the pitch-black, cramped room, a rectangular screen as tall as a man shines over a monster of an audience, over a crowd bewitched by this white eye with its fixed gaze."[56] In this depiction, the eye of the screen and the fixed stare of the members of the audience are fused—a condition that Marshall McLuhan called sensory extension and that Friedrich Kittler described as a projection of the central nervous system. What was once theorized as the interior soul or spirit of the individual is radically externalized as material visions, much as Hofmannsthal later argues in "The Substitute for Dreams." What is therefore significant about Döblin's formulation in "Ordinary People's Theater" is not whether he approves or disapproves of film, but more radically, how he thinks film changes the terms of representation more generally.

In Döblin's formulation, a literary *Kinostil* is marked by specific traits closely allied with the formal qualities of the film essay of 1910 and reiterated in the "Berliner Programm" manifesto of 1913: the dissolution of the inner self or unified subject, the rejection of a linear plot in favor of a montage-like text, and the inclusion of actual documents or preexisting material within the text (the 1910 essay, for example, reproduces copy from a theater program). In the "Berliner Programm," Döblin roundly criticized his contemporaries for (among other things) the overpsychologization of the novel and the "inwardness" of their prose. In his view concepts like "anger," "love," and "contempt" are nothing more than linguistic conveniences, "primitive and tasteless bunches of letters" that in the final analysis tell us nothing at all.[57] For Döblin, the subject matter of the novel should be precisely that rendered by the screen:

"a reality without a soul [*entseelte Realität*]."⁵⁸ The novelist should draw from external, documentable facts, and material elements, not interior fabulations. Döblin ultimately insists that a properly modern art is one that is hybrid: "Fantasy of fact! The novel must go through a rebirth as work of art and modern epic."⁵⁹

A provocative example of Döblin's manifesto is a short story published three years before *Berlin Alexanderplatz*. The story, "Die Zeitlupe" (Slow-Motion), was Döblin's contribution to a thought experiment posed by the editorial staff of the *Vossische Zeitung*. Six established authors were asked to address this cinematic special effect of slow motion photography either "lyrically, novelistically, dramatically, or philosophically."⁶⁰ Döblin's story dramatizes events that occur when a camera that records (and replays) actions in slow motion falls into the wrong hands. A baboon at the zoo first picks up the apparatus after a professor who has visited inside the cage inadvertently leaves it behind. With one eye peering through the lens of the device, the animal sees the two men again moving slowly through the cage although they remain permanently out of his grasp; with his other eye (another split screen) the animal contemplates the contradiction of the (in reality) empty cage. The zookeeper wrests the camera from the animal, only to likewise relive the baboon lunging for him at an excruciating pace. Next, the instrument is inadvertently given to the wrong man in a crowded bar who lifts it to his eyes while helping his wife on with her coat; he spends the next four hours reliving the act of reaching to arrange her collar. Finally he is escorted home, only to discover that his angry wife has spent the interim sleeping with his best friend. When she holds the device up to her own eyes, she repeatedly witnesses her husband's agonizing and pleading stare. The professor of the first scene finally arrives to reclaim the camera and laughs at how easily they had been duped by the manipulation of space and time: You can see your great-grandmother at her wedding, he cries, or turn it around and your children will come tumbling out the other end.

Döblin's story reads like a bit of early slapstick. The prose moves rapidly, cutting between distinct scenes and various visual and temporal levels. There is very little dialogue, only sporadic exclamations typical of intertitles in a silent film. It reveals his fascination with cinematic devices and particularly the manner in which time and space are radically reorganized. The characters are totally taken in by the visual illusion, which overwhelms their other sensory capacities. They could not have been more frightened if they had seen a ghost, for this is a rearrangement of reality itself. Because of the use of the split screen, the image is contiguous with reality and not merely a representation in which one could easily distinguish between the two. Movement is presented as fantasy; however, this is no false image, as irrational as it may appear to a consciousness unprepared for this level of apprehension. The baboon, who first seizes the camera, is perhaps most aware of this split. Because of his large facial features, one eye views the image presented by the slow-motion device, while the other still gazes around at the "reality" of the empty cage.

One is reminded here of Benjamin's comments in the "Artwork" essay when he describes the unique quality of film as the "equipment-free aspect of reality": "In the studio the mechanical equipment has penetrated so deeply into reality that its pure aspect freed from the foreign substance of equipment is the result of a special procedure, namely, the shooting by the specially adjusted camera and the mounting of the shot together with other similar ones."[61] Paradoxically, the scene that is most penetrated by the technological apparatus (in the form of deliberate cinematography and editing decisions) appears to the spectator as the least mediated. In other words, reality and its illusion, or the duplication of reality, correspond so closely that one can no longer distinguish the one from the other. Surely this is already what Döblin had in mind when he called for "fantasy of fact" (*Tatsachenphantasie*) when referring to his own proposed cinema-style. To achieve this result, and in an inversion of Paul Wegener's mandate, Döblin puts the poet in the place of the camera, comparing the technician of the print medium to contemporary technological developments in film and television: "*The true poet was always himself a fact.* The poet must demonstrate and prove that he is a fact and a piece of reality and as good and factual as the great inventions of the 'Triergon' or the 'Karolus-Zelle.'"[62] In other words, the epic novelist should record reality in a manner analogous to that afforded by recent developments in sound recording in film and image transmission in television.[63] The cinematic effects described by Benjamin have repercussions beyond the immediate audience in the theater and go to the core of Döblin's formulation of literary representation itself.

Döblin's *Tatsachenphantasie* is more fully developed in the 1929 essay on the epic novel, "Construction of the Epic Work." He begins by comparing a passage from Arthur Schnitzler's novel *Therese: Chronik eines Frauenlebens* (1928) with an extract from a newspaper page. Schnitzler's prose describes a family sitting down to breakfast in their rented house in the countryside; the newspaper report describes a motorcycle accident in the city and details the riders' injuries. Döblin contrasts these two texts in order to introduce several essential points about the epic novel: its formal structure, its content, and its relationship to time. Although both Schnitzler's text and the newspaper are described as "reports" (*Berichte*), the newspaper text is an *actual* report of actual events whereas the novel only *imitates* a report. Therefore they differ in their respective relationships to reality, and it is, above all else, the epic author's task to construct reality, even though he may still be writing fiction. "I do not need to point out that the achievement of this exemplary and simple sphere distinguishes the epic artist from the writer of novels for whom writing is a solid bourgeois, useful, commercial pursuit. The novelist imitates some of the superficialities of reality without penetrating or even piercing reality. The truly productive one must, however, take two steps: he must approach reality very closely, its materiality, its blood, its odor, and then he must pierce it, that is his specific task."[64] Unlike the novelist the epic writer does not merely imitate reality, he simulates it—the world is not represented, but presented. Again, Benjamin's "Artwork" essay proves helpful in clarifying this distinction, specifically when he contrasts the painter's method with that of the cameraman: "The painter maintains in his work a natural distance from reality, the cameraman penetrates deeply into its web. There is a tremendous difference between the pictures they obtain. That of the painter is a total one, that of the camera man consists of multiple fragments which are assembled under a new law."[65] This new law is one of simulation as opposed to imitation, and its effects directly impact the perceptions of the spectator. This is manifested, for example, in a particular temporal order. In the two quotations that Döblin compares at the outset of his essay, both Schnitzler's novel and the newspaper article are written in the past tense; however, Döblin asserts that they have a different relationship to time—the novel narrates or represents past and complete events as passed; the newspaper and the epic present events (no matter the choice of verb tense) as occurring in real time: "The epic does not narrate something as past [*Vergangenes*], but rather presents [*stellt dar*]."[66] *Darstellen* literally means "places before" or shows. Further: "All epic works are concerned with developments and events, and thus it is appropriate that the epic report is not submitted as something finished, whizzing by as if shot out of a pistol, instead the reader experiences it *in statu nascendi*."[67] The epic does not synthesize or distill events, but offers the event itself as simulated present.

A conception of film as a medium that makes present and simulates, rather than represents or narrates, goes back to a tradition of film theory found initially in the work of Hugo Münsterberg and reiterated to some extent in the writings of Béla Balázs. Munsterberg, a psychologist and philosopher by training, published *The Photoplay* in 1916, one of the first attempts to establish a major film theory that distinguished film from the traditional arts. Because film employs the "scientific principle" by which "isolated pictures presented to the eye in rapid succession but separated by interruptions are perceived not as single impressions of different position, but as a continuous movement," film is directly linked to the active powers of the mind that make sense out of distinct stimuli.[68] According to Münsterberg, the mind resolves the chaos of undistinguished stimuli into a virtual world of objects, events, and emotions in which each of us lives. Film records this process or the neurological data flow itself, and presents spectators with their own processes of perception. For in Münsterberg's view film does not exist on celluloid as such, or even on the screen, but only in the mind that actualizes it by conferring movement, attention, memory, imagination, and emotion on a dead series of shadows. Moving pictures are realized as processes of the imagination. And if reality is characterized by the primary orders of time, space, and causality, then these are precisely the categories of experience that the filmmaker is able to displace through the use of editing techniques.

Balázs addresses a similar point in his *Theory of the Film* (1930) when he distinguishes between film as mere photographed theater and film as art. In the former, the spectator sees the enacted scene as a whole in space: the stage is at a fixed distance and the angle of vision does not change. However, in the latter, the distance between spectator and image varies within the same scene, the once integral picture is divided into shots, and the angle, perspective, and focus of the shot constantly changes. This is why montage is so fundamental to those films which Balázs considers art.[69] As a result, we see things on the film screen that one could never have seen in the studio while the film was being made, which means that cinematic effects are produced on celluloid and in the act of projection. In this way, the film does not reproduce but actually produces an event. Or as Balázs put it: "There is no original to reproduce in this phase of film creation, not even as much as the painter has in his model. Montage, the mobile architecture of the film's picture-material, is a specific, new creative art.... Pictures have no tenses. They show only the present—they cannot express either a past or a future tense."[70] As Döblin wished for his epic novel, one experiences them *in statu nascendi*.

Ample evidence exists of Döblin's active engagement with the film industry. Between 1920 and 1935, Döblin wrote three original screenplays and cowrote the screenplay for *Berlin Alexanderplatz* with Hans Wilhelm. (The *Alexanderplatz* screenplay will be discussed at length later.) During World War

II, Döblin and his wife emigrated to the United States where he worked as a scriptwriter for Metro-Goldwyn-Mayer for approximately one year.[71] While at MGM, Döblin participated in the development of six screenplay ideas, two of which became full-length scripts and were eventually produced and distributed (although Döblin's name does not appear in the credits).[72] With the exception of the screenplay for *Berlin Alexanderplatz*, Döblin's "Die geweihten Töchter" (The Consecrated Daughters) is the most complete of his works in this genre. (Some of his screenplays consist of little more than an outline.) The screenplay was composed in 1920, and is written in five acts, with a total of ninety-one individual scenes, plus introductory comments and a brief summary of the film's story. The film was never produced. Briefly, the film portrays a count who returns to his homeland with his daughter. Through a series of flashbacks we learn that the count had raped the child's mother, who stabbed herself after the child was born. Back in his native town, the count imagines that he sees the devil everywhere among the perpetual partygoers and revelers. He seeks help from a group of nuns (the *geweihten Töchter* of the title); however, the citizens of the town have mobilized the police against them. In the final battle between the townspeople's debauchery and the pure love of the nuns, the daughter (who has in the meantime joined the sisterhood) is killed and her father takes up the torch to continue her fight. Although the story itself is highly melodramatic and the screenplay perhaps uninteresting in and of itself, read within the context of Döblin's later novelistic output and his specific remarks on the film medium, the document proves extremely valuable.

Döblin's introductory remarks to the screenplay (published along with approximately one-quarter of the film's scenes in *Das Dreieck* in 1924) reveal what he considered the two most important, interrelated elements of the film medium: the editing process and the uniquely visual qualities of the medium. "As a general rule, the random flow of scenes will be avoided. Groups of scenes will be constructed like a chapter of a novel and individual passages. A film sequence is a particular piece of the story; transformations connect the scenes. When the scene changes, the milieu or individual plot supports dissolve or disappear on the film strip; the leading figure or figures carry over throughout the entire cut."[73] And: "The principle of film: the absence or a minimum of words. In this film, there are a total of two phrases and two titles. Totally optical thinking and fantasy—not, however, in the sense that the fundamental psychic processes are left to the gestural delivery of the actors—rather a truly optical expression which makes use of the inherent properties of optical fantasy."[74] Döblin emphasizes here that the shots will be assembled to produce a particular effect; they will not merely be strung along in a stream of images that enhance the plot. The organizational principle of the film is montage. Further, Döblin clarifies what he means by "optical thinking" or "optical fantasy," a phrase that also appeared in the "Berliner Programm." It is not merely the absence of words (although this is a common criticism of film at the time), nor is it merely an emphasis on the rich imagery or pantomime of individual shots. More important, Döblin emphasizes here that optical thinking and optical fantasy refer to the psychic effects produced by the way the film is edited. Montage does not refer to the simple flow of images, but is the conscious product of two images that have been deliberately juxtaposed.

Die geweihten Töchter is marked by a number of optical curiosities that demonstrate how these ideas would be carried out in practice. For example, in the first scene the count stands in the waiting room of a government minister; this shot dissolves into a shot of the count standing inside the minister's office. The count remains in the same position, only the scenery around him changes. Further, Döblin makes extensive use of close-ups and cuts to symbolic imagery such as flowers or fire. Döblin even devises a film within the film, when he splits the screen so that the "actual" events occur on one half of the screen, and fantasy or surreal imaginings are projected on the other half. For example, while riding in a train compartment, the count stares across at the blank wall facing him. Onto this wall the count's fantasies of his daughter's mother are projected and then fade again. Through the use of this film within a film, Döblin reveals the workings of the medium itself. In addition, he reveals some of the techniques he will employ when he begins composing *Berlin Alexanderplatz* a few years later. When *Die literarische Welt* republished scenes from *Die geweihten Töchter* in 1930, the accompanying editorial remarks read: "Alfred Döblin once wrote a screenplay that was never produced. We are publishing some of the scenes here, primarily because of Döblin's remarkable image-based association technique . . . whose irrational loose linkages suggest a preliminary stage of the technique of the *Alexanderplatz*."[75]

TEXTUAL VELOCITIES

In his review of Döblin's "Die Ermordung einer Butterblume," Joseph Adler compared the text not only to film, but also to accelerated forms of modern transportation. How do transportation systems function like a medium through which the subject relates to one's environment? Forms of urban transportation and mechanized movement are foregrounded throughout *Berlin Alexanderplatz* (beginning of course with the title itself). Indeed, the novel opens with Franz Biberkopf reluctantly boarding the tram from Tegel prison to the city center, sitting in his seat, and feeling a newspaper brush across his cheek:

> He shook himself and gulped. He stepped on his own foot. Then, with a run, took a seat in the car. . . . He turned his head back towards the red wall, but the car raced on with him along the tracks, and only his head was left in the direction of the prison. The car took a bend; trees and houses intervened. Busy streets emerged, Seestrasse, people got on and off. Something inside him screamed in terror: Look out, look out, it's going to start now. (5)

It? Is the reference here to a roller coaster, a film, life? Like the filmgoer who cannot arrest the fleeting images before him on the screen, Biberkopf is unable to stop the movement of the vehicle. He is visually assaulted by the series of disconnected images that fly by and can only be briefly glimpsed through the frame of the window but never grasped for studied contemplation. In a lecture given before the screening of a film in 1912, Egon Friedell's description of cinematic experience matches Biberkopf's from the train: "[The film] is short, quick, at the same time coded, and it does not stop for anything. There is something concise, precise, military about it. This is quite fitting for our time, which is a time of extracts. In fact, these days, there is nothing which we have less of a sense for than that idyllic relaxation and epic repose with objects which earlier stood precisely for the poetic."[76] The passenger's view from a rapidly moving vehicle has often been compared to a kind of cinematic perception. Wolfgang Schivelbusch, for example, makes this comparison on two grounds: the images fly by at high speeds, and the viewer no longer belongs to the same space as the objects he perceives.[77] When Biberkopf finally descends from the tram at the Alexanderplatz, it is not to exit this rapid transit theater, but only to continue his experience of the city as if viewed on a movie screen. As he stands in front of "hundreds of polished window-panes" (5), he confuses the mannequins behind the shop windows with the reflection of the city on the shop windows—the activity of the metropolis is thus first observed as a series of moving images on a static, glass screen.[78] And in a bit of cinematic quotation, Biberkopf's perception of the architecture of Berlin, or more specifically, the precipitously tilting rooftops that threaten to slide down on him, resemble the unstable and menacing urban landscape of *The Cabinet of Dr. Caligari* (dir. Robert Wiene, 1919) and the looming building of the hotel in *The Last Laugh* (*Der letzte Mann*, dir. F. W. Murnau, 1924). Murnau's masterpiece is especially instructive because spatial disorientation is transferred from the protagonist to the film spectator through the use of Karl Freund's unchained camera, as opposed to static film sets.

If Biberkopf's eye is trained to cinematic perception and the fleeting and disconnected images observed from a mobile window, the eye of the modern reader is no less programmed. Indeed, in "Literatur und Rundfunk," Döblin characterized the reading eye as the "express train" that travels the page.[79] Stylistically, Döblin's novel registers or responds to these alternate cinematic means for recording experience, which is not to say that the novel can be directly transferred to the screen. The multitude of simultaneous happenings in the textual and physical makeup of the Alexanderplatz communicate a chaos that fractures any linear, continuous flow of the novel. One could say that the illusion of narrative continuity in the novel imitates the illusion of movement in film. For example, the chapter "Local News" reports in rapid succession a lover's suicide pact, a streetcar disaster, stock market figures, and the description of a theater poster. The speed of the prose contributes significantly to this cinematic quality or *Kinostil*, not in terms of how quickly or slowly one might read, but in the abruptness and sudden reversals of the prose. Linguistic images appear from nowhere and are never pursued. The novel accelerates the word-images that flow across the page, seemingly disconnected except for the fact that they appear in succession, creating an illusion of narrative movement corresponding to the illusion of physical movement created by film's presentation of twenty-four still images a second.

The city is thus not described but made present. These information flows, however, cannot be ordered, contained, or predicted by the narrative itself. Rather (as Benjamin already indicated), they explode the novel. In this respect, Döblin's novel stages a confrontation between two different ways of making meaning of the world: the *database* and the *narrative*. Lev Manovich has distinguished database from narrative in the following terms: "As a cultural form, the database represents the world as a list of items, and it refuses to order this list. In contrast, a narrative creates a cause-and-effect trajectory of seemingly unordered items (events). Therefore, database and narrative are natural enemies."[80] Although the subtitled "Story of Franz Biberkopf" follows a linear progression, the excess of simultaneous information presented in *Berlin Alexanderplatz* cannot be resolved or definitively located in this narrative space. Döblin's description of a tram ticket serves almost as a microcosm of this effect:

> Those mysterious long tickets on which is written: Line 12 Siemensstrasse D A, Gotzkowskistrasse C, B, Oranienburger Tor C, C, Kottbuser Tor A, mysterious tokens, who can solve them, who can guess and who confess them, three words I tell you heavy with thought, and the scraps of paper are punched four times at certain places, and on them there is written in that same German in which the Bible and the Criminal Code are written: Valid till the end of the line, by the shortest route, connection with other lines not guaranteed. (221–22)

If this is indeed the case, if these tickets as text cannot be "solved," if one cannot "guarantee" their "connection" to or cohesion with any other structural element, then what does that reveal about other texts that may be "written in the same German"? Including the book we hold as we read that line?

This excess of information which cannot be resolved into the structure of the novel's plot (indeed functions sometimes, like noise, as an impediment to our reception of the clear signal of a plot), is a stylistic device by which Döblin pushes his text to the limit of the print medium in an attempt to record an experience that other, mechanical media were just beginning to deliver with ease: the passage of time.[81] In his "Literatur und Rundfunk" lecture, Döblin asserted that the printed text is silent, and its readers mere mutes. In terms of reception, this silence is the result of so-called silent reading. We read with our eyes, not our mouths and ears. In terms of production, however, these texts are silent because something cannot be and has not been recorded within them, and this omission only becomes evident once the recording is successfully obtained in another medium.

In the introduction to *Gramophone Film Typewriter*, Kittler distinguishes the three media of his title not only by their various operations of acoustic, verbal, or visual recording, but also their relationship to the recording of time. "What phonographs and cinematographs, whose names not coincidentally derive from writing, were able to store was time: time as a mixture of audio frequencies in the acoustic realm and as the movement of single-image sequences in the optical. Time determines the limit of all art, which first has to arrest the daily data flow in order to turn it into images or signs. . . . To record the sound sequences of speech, literature has to arrest them in a system of 26 letters, thereby categorically excluding all noise sequences."[82] In other words, something drops out in the process of symbolic mediation and the production of sense. What Kittler terms the "bottleneck of the signifier" is what in effect silences noise and the simultaneity of information networks and arrests time.[83] The novel as a print medium proceeds according to the atemporal symbolic of the technology of the letter.

This atemporality of the signifier is perhaps most clearly described in Ferdinand de Saussure's *Course in General Linguistics*.[84] In a radical theoretical shift, Saussure rejected the diachronic or historical study of language as practiced in the nineteenth century. He asserted that language is constructed along two planes: the one diachronic and including occurrences of individual acts of speaking (*parole*), and the other a synchronic slice that reveals the system or structure from which all of those acts of speaking can emerge (*langue*). As the condition of possibility of all acts of speaking, Saussure concludes that *langue* is the true object of his scientific linguistic study, thereby privileging the atemporal system over embodied moments of speaking. This distinction is, as Jonathan Culler has pointed out, "a logical and necessary consequence of the arbitrary nature of the sign and the problem of identity in linguistics."[85] For if the sign is arbitrary, then it is a purely relational entity, and these relations can only be distinguished by looking at the entire system from which they emerge. Saussure thus required a synchronous structure, or what Foucault called a *tabula*, in order to provide a space for the juxtaposition of every signifier with every other.[86] Because no sign inherently possesses any meaning, its significance is generated only through the simultaneous absence of every other possible signifier, which is to say that signs generate meaning only *in absentia*. The separation of *langue* from *parole* implies, then, a separation of the essential from the contingent, or as Saussure calls it, "the more or less accidental."[87] The symbol of the letter is thus "timeless" because its appearance has always already been predicted or set forth by the overriding synchronic system. Timeliness, or the event, is eliminated from the outset.

However, in order for it to become apparent that literature, or the letter, is unable to encode, or to write down, time, it is necessary, to employ Kittler's borrowing of Lacan's terminology, for something else to "cease not writing itself." Literature's silence on the nature of real time was only recognized as such when something else began to record it or to write it down. What happens to a text, then, that is written in an age when the acoustic and the optical realm are broadcast as sound waves and recorded on tape and film, that is, when the "accidents" in time are encoded as a sound or a light wave and not encoded in the letter? It is within this context that I offer that the "informational content" of Döblin's novel does not function as a symbol that could be interpreted from the closed structure or system of the novel itself. Its words are not the transparent signifiers of a higher or more comprehensive meaning, but rather serve to convey the timeliness of a material world into the inadequate and incompatible boundaries of a necessarily immaterial and atemporal symbolic of the letter. In this regard, one might begin to think of Döblin's text as intentionally jeopardizing the stable symbolic structure of the letter by introducing the notion of the indexical into the letter.[88] With the index, time is reintroduced into the narrative event. Charles Peirce's terminology of the "index" is appropriate here because his semiotic theory does not presuppose meaning or any other *a priori*, but begins with the image itself and is deliberately temporally structured. The index is evidence of an actual event. Two of his more famous examples include the smoking chimney and the bullet hole. One might, however, provide two more relevant examples here: the grooves in a phonograph album or the needle of a dial indicating radio frequency (two technologies that are cataloged in Döblin's novel). With the term "index," we introduce the possibility that in *Berlin Alexanderplatz*, the evidence to be indexed is the event of real time. The novel indicates its own threshold, then, where it might function as an index of timeliness, as opposed to the timeless symbolic.

The text serves as a collection of the verbal data flow of radio transmission: news items, hit songs, weather reports, political slogans. And these words not only impact the organs of the body, but also the body of the text. The text does not proceed linearly to an increasingly refined state of resolution, but "piles up," "accumulates," "rolls," and "shifts," to employ Döblin's descriptors from his theory of the novel.[89] The novel is thereby rendered a highly unstable site. Its instability at the stylistic level reiterates the literal instability of the geographic terrain of the city of Berlin, for Döblin makes repeated reference to the ongoing subway construction in the city. In this text, we read endless lists of traffic plans, streetcar routes, and times of arrival and departure. Streets are dug up and buildings demolished to make way for more rail. Indeed, in his "Bau des epischen Werks," Döblin's description of the structural parameters of the text is oddly similar to the transportation lines that span the city, and the construction of the novel resembles Berlin as construction site: "I am talking about an electrical network, a dynamic net, that extends by degrees over the whole work, becomes attached to certain concepts, and in which storyline and characters are embedded. And you will recognize that epic works of this sort are similar neither to the boundless ancient epic nor to the inferior modern dramatic novel."[90] Indeed, "Berlin" is not some abstract concept that reveals some sort of spiritual essence of the city. This space is defined through its transport systems: "Berlin: 52 31' North Latitude, 13 25' East Longitude, 20 main-line stations, 121 suburban lines, 27 belt lines, 14 city lines, 7 shunting stations, street-car, elevated railroad, autobus service" (625–26). The coordinates of station stops plot a map of the city, and tracks are endlessly played and replayed as the schedule permits. But the question remains: Why is this in the text? What might the relationship of these straight lines and *Haltestellen* (literally, stopping points) be to the lines of text printed across the page? How is this *Umbau* or reconstruction of the city simultaneously an *Umbau* of the novel? "The words come rolling up to us, we must be careful not to get run over; if we don't watch out for the auto-bus, it'll make apple-sauce out of us. I'll never again stake my word on anything in the world" (633). And of course, Biberkopf is not only assailed by words, but is quite literally run over by a car.

In *Berlin Alexanderplatz* Döblin isolates, among other things, mechanized traffic as constitutive of our model of experience. Under conditions of mechanical movement, the commuter is dislocated from the images rushing past the window. The images themselves are fractured and constantly changing, rendered into what one critic has called a "useless spectacle," and producing the illusion of continuity only because of the speed of their succession. The traffic of the city is presented through the traffic of the text itself. In German, *Verkehr* refers not only to traffic in terms of moving vehicles, but also to movement and exchange more generally, whether that be commerce, sexual intercourse, or communication. In addition to film and transportation networks, the novel's formal construction thus also imitates modern communications technology, especially the telegraph, which was critical to the growth of rapid transit (the first telegraph stations were located at train stations to coordinate the arrival and departure of trains).

In an extended aside in the novel, Döblin compares the communications technologies of the early twentieth century with that of the ancients. When Troy finally fell to the Greeks, signal fires were lit all the way to Athens, proclaiming the victory: "How splendid, be it said in passing, this flaming message from Troy to Greece! Isn't that grand, this march of fire across the sea, this is light, heart, soul, happiness, rejoicing! . . . It burns, it blazes, it speaks, it feels, at *every moment*, in *each place*, and the joy is *general*" (125–26, my emphasis). The torch is a perfect and continuous translation of interior thoughts, spiritual hopes, and invisible longings into the visible realm. It "speaks" and "feels"; and everyone who looks at it, the tens of thousands along its path, share in this expression, this inward joy taking outward form. The symbol of the torch is therefore, as it were, suspended in time. How, then, does this compare to the technological regime under which the modern author writes?

> We telegraph by wireless. We produce high frequency alternating currents through transmitters in big stations. We produce electric waves by oscillations of a vibrating circle. The vibrations spread out spherically, as it were. And then there is also an electron-tube of glass and a microphone the disk of which vibrates in alternating degrees, thus reproducing tones, precisely as when they entered the machine, and that is astonishing, clever, tricky. It's hard to get enthusiastic about all this; it functions, and that's all. (126)

In several passages, Döblin similarly describes words or communications as material objects or the product of the sound waves that are the index of their having been spoken as opposed to the meaning they evoke. "Words, resounding waves, noise-waves, full of content rock to and fro through the room, from the throat of Dreske, the stutterer, who smiles at the floor" (105). The message is not an exteriorization of a romantic idea or ideal, but only electric waves. And how is this message, as sound wave, interpretable? How can it be subject to further analysis? Words are not considered mysterious conveyers of signification, but are simply waves of noise that spread out, bumping into things like the fragile bones of the inner ear. Sound waves are transported along a route from transmitter to receiver, station to station. With the recognition of the materiality of the word as sound wave, its former lofty position as transparent conveyer of an absent, though perfectly substitutable, signified is cast in doubt. And even the words of Death, who visits Biberkopf in the asylum, do not immediately communicate a spiritual truth but are dismissed as the recordings of "a mere talking-machine, a phonograph" (603).

Döblin employs the medium of the novel to foreground its material organization and to draw attention to both the possibilities and limits of print. The novelist writes with letters on paper; he does not inscribe grooves on vinyl discs. Nonetheless, the reader is immediately struck (if not stymied) by the nontraditional orthography that Döblin employs in an attempt to reproduce the dialect of eastern Berlin. In this fashion perhaps, the author permits the text to speak again, for the reader must abandon silent reading, lest the combination of letters appear as mere gibberish. Once spoken, the words become, again, a sound wave in time as they enter the reader's ear. Even spoken, however, the words are often without sense or referent. The text proceeds associatively, offering the materiality of the words as events in and of themselves, tumbling along through alliteration, rhyme, and puns: "Her luminous eyes roamed blazing through the darkness, and her lips trembled, colon, quotation marks, Eleanore, dash, Eleanore, dash, quotation marks, quotation francs, quotation dollars—going, going, gone!" (89–90).[91] Any meaning generated here is merely incidental, secondary to free association and the sensory aspects of the printed words.

Döblin speaks of the liberation of the epic novel from the medium of the book as a difficult, and quite probably impossible, task but a useful goal nonetheless for comprehending modern experience within print. *Berlin Alexanderplatz* is and remains a book despite the subsequent radio play and two films of the same name, and Döblin continued to write books for the rest of his life. Although the novel is constrained by the characteristics of the print medium, it nevertheless evokes other media. The book insists on being read in its competing dynamic with other media, and with the experiential knowledge of the radio-listener and the filmgoer. As a result, it cannot be strictly interpreted within the confines of its covers but as a medium that engages the larger mediascape.

FILM-TEXT BERLIN

Despite the explicit relationships Döblin draws between writing and film in his theoretical essays, and the overt manner in which these ideas are manifested in *Berlin Alexanderplatz*, the screenplay of the novel that he cowrote with Hans Wilhelm, a well-known screenwriter, and the subsequent film that was produced are decidedly uncinematic. How can a film be less cinematic than a novel? Why, given the chance, was Döblin unable to transpose his work across media? Following the premier of the *Alexanderplatz* film, Döblin was asked in an interview why he participated in the film adaptation of the novel:

> I realized that it would not be possible to write a theatrical play from the Alexanderplatz material because Biberkopf's line of fate, or better, his melody of fate could not be molded appropriately for the stage. The stage play—whose form requires division into scenes and acts and an ending where an iron curtain comes down—just wouldn't do. It could only become a radio play or a film. Precisely the mechanics of film, which give the sound film an advantage over the stage, could help here.

Photographic images that accurately reflect the atmosphere and local color of the Alexanderplatz neighborhood; second, the language that Franz Biberkopf can speak unmediated, making it acoustically more authentic than the novel; and third, the musical accompaniment that underscores and expresses particularly effectively the constant flux of Biberkopf's fate.[92]

The film premiered on October 8, 1931. The critical reception ranged from lukewarm to negative, and the negative critiques were largely formulated around a comparison of the film with the novel from which it had been adapted. The choice of words used by the critics is particularly instructive here, for this is not the common and by now timeworn complaint that a film does not "do justice" to a novel's story or setting or mood. Instead the film is criticized for being too *novelistic*, whereas the novel itself was already a film. Siegfried Kracauer wrote in *Die Neue Rundschau*, December 1931: "The example is that much more instructive because Döblin's book presented the opportunity to produce a film that would convey situations in an epic manner. They let this opportunity slip away and confined the loose web of associations to a contained fable of the underworld, just as it's always done.... In short, a series of concessions spoiled the concept, and out of these circumstances, a work of literature that gestured toward film became a film that turned away from it."[93]

Herbert Ihering wrote in similar terms for the *Berliner Börsen-Courier* in October 1931: "This film can hardly be called *Berlin Alexanderplatz* after Döblin's novel.... Döblin's novel traces out the form of film. It was, to exaggerate a bit, a written film.... Inexplicably, Alfred Döblin got together with Hans Wilhelm only to turn the novel, *Berlin Alexanderplatz*, into the film, *Heinrich George as Franz Biberkopf*.... A crucial aspect is missing, and that is the connection to cinematic form."[94] The film by and large presents only half of the story, the "Story of Franz Biberkopf." In other words the film recoups precisely that narrative which the novel avoided through its adoption of nonnarrative strategies borrowed from alternative media sources. The radio play reveals its own inconsistency with the novel from the outset: it was titled simply, "Die Geschichte vom Franz Biberkopf." The radio play includes only infrequent interpositions of voices calling headlines, reading advertisements, and the like. Otherwise, "realistic" or documentary elements are limited to sounds that designate the location of narrative action (i.e., automobile horns or glasses clinking and drunkards singing). They are secondary to and exist only for the plot or storyline itself, while in the novel, Döblin expressly rejected the incorporation of the extraneous detail of the Alexanderplatz into Biberkopf's thin story line or the subordination of material effects to the diegetic narrative. In Döblin's actual film and radio play, the city is merely décor, anchoring the representation of a moralistic fable; in the novel, however, the city is presented directly.

It is, I think, important to note the so-called failure of these projects because they underscore the fact that Döblin was not a thwarted filmmaker, sidelined into the medium of print. On the contrary, the writer Döblin took stock of the situation of the novel and its position relative to the new media of the period and modern experience more generally. The emerging mechanical media reorganized both the construction and the reception of the textual medium. Through the phonographic and filmic strategies adopted by the text, *Berlin Alexanderplatz* stakes its modern claims, and the "mute" language of print registers the emergence of something new into legibility. The novel serves almost as testimony to something that it is not. Indeed the novel is not a film, but then again, no film is ever a novel, either. In light of the narrative restructuring of spatial and temporal experience, the text insists on a reevaluation of the questions: What is the relationship of technology to writing? And what are the limits or boundaries of individual media? This media competition is important because it reveals the spaces or gaps in which writing is not the perfect trace or univocal recording of experience, but rather must redefine its own communicative structure by pointing to other experiential modes—a media competition that Döblin himself called the *Dauerkrieg* of technology.

Or perhaps it is simply the case that the wrong filmmaker was selected. In his review of Döblin's novel, Axel Eggebrecht, a literary essayist and occasional screenplay writer, connected *Berlin Alexanderplatz* to Walter Ruttmann's film *Berlin, Symphonie der Großstadt* (Berlin, Symphony of a City), produced two years earlier in 1927: "Döblin's powers of observation are extraordinary. If we had an enterprising film industry, it would have seized on this book. Ruttmann's daring Berlin-film, in which the humanity of Berlin disappears behind a montage of technology and traffic could serve as a preliminary study."[95] Considering the critical failure of Döblin's own screenplay of *Berlin Alexanderplatz* and its inability to make good on the expectations produced by the novel, Döblin might have done well simply to have retitled Ruttmann's film as his own. *Berlin, Symphonie der Großstadt* is divided into five acts and covers a day in Berlin, from the first images of a train rolling into the city at dawn to fireworks exploding over the city's nightscape. As Ruttmann's title indicates, he constructed the film, not on a literary model, but rather on a musical one. In his "Bau des epischen Werks," Döblin similarly compared his epic model with the composition of a symphony: "Were one to ask for a comparable work with these formal parameters, the preceding analysis has surely revealed it already: symphonic works."[96] Although extremely brief "mini-narratives" are occasionally played out in Ruttmann's film, the film as a whole has no unified storyline or protagonist. Rather, like *Berlin Alexanderplatz,* it presents the city directly by simulating the sensory overload that is its defining characteristic—a characteristic often cited in conjunction with the reception of cinema itself. In presenting the city as a cinematic spectacle, the film doubles the experience of the masses in the street. As Siegfried Kracauer wrote in his illuminating statements on Berlin's picture palaces: "Here, in pure externality, the audience encounters itself; its own reality is revealed in the fragmented sequence of splendid sense impressions."[97] As a surface effect, the film revels in the visuality of Weimar culture and in the fragmented and varying sites of exchange, desire, and traffic.[98]

Before producing *Berlin, Symphonie der Großstadt,* Ruttmann was already established as a painter and experimental filmmaker. In his essay "Malerei mit Zeit" (Painting with Time), Ruttmann claimed that he turned from painting to film precisely because the aesthetic conventions of painting could not accommodate his understanding of dynamic events. This is clearly evidenced in his 1922 film, *Opus I,* which consists only of hand-colored geometric shapes that move in varied patterns and tempos across the screen. Similarly, in *Berlin, Symphonie der Großstadt,* elements of the physical landscape of Berlin are assembled to simulate the dynamic movement of the city. And if the rapidly changing sense impressions of the actual city are analogous to the montage effect of film, then Ruttmann's work presents the viewer with the cinematic quality of everyday life. Indeed, it reveals how Benjamin's "equipment-free aspect of reality" might not only be a function of the cinema but a more general characteristic of urban experience. Several points of comparison can be made between Ruttmann's film and Döblin's work, including montage sequences, the use of documentary material of the city, and the network of streets and passages that function as a predominant motif. For example, Ruttmann crosscuts shots of the legs of workers hurrying to work in the factories with the hooves of cattle being driven, presumably, into the slaughterhouse. Likewise, Döblin records in excruciating detail a slaughterhouse in a Berlin suburb, and occasionally inserts images of this scene with images from the narrative text. These montage sequences are highly evocative of Eisenstein's own filmmaking practices.

The primary documentary source of Ruttmann's photographic footage is exterior shots, and among these, the dominant scenes are streets and transportation lines. The film opens with a series of cuts: from the ripples on the surface of a body of water, to the movement of abstract lines, the crossing bars signaling the approach of a train, and finally the tracks themselves. The remainder of the opening sequence is shot from the interior of the train, culminating in the arrival at the city's main rail station. In a similar move, as we already noted, Döblin's novel opens as Franz Biberkopf boards a tram from the suburbs into the city center, and throughout the novel, forms of urban transportation and mechanized movement are foregrounded. Ruttmann's film, too, highlights systems of conveyance: streets and gutters, underground sewage systems, rails and streetcars, trains and automobiles. As Wolfgang Natter notes in his essay on the film, "Apart from its function in setting place, the street, as pure circulation and movement, defines the essence of the modernist city."[99] This movement is not limited to the circulation of people and vehicular traffic, but also commodities and, especially, information. The city is a textual space of newsprint, signage, posters, memoranda, type, telegraph messages, and telephone conversations. In other words, *Berlin, Symphonie der Großstadt* and *Berlin Alexanderplatz* both present us with the confluence of the city, the cinema, and print, as interpenetrating medial effects.

One of the opening passages of the second "book" of Döblin's novel, "The Rosenthaler Platz Entertains Itself," reads almost like a list of the shots of any of a number of sequences in Ruttmann's film. Here, over the course of several pages, one reads in rapid succession: a weather report (one of the many Döblin transcribed directly from the newspaper); the stops for Tram No. 68; the fares and regulations for any of the three systems of public transportation in Berlin; a near-accident as a man descends the tram into busy traffic; advertisements; the numerous divisions of the sprawling A.E.G. enterprise; snatches of conversation overheard on the street corner; a rundown on the commercial occupants of a block of city buildings; and brief descriptions of the occupants of a streetcar. This last enacts a vertical cut in the temporal fabric as the entire life story of fourteen-year-old Max Rüst is briefly accounted for up to and including the formulaic prose of his obituary. These rapid cuts, similar to those in Ruttmann's film, present the city to the reader as an unending information stream, as multiple and complex as the physical location itself. There is no synthesis or analysis of the city, however; it is simply presented to us. As

Döblin notes in the novel when describing the teeming throngs of people hurrying rapidly along the streets:

> They have the same equanimity as passengers in an omnibus or in streetcars. The latter all sit in different postures, making the weight of the car, as indicated outside, heavier still. Who could find out what is happening inside them, a tremendous chapter. And if anyone did write it, to whose advantage would it be? New books? Even the old ones don't sell, and in the year '27 book-sales as compared with '26 have declined so and so much per cent. Taken simply as private individuals, the people who paid 20 pfennigs, leaving out those possessing monthly tickets and pupils' cards—the latter pay only 10 pfennigs—are riding with their weight from a hundred to two hundred pounds, in their clothes, with pockets, parcels, keys, hats, sets of artificial teeth, trusses, riding across Alexanderplatz. . . . (221)

In other words, all one can record of these people on the street, shopping, going to work, eating, talking, laughing, is the documentary material that the film itself captures.

Which is not to say that the "documentary" is unmotivated or arbitrary. Kracauer criticized Ruttmann's film for "instead of penetrating his immense subject-matter with a true understanding of its social, economic and political structure [he] records thousands of details without connecting them, or at best connects them through fictitious transitions which are void of content. . . . This symphony fails to point out anything, because it does not uncover a single significant context."[100] However, what Ruttmann's film and Döblin's novel reveal is that one may no longer be able to speak of "content" or "significant context" as a function of twentieth-century experience. Thus a film or a novel that has "adapted itself to the age" can no longer adhere to systems of representational closure, unity, and harmony. In the early discourse on film, a subtle confusion exists between "objective" reality and its representation, or between reality and fantasy. Does film merely record what is placed before the camera, or does the act of filming itself reorganize the flow of information? How is one's perception of everyday life affected by these visual manipulations? These questions are perhaps no more apparent than in the discourse that merges film and the city. As is the case with Ruttmann's film, in *Berlin Alexanderplatz*, the space of writing involves the negotiation of transport and communications technologies, modern systems of conveyance and transfer. In this sense, the greater criticism to make of the film and the novel may not be their failure to penetrate social, economic, and political themes per se, but to recognize and to reflect on the role of the modern mediascape in the perpetuation of social, economic, and political forms. In other words, the cinema does not merely offer a new way of recording the world but in so doing already participates in the construction and apprehension of so-called social reality. The medium is no neutral repository of sensorial effects but functions within a far-reaching program of social organization.

five

From Wordminded to Eyeminded: John Dos Passos's Image-Text

> The professional writer discovers some aspect of the world and invents out of the speech of his time some particularly apt and original way of putting it down on paper. If the product is compelling, and important enough, it molds and influences ways of thinking to the point of changing and rebuilding the language, which is the mind of the group. The process is not very different from that of scientific discovery and invention. The importance of a writer, as of a scientist, depends upon his ability to influence subsequent thought. In his relation to society a professional writer is a technician just as much as an electrical engineer is.
>
> JOHN DOS PASSOS, "THE WRITER AS TECHNICIAN" (1935)

In his contribution to the published proceedings of the American Writers' Congress, a convention of radical writers meeting in April 1935, John Dos Passos drew a correspondence between writing and electrical engineering. Just as the electrical engineer deals with the practical application of electricity to the construction of machinery, power supplies, and circuitry, Dos Passos saw the writer as dealing with the application of the language of his time to the construction of texts. As he went on to note, however, questions of writing, of who the writer is, and of what is being produced are increasingly difficult to sort through: "The whole question of what writing is has become particularly tangled in these years during which the industry of the printed word has reached its high point in profusion and wealth, and, to a certain extent, in power."[1] For the designation "professional writer" refers not only to the novelist, of course, but also to the journalist, ad-man, screenplay writer, speech writer, political propagandist, historian, scientist, songwriter, and poet. All are technicians of words, and all add to the proliferation of printed and broadcast verbal constructions encountered at any moment of the day or night. Of all technical occupations with which to compare writing, Dos Passos's focus on one that works with electricity is telling: both employ networks of distribution. And it is largely inventions of the late nineteenth and early twentieth centuries that account for the "particular tangle" to which Dos Passos refers. Twentieth-century "technical writers" must therefore be finely attuned, not only to infinitely varied and varying registers of speech and language, but also to the new media through which both speech and images are composed, transmitted, and received. The writer is not simply passively affected by the modernization of the world, but is actively engaged in the ongoing processes of modernization: "changing and rebuilding." As a technician, the writer takes technology into account at every level—from the way in which it alters industrial and social behavior, to economics, politics, and especially, words on the page.

Dos Passos further specified both how and why visual and literary artists engage in this process of modernization in "Grosz Comes to America" (*Esquire*, September 1936), an essay on the German-born painter and graphic artist. Dos Passos opens the essay by claiming there is a fundamental distinction between conceptual and perceptual processes in the new century and the preceding one:

> From being a wordminded people we are becoming an eyeminded people. As I remember how things were when I was a child, the people my parents knew had hardly any direct visual stimulants at all. There were engravings on the walls and illustrated magazines and reproductions of old masters even, but the interest in them was purely literary. The type of drawing current in the late nineteenth century had such meager conventions of representation that it tended to evoke a set of descriptive words instead of a direct visual image. I am sure that my parents enjoying a view from a hill say, were stimulated verbally, remembering a line of verse or a passage from Sir Walter Scott, before they got any real impulse from the optic nerve.[2]

Dos Passos argues here that the twentieth century is marked by a systematic reorganization of perception itself. Further, he attributes this change in no small part to the mass cultural images encountered every day: "Display advertising and the movies, though they may dull the wits, certainly stimulate the eyes. In New York the visual attack of the showwindows of Fifth Avenue stores almost equals in skill and scope that of the windows of the picture dealers on the Rue de la Boètie in the heyday of the school of Paris."[3] But what does this mean to think in a "literary" fashion and to encounter even visual images through a "literary" interest? And what has occurred for Dos Passos to date this change to the beginning of the century, at least from an American perspective? With his phrase, "visual attack," twentieth-century images are described as an assault on the observer through a kind of direct and tactile communication, as opposed to the visual images of the nineteenth century, which communicated only indirectly, after undergoing a linguistic transposition on the part of their observer. Indeed, Dos Passos does not limit the indirect visual experience to artistic representation (for the parents' generation responds in a similar manner to the view from the hill), but maintains that this linguistically mediated encounter with the visible world is an essential characteristic of nineteenth-century understanding. The primary difference that Dos Passos articulates in the passage is that in a "wordminded" culture, experience is filtered through a storehouse of learned intellectual and cultural material (the parents who quote Sir Walter Scott in response to a landscape), whereas in an "eyeminded" culture the body is impacted directly (the "real impulse from the optic nerve" and the "visual attack of the showwindows"). The distinction between "wordminded" and "eyeminded" also relates to the epistemological distinction Jonathan Crary has made between different technologies of vision, such as the camera obscura and photography, as discussed earlier. The correspondence between Dos Passos's statements here and Crary's later theorization of the turn in optical techniques is particularly noteworthy with regards to the "decorporealization" of vision that Crary claims is in part modeled on the camera obscura, and the "recorporealization" and subjectivization of vision surrounding the discourse on photography. In a certain sense then, Dos Passos's "wordminded" culture is the culture of the camera obscura, whereas his "eyeminded" culture corresponds to the age of photography.[4] In Dos Passos's work, a dichotomy is established between words and the eye that underscores changes in both physical perception and representational models. Furthermore, this change is tied directly to the advent of new media, which function differently from the printed texts of his parents' literary models. With this claim, Dos Passos anticipates Friedrich Kittler's statement that "media determine our situation." Modern artists, and in Dos Passos's example George

Grosz in particular, play a necessary and pivotal role in this increasingly "eye-minded" mediascape by inventing "new ways of seeing" that respond to this change in situation:

> Experiments in the visual arts (the invention of new ways of seeing things), are made because, due to the way the apparatus that makes up the mind is made, old processes and patterns have continually to be broken up in order to make it possible to perceive the new aspects and arrangements of evolving consciousness. The great enemy of intelligence is complacency. The satirist in words or in visual images is the doctor who comes with his sharp and sterile instruments to lance the focusses of dead matter that continually impede the growth of intelligence.[5]

Dos Passos echoes here sentiments frequently associated with what it means to be "modern," through his insistence on the "new" as opposed to the "old," and his even more direct image of the doctor piercing the body with a scalpel in order to remove the "dead matter."[6] Although Dos Passos was himself not strictly a satirist, as I will show, it is clear that his work is similarly an "experiment" in which a new literary form would be invented that would enable the reader to perceive the "new aspects and arrangements" of modern life and the role the media play therein. This definition of what it means to be modern, of the relationship of the work of art to the modern mediascape, recalls for us Robert Musil's call for a revitalized theory of art, and especially literature.

In the foreword written for his translation of the French poet Blaise Cendrar's collection *Panama; or, The Adventures of My Seven Uncles* (1931), Dos Passos situates himself in a direct line with European art and literature from the turn of the century, citing all of the major movements of that period:

> Under various tags: futurism, cubism, vorticism, modernism, most of the best work in the arts in our time has been the direct product of this explosion, that had an influence in its sphere comparable with that of the October revolution in social organization and politics and the Einstein formula in physics. Cendrars and Apollinaire, poets, were on the first cubist barricades with the group that included Picasso, Modigliani, Marinetti, Chagall; that profoundly influenced Maiakovsky, Meyerhold, Eisenstein; whose ideas carom through Joyce, Gertrude Stein, T. S. Eliot (first published in Wyndham Lewis's "Blast"). The music of Stravinski and Prokofieff and Diageleff's Ballet hail from this same Paris already in

the disintegration of victory, as do the windows of Saks Fifth Avenue, skyscraper furniture, the Lenin Memorial in Moscow, the painting of Diego Rivera in Mexico City and the newritz styles of advertising in American magazines.[7]

The quotation reveals the degree to which Dos Passos considered these different movements as interconnected in their impulse: the explosion in the arts scene changed how one thought about and understood art, much like Einstein's physics forced a rethinking or a restructuring of conceptions of time and space dating back to Newton. And the reference to Einstein is, of course, not accidental, for the fixed relationship of the human subject to time and space is similarly challenged by the artists Dos Passos cites. A particularly impressive aspect of this list is its breadth, beginning with French poetry and European painting, and spanning to include Russian filmmakers, Anglo-American authors, music, dance, and even mass-cultural artifacts, such as store windows, industrial design, and the graphics of print advertising. Dos Passos includes examples from the visual, linguistic, and kinetic arts, suggesting their mutual influence and interaction, and more specifically, the degree to which they have informed his own ideas about art. In Dos Passos's view, they are all examples of "new ways of seeing," both responding to and provoking change at every level of the artistic and commercial spectrum.

If we transfer our attention from Germany to the United States, we can gain insight into a shift from a preoccupation with media effects as such to a more detailed apprehension of the "realities" differentiated media create. It is the modeling of the text on the various networks of the city itself that suggest the strongest comparison between Döblin's novel and the work of his American contemporary, John Dos Passos. In both Döblin and Dos Passos's novels, explicit reference is made to the new technologies of the twentieth century (or what Egon Friedell called the "signature" of modernity): elevated trains, streetcars and subways, the telegraph, the telephone, and film.[8] However, these mechanical means are not only described as objects in the world, rather these technologies are constitutive of a text that cannot be read outside the modes of perception and experience that new media have introduced or created within the human psyche. In other words, these technologies are constitutive of a text that cannot be interpreted as such, but must be read after the materiality, as opposed to the transcendental meaning, of the word has brought the hermeneutic project to an end. The contemporaneous technological regimes thus affect the narrative strategies of representation when so-called technological metaphors function in excess of themselves—these technologies are "transported" into the novel—and the structure of the text reveals new strategies to adapt itself to the times and the logistics of alternative medial possibilities and the social realities they construct.

We can view Dos Passos's project as a writer as a particular response to the question of how one writes as a participant in and a producer for an "eye-minded" culture. In this sense, his project is essentially similar to that of his European contemporaries. For he too uses the medium of print, and more specifically the novel, to explore the question of how the emerging technological environment influences the human sensorium and consciousness, and further, how the author can continue the project of writing in this changing environment. In other words, he uses his texts—and I focus here on *Manhattan Transfer* and the *U.S.A.* trilogy—to reflect on those characteristics of print which distinguish it from other media. *Manhattan Transfer* can be, and has been, read as articulating impulses and motifs similar to those found in Döblin's *Berlin Alexanderplatz*, and Dos Passos was quite clear concerning his own debt to cinematic montage. *Manhattan Transfer* exploits alternative media to construct a text about a city that reveals the extent to which the city is defined by the competing networks of media found in it. Examining Dos Passos's use of what he termed the "Camera Eye" in *U.S.A.* will permit us to return to some of the questions concerning photography and poetic language that were raised earlier with respect to Rilke's work, and more specifically how the figure of the photograph becomes a privileged technological vehicle through which to work through the paradoxical impulse of modernity. By exploring the manner in which the writer in these first decades of the century confronts alternate media of recording, transmission, and reception, one finds strong indications that modernist literature is deeply concerned with the question of literature as a *medium* among other media, and further, one realizes that the emerging technological environment or mediascape is an implicit characteristic of the notion of modernity itself.

MONTAGE CITY

Reflecting back on his novel over thirty years after its publication, Dos Passos recalled that "*Manhattan Transfer* . . . was an attempt to chronicle the life of a city. . . . I wanted to find some way of making the narrative carry a very large load"; and "I felt that everything should go in: popular songs, political aspirations and prejudices, ideals, hopes, delusions, crackpot notions, clippings out of the daily newspapers."[9] Published in 1925, *Manhattan Transfer* presents New York City and a cross-section of its inhabitants during the first two decades of the twentieth century. Divided into three sections and eighteen chapters, the novel is composed of well over one hundred narrative segments that splice together the lives of Bud Korpenning, a fugitive from upstate who finds no salvation in the city and ultimately commits suicide; Ellen Thatcher, an actress who uses marriage for upward mobility; Stan Emery, a playboy drunk; Gus McNiel, a former deliveryman who rises from obscurity to power and authority as a result of a freak though fortuitous accident; George Baldwin, a lawyer whose career is launched by the McNiel lawsuit; Jimmy Herf, a sometime journalist; Congo Jake, a bootlegger; and many, many more. Their stories are interspersed with popular songs, advertisements, billboards, political slogans, the rattle of elevated trains, and the glare of sunlight reflected from the windows of towering skyscrapers. Together they record and broadcast the multitude of acts, sights, and sounds of the city gloriously proclaimed the "World's Second Metropolis" in a newspaper headline cited in one of the opening passages of the novel.[10]

The most obvious similarity between *Manhattan Transfer* and *Berlin Alexanderplatz* is, of course, their titles. Both refer to major transit stops at which several transportation lines come together, and both announce the city that is their subject. This coincidence should, however, not be surprising, for both novels employ the setting of the metropolis as emblematic of modern experience, and further, both construct a textual presentation of their respective cities through networks of circulation. Further, both novels record the city through an amount of detail so overwhelming that it frustrates traditional models of narrative composition.[11] As in Döblin's novel, the extensive use of verbal documents from a variety of sources in *Manhattan Transfer* interrupts the development of linear plot, resulting in multiple perspectives that do not fit easily into a static or unified framework. Both novelists employed this stylistic device to indicate that traditional narrative forms were inadequate to the representation of the metropolis. As Dos Passos once asserted, "There was more to the life of a great city than you could cram into any one hero's career."[12] Sensitive to being labeled an imitator, Döblin maintained that a major distinction between his work and *Manhattan Transfer* was that he had written a "homophonic" novel, whereas Dos Passos's work was "polyphonic."[13] This statement is at first glance difficult to reconcile with the vast linguistic scope and multiple verbal genres of which *Berlin Alexanderplatz* is composed; one might surmise that Döblin was referring to the fact that his own novel is primarily the story of a single protagonist, Franz Biberkopf, whereas Dos Passos's novel pursues the stories of multiple characters throughout the narrative. One gains here a first sense of a possible weakness of Döblin's text in which a "homophonic" novel might (even if unwittingly) serve to duplicate a system of discourse that a "polyphonic" novel attempts to critique. I will return to this question in my conclusion. Whatever the stakes of this distinction, both novels make clear that the modern metropolis could be only inadequately represented through a closed, diegetic narrative. In these novels, early twentieth-century urban experience is reformulated through radically divergent categories of representation that had been introduced by the new, non-print media.

Early reviews of Döblin's novel noted the correspondence with Dos Passos when *Berlin Alexanderplatz* was first published. In his review in the *Berliner Tageblatt* (October 18, 1929), for example, Hans Sochaczwer introduces Döblin's text with the statement: "This novel will bewilder those who are not familiar with the new literature coming out of America; influences of a formal nature are perceptible, such as has not yet been seen in any other German novel."[14] The comparisons to Dos Passos were never as numerous as those to James Joyce (and Döblin did not deny the suggestion of a similarity to Dos Passos's work as vehemently as he did comparisons with Joyce); however, a body of scholarship exists that seeks to document exactly when Döblin may have read the work of his literary contemporaries and to identify points of correspondence among *Berlin Alexanderplatz, Manhattan Transfer,* and *Ulysses*.[15] In his study, for example, Joris Duytschaever goes into great detail concerning the German publication of both English-language authors, noting how far along Döblin was in the preparation of his own manuscript, and concluding that Döblin must have read Dos Passos whenever works from both men happened to appear in the same periodical.[16] However, it seems almost beside the point to argue about direct or indirect influences or imitations, or at exactly what point Döblin read these other authors. Rather, their very similarity lends strength to the notion that the emerging media technologies surrounding all three men had a pronounced effect on their output as literary "technicians," and that the influence of media technologies was not limited to Germany, but was a critical factor in the evolution of literary writing in both Europe and the United States.

One of the strongest points of convergence between Döblin and Dos Passos lies in their admiration of certain film techniques, and in their explicit reference to filmmaking methods in connection with their own writing techniques.

We will recall from the previous chapter that Döblin had already published on this subject some ten years before *Manhattan Transfer* was published. Like Döblin, it is clear that Dos Passos's interest in film was foremost an interest not in the movie industry, per se, which is scathingly criticized in *The Big Money*, the final installment of his *U.S.A.* trilogy, but in film's techniques of representation. Dos Passos's single foray into Hollywood was disastrous in terms of the screenplay he was ostensibly contracted to produce and only provided material for his novel.[17] If anything, Dos Passos was more explicit than Döblin in acknowledging the direct influence of film on his work, singling out the filmmakers D. W. Griffith and, especially, Sergei Eisenstein, and their use of montage. Asked in an interview in 1962 whether he had been "trying to create an entirely new kind of novel" with *Manhattan Transfer*, Dos Passos replied:

> I don't know how this question can be answered. I was trying to get a great many things in to give a picture of the city of New York because I had spent quite a while there. I was trying also to get a certain feeling in. Precedents? I don't think so. I never went in much for theories of that sort. At the time I did *Manhattan Transfer*, I'm not sure whether I had seen Eisenstein's films. The idea of montage had an influence on the development of this sort of writing. I may have seen *Potemkin*. Then, of course, I must have seen *The Birth of a Nation*, which was the first attempt at montage. Eisenstein considered it the origin of his method.[18]

It is striking that in response to the interviewer's question Dos Passos rejects any literary precedents for his work and refers only to influential developments in a totally different medium.[19]

One can piece together Dos Passos's concept of montage from various statements he made in later years concerning the stylistic impulse behind his composition of *Manhattan Transfer*. Major terms that emerge from these passages include simultaneity, fragmentation, contrast, and juxtaposition. These terms closely echo Eisenstein's own writing on the subject, as discussed earlier:

> Conflict lies at the basis of every art. (A unique "figurative" transformation of the dialectic.)
>
> The shot is then a montage cell. Consequently we must also examine it from the point of view of *conflict*.
>
> Conflict within the shot is:

potential montage that, in its growing intensity, breaks through its four-sided cage and pushes its conflict out into montage impulses between the montage fragments....

If we are to compare montage with anything, then, we should compare a phalanx of montage fragments—"shots"—with the series of explosions of the external combustion engine, as these fragments multiply into a montage dynamic through "impulses" like those that drive a car or a tractor.[20]

We also note again the convergence of film and transportation technologies. Both Eisenstein and Dos Passos maintained that a new dramatic principle is introduced through this technique: the juxtaposition of disparate elements leads to "the emergence of a concept, of a sensation" that could not otherwise be depicted.[21] In other words, montage provides a new way of seeing. The presentation of simultaneity is simulated through the use of montage, which results in "the emancipation of closed action from its conditioning by time and space."[22] Dos Passos explicitly breaks with a linear time sequence, for example, in the first section of *Manhattan Transfer,* by pursuing divergent temporal sequences in the juxtaposition of multiple narrative fragments. Both Eisenstein and Dos Passos echo Döblin's concept of a literary cinema-style discussed in the preceding chapter. The *Kinostil* is an attempt at the linguistic representation of simultaneous events even as the text is read progressively in time. With this move, events are presented as "actual and existing" (Döblin) instead of something merely talked about. The deployment of what one might call literary montage is not far afield from Eisenstein's own ideas, for as he stated in his argument against the comparison of film with other visual arts: "Why then should cinema in its forms follow theatre and painting rather than the methodology of language, which gives rise, through the combination of concrete descriptions and concrete objects, to quite new concepts and ideas? It is much closer to film, than, for instance, painting, where form derives from *abstract* elements (line, colour)."[23]

Dos Passos described the impulse behind his work as a desire to create a "novel full of snapshots of life like a documentary film"; and he maintained that "the artist must record the fleeting world the way the motion picture film recorded it."[24] Like Döblin, Dos Passos does not engage for the most part in psychological portraits of his characters. There is no narrator who intervenes to postulate what motivates their actions or to voice the characters' inner thoughts for us. Comparing the novel to a film, D. H. Lawrence wrote, it is "like a movie picture with an intricacy of different stories and no close-ups and no writing in between. Mr. Dos Passos leaves out the writing in between."[25] The novel records only movement and dialogue, that which is seen and heard, as if a recording apparatus were placed in various locations of the city. And like that recording apparatus (and similar to the effect discussed earlier of Rilke's *Notebooks of Malte Laurids Brigge*), there is no filter for the recording: all of the debris, the noise, and the incidental and accidental artifacts of the city are dutifully recorded along with the actions of the primary characters. Henry Longman Stuart thus made justifiable reference to a recording apparatus in his review of the novel in the *New York Times Book Review* (November 29, 1925): "The sensitized plate records [everything] with a mechanical impartiality."[26] The novel presents the unremitting immediacy of information circulating in the city and simultaneously reveals that this information stream defies categorization or classification.

The city is established from the outset as a chaotic scene of partially connected networks of circulation and movement. This idea is highlighted by the five chapter headings of the first section—Ferryslip, Metropolis, Dollars, Tracks, and Steamroller—for all refer to various types of circulation in the city. The ferry is, of course, what brings people into the city, and the image is continuously repeated as a site of arrival and departure. Both Bud Korpenning and Jimmy Herf arrive in Manhattan on the ferry (as do the countless numbers of faceless immigrants); Jimmy Herf will make his final departure on the ferry at the novel's close. The metropolis itself is teeming with a vast circulation network of vehicles and people. Characters are forever walking the grid of streets and going in and out of restaurants, hotels, and office buildings. Dollars highlight the circulation of currency, the fruitless quest of so many of the characters encountered, and the threshold for social opportunity. Tracks refer to the countless railway trains, streetcars, and elevated lines that crisscross the geographic space. And the steamroller that appears infrequently—and always in association with death (the boy who murders his mother, or Herf's mother's funeral)—is laying pavement for the circulation of an increasing number of automobiles. Other chapter headings include Fire Engine, Rollercoaster, and Revolving Doors, all of which further emphasize the notion of change and motion, as does the title of the novel as a whole. Foremost, however, the city is marked by the circulation of print—newspapers, billboards, advertisements, popular slogans, and songs—all dutifully recorded by the author in an endless transcription of verbal communication (an aspect of the text that will become even more accentuated in the *U.S.A.* trilogy through the Newsreel sections that are spliced in throughout the books). The inclusion of these various forms of printed matter mimic the linguistic chaos of the city itself and its multiple, and often conflicting, grids of intelligibility. When we read the novel, we do not merely read *about* a city, we read the material city itself.

This technique is foregrounded in Dos Passos's insistence that "the narrative must stand off the page."[27] The author means, here, that the narrative should, like the advertisements, movies, and show windows described in the Grosz essay, impact one directly, "attack" the reader and enable her to perceive the new patterns and arrangements of modern life. By inventing "new ways of seeing things" through the literary text, Dos Passos explicitly associates the text with a visual, material dimension. And with this move, Dos Passos suggests how the experience of the text duplicates the physical experience of the city. The author demonstrates this through the inclusion of vast amounts of printed matter that is recycled and circulated throughout the novel. If we take him at his word, that he records in the same fleeting manner as the movie camera, then clearly what the novelist most has access to is the printed matter that circulates in the city.[28] If the city is a medium, then the print medium is one compatible data channel, and the New York of *Manhattan Transfer* is described as "the city of scrambled alphabets" (351).[29] We might say the same for the novel as a whole. The city, no less than the book, is a discourse network, and both the geographical and the textual Manhattans reveal the constraints on media that determine what data are selected, stored, and transmitted from the vast background of noise. Moreover, and this is a critical point, the book shows that media do not function within a vacuum of their own technical making, but are components of a complex array of social, political, and economic forces. In this regard Dos Passos can be contrasted with Döblin, who, although he presents political content, does not reflect on the role of the media in its formulation. Döblin shows concern for and attention to questions of aesthetics and the work of art; Dos Passos, however, connects these questions to sociopolitical concerns.

A scattering of examples from the text gives evidence to this effect. Broadway, for example, is presented as "the furnace of beaded letter cut light" (249). And in the opening imagery of the chapter, "Nine Days' Wonder," the city is presented as "Pink sheets, green sheets, gray sheets, FULL MARKET REPORTS, FINALS ON HAVRE DE GRACE. Print squirms among the shopworn officeworn sagging faces, sore fingertips, aching insteps, strongarm men cram into subway expresses. SENATORS 8, GIANTS 2, DIVA RECOVERS PEARLS, $800,000 ROBBERY" (169). The young Jimmy Herf, who will eventually reject his uncle's offer of a promising banking career to pursue the life of a journalist, finds no pleasure in children's stories, opting instead to read the *American Cyclopædia,* beginning with "A the first of the vowels" (86). As he later states, "Print itches like a rash inside me. I sit here pockmarked with print" (354). The movement in and out of various linguistic registers makes it difficult for the reader to establish where Dos Passos's use of documentary material ends and his fictional narrative recommences, so thoroughly intertwined are the various components of the prose. This aspect of the prose is taken up in a highly self-reflexive passage in which the fictional narrative of Francie and her boyfriend Dutch, who turn to a life of crime in order to escape poverty, is continued in a newspaper article on their capture that Jimmy Herf reads, and finally concludes with the legal jargon of a courtroom scene. Newspapers and office reports are of course not the only source of this linguistic debris, the city (and the novel) is strewn with advertisements, exemplified most pointedly by the woman on the white horse who does not ride around the city pleading for tax relief, but in order to advertise "Danderine," a dandruff shampoo.

The verbal elements of which the novel is composed function individually on the order of discrete and fragmented pieces of information. Reassembled as constituent parts of a textual montage, however, they communicate a complex emotional message of desire, loss, ambition, and love. Eisenstein described his own method of montage in similar terms. The novel incorporates actual elements of the city—its verbal material—but recombines and reorganizes their presentation in order to produce a whole work directed to instruct and to aid the reader in new ways of seeing and of critiquing various technologies of representation, and to communicate a message that is felt like a physical shock to the body through the eyes. By working with his linguistic material in this manner, Dos Passos makes explicit the characteristics of the medium of print itself. The discrete letters and complexes of words bump against each other (sometimes quite literally, in Dos Passos's frequent coining of neologisms and run-ons), producing a reading effect that denies the possibility of stable or at least consistent sites of linguistic reference.

In Dos Passos's view, this formal experimentation with the text is necessary because the mediascape of the early twentieth century does not permit the writer the same faith in language that previous generations enjoyed: "In a time of confusion and rapid change like the present, when terms are continually turning inside out and names of things hardly keep their meaning from day to day, it's not possible to write two honest paragraphs without stopping to take crossbearings on every one of the abstractions that were so well ranged in ornate marble niches in the minds of our fathers."[30] The author echoes here the linguistic crisis that was already (ironically) verbalized in Hofmannsthal's writing from the beginning of the century as discussed earlier. However, Dos Passos uses his literary montage to render the familiar aspects and connotations of the words he uses unfamiliar—shocking the reader into a new way of reading, a new way of seeing. It is thus perhaps no coincidence that one of the most telling similarities between Döblin's *Berlin Alexanderplatz* and Dos Passos's *Manhattan Transfer* has to do with the negotiation of and, in the case of the two protagonists Franz Biberkopf and Jimmy Herf, an ultimate disavowal of linguistic certitude. Biberkopf makes explicit the connection between physical traffic in the city and the circulation of words, concluding: "The words come rolling up to us, we must be careful not to get run over; if we don't watch out for the auto-bus, it'll make apple-sauce out of us. I'll never again stake my word on anything in the world" (*Berlin Alexanderplatz*, 633). And prepared to leave the city after a brief, unsuccessful career as a journalist, Jimmy Herf can only lament, "If I still had faith in words" (*Manhattan Transfer*, 366).

It is by now commonplace, perhaps, to remark on the notion of linguistic incertitude when referring to this literary period, or to speak of the crisis of language that is inscribed in the language of the text. However, the effect in a novel like *Manhattan Transfer* is not ultimately one of a rejection of the literary medium of print, but rather, as Dos Passos states, one of taking "crossbearings" on the problem of language and communication itself, and that particularly with respect to the representation of a city like New York or Berlin. For the experience of those cities upsets traditional modes of representation and communication. Both Döblin and Dos Passos suggest that the city cannot be properly synthesized or narrated through any kind of unified composition. The city must be presented directly—an idea that both men explicitly linked to the sensorial effects of the film medium. Rather than turn their artistic attention to film (with the exception of a few screenplays neither man pursued a career in the film industry), they investigate how their work in the linguistic medium can imitate some of the effects of the technical one. The text *on* the city must simulate the text *of* the city, presenting the metropolitan imagination itself as a dynamic event. In this manner the literary text inscribes in its own language the effects of other media. Although a common perspective on the period before the cinematic sound era posits traditional cultural forms such as literature or the fine arts as the standard from which new media are analyzed, Dos Passos's and Döblin's writing embrace and illustrate the role that emerging recording technologies played in a new theorization of literary prose.

CAMERA EYE AND THE RECORDING OF MODERNITY

Dos Passos considered *U.S.A.* in many ways an extension and refinement of some of the formal prose experiments initiated with *Manhattan Transfer*, especially in the refinement of techniques invented to simulate cinematic montage: "I was trying to develop what I had started, possibly somewhat unconsciously in *Manhattan Transfer*. By that time I was really taken with the idea of montage. I had tried it out in *Manhattan Transfer*—using pieces of popular songs. By the time it evolved into such compartments as the camera eye of the *U.S.A.* trilogy it served a useful function."[31] Film is not the only recording medium evoked in the novel, however. With the Camera Eye, Dos Passos explicitly foregrounds both photographic techniques and the possibility of a photographic discourse. *U.S.A.* is the title of the trilogy composed of *The 42nd Parallel* (1930), *1919* (1932), and *The Big Money* (1936). All three novels incorporate the weaving together of four distinct methods: Camera Eye, Newsreels, biographies of famous citizens, and narratives of a primary set of fictional characters (twelve in total across the three novels). In his introductory note to the 1937 edition of *The 42nd Parallel,* Dos Passos described the function of each of these elements: "In an effort to take in as much as possible of the broad field of the lives of these times, three separate sequences have been threaded in and out among the stories. Of these *The Camera Eye* aims to indicate the position of the observer and *Newsreel* to give an inkling of the common mind of the epoch. Portraits of a number of real people are interlarded in the pauses in the narrative because their lives seem to embody so well the quality of the soil in which Americans of these generations grew."[32] By combining these different elements, Dos Passos sought not only to broaden the perspective and scope of the novel but also to provide contrasting formal possibilities. With the exception of the biographies, the different elements are spliced together roughly chronologically, from 1900 (the date with which *The 42nd Parallel* opens) to approximately 1930. So for example, in addition to providing the background noise or "clamor"[33] of the period, the Newsreels serve to locate the story in time (political slogans from a particular campaign year, the sinking of the Titanic, and so forth). The Newsreel sections are probably the most familiar aspect from *Manhattan Transfer* in terms of their formal composition, for the narrative sequences in *U.S.A.* are much more self-contained and expansive than the brief fragments of which *Manhattan Transfer* is composed.

The most striking distinction between the earlier novel and the later trilogy, however, is the inclusion of the Camera Eye sequences. Dos Passos always maintained that the function of the Camera Eye was to provide a subjective outlet so that the other components of the novel could be more properly objective. Through the Camera Eye, Dos Passos wanted to "distill my subjective feelings about the incidents and people described. My hope was to achieve the objective approach. . . . In the biographies, in the newsreels, and even the narrative, I aimed at total objectivity by giving conflicting views—using the camera eye as a safety valve for my own subjective feelings. It made objectivity in the rest of the book much easier."[34] The correspondence between the events alluded to in the Camera Eye sections and biographical elements drawn from Dos Passos's life has long been noted.[35] The Camera Eye runs parallel to the chronology of events portrayed in the trilogy as a whole: allusions to the Boer War in the first Camera Eye in *The 42nd Parallel* date it to 1900; the last Camera Eye of *The Big Money* refers to Dos Passos's visit to Harlan County, Kentucky in the fall of 1931. As a result, the Camera Eye sections have sometimes been read as "a story of maturation" delineating the artistic, sexual, and biographical trajectory of the author himself.[36]

Less frequently in these readings, however, do critics reflect on the technology and recording medium referred to by name: Camera Eye. In her study, Gretchen Foster points out the correspondence between Dos Passos's heading and the Russian filmmaker Dziga Vertov's name for his documentaries, "Kino-Eye." However, as she concedes, there is a problem with this comparison since Vertov used his term to refer to a method of documentary filmmaking that assembles fragments of seemingly objective visual material into a new and meaningful whole, whereas Dos Passos insists on the subjectivity of his device from the outset. Foster properly maintains that Vertov's "Kino-Eye" corresponds more closely to Dos Passos's Newsreel sections in *U.S.A.*, and I would add, to the initial motivation behind the verbal experiments in *Manhattan Transfer* (in order to read "like a documentary film"). In light of this contradiction, Foster concludes: "If Dos Passos was aware of its connotations, why did he use camera eye for his novel's most subjective sections? Most likely, he had heard the term somewhere and, with his keen sense of the author as 'the best possible type of moving picture machine contrived to focus the present moment on the screen of the future,' saw no contradiction in using a documentary term to record his private consciousness."[37] This conclusion, however, vastly oversimplifies the conceit of the Camera Eye, ignoring Dos Passos's recognition that photography was anything but an objective exercise. The photographic image is no mere capture of external reality but a highly subjective experience through which we organize our experience at the personal level and construct social reality at the public level. This emphasis on the social function, if not the ideological construction, of seemingly objective media practices marks a critical distinction in the conception of the mediascape as it is taken up by the German literary authors in our study. Further, Foster's reading reduces the Camera Eye sections to the mere recording of the author's thoughts, much like a journal or diary, and thereby ignores the explicit manner in which the Camera Eye records from the position of the observer an external world of images. In effect, Foster's conclusion resituates the Camera Eye in a "wordminded" culture. It is, however, distinctly "eyeminded."

This distinction is critical, for Dos Passos's creation of the Camera Eye suggests an alternative approach to some of the questions concerning the relationship of poetic writing to photography discussed earlier with regard to Rainer Maria Rilke's own city novel. For Rilke, we recall, the photographic plate is emblematic of the poet's temporal and spatial disorientation and his struggle to create the eternal art object in the midst of a rapidly modernizing world. Rilke struggled with the question of how the medium of photography as an alternative means of material recording problematizes the presupposition and possibility of poetic writing as transcendent; Dos Passos, however, uses the Camera Eye, and by extension a theorization of photographic recording, to show how one can employ the epistemological considerations introduced by the fact of photography precisely in order to go on writing (recall Dos Passos's claim that the other three sections of *U.S.A.* require the inclusion of the Camera Eye so that they can stand). Dos Passos thus unwittingly shows himself the heir to Rilke (and through Rilke, to Baudelaire). In a sense, Malte's apprenticeship in vision in *The Notebooks of Malte Laurids Brigge* ("I am learning to see") was his initiation into what Dos Passos would later identify as an increasingly pervasive "eyeminded" culture. The subject of Dos Passos's Camera Eye sections is explicitly a subject who sees and who in seeing, records. The Camera Eye sections are not written from the point of view of the adult author reflecting on, for example, his experience as a four-year-old (the observer's age in the first Camera Eye of *The 42nd Parallel*), but rather serve to retransmit what was directly perceived and recorded at a moment past onto a moment future: "She's walking fast and we're running her pointed toes sticking out sharp among the poor trodden grassblades under the shaking folds of the brown cloth dress   Englander   a pebble tinkles along the cobbles."[38] One must take the author literally when he states: "I cannot see how even the most immortal writer is more than the best possible type of moving picture machine contrived to focus the present moment on the screen of the future."[39] With this statement (which Foster also quotes only to oversimplify as the author's documentary impulse), Dos Passos makes clear the inherent paradox of *modernity* and its contradictory relationship to temporality. For on the one hand, the author seeks to record the "present" as a unique and instantaneous moment, divorced from its linkages to the past; however, this recording is concurrently incorporated within a temporal chain, directed to a future in which that present is already past. As a result, the instantaneity of the present is always coupled with its representation ("on the screen of the future"). The camera becomes the chosen analogy by which to express the untenable position of this paradoxical link.

In two notebook entries preceding the composition of *U.S.A.*, Dos Passos made early attempts to explain the function of the Camera Eye section:

> Camera eye
> The upside down image in the retina
> piece by piece immediately out of color
>   shape
> remembered bright and dark rebuilds the city
> [Sunday] sunlight on the downtown streets
> [Stained uneven] pavements—Truck cluttered
> streets—Terrible dead city on the make—

And:

> Camera Eye—the careful clipping out of
> paper figures the old photographs   the
> newspaper cartoons shall I make this
> one up—Newspaper photographs of old
> photographs in a trunk the pathetic
> enthusiasm—...
>   how could you warp the paper figures
> to simulate growth—twist cut out a
> pack and [tickle] whittle it up to eighty

>   —shove him through the terribly various
>   velocities of time. Imagine paper boats
>   that will indicate the swirls and
>   eddies of the stream.[40]

In these two poems on the Camera Eye, we find a wealth of imagery that goes far beyond the simple idea offered by Dos Passos in interviews that the Camera Eye functions as an outlet of the narrator's subjective experience in time and is replayed in parallel to the action of the three otherwise objective sections of the novels. The use of the Camera Eye goes rather to the heart of complex questions of temporality and experience, and of objectivity. As we saw in Rilke's writing from almost two decades earlier, Dos Passos conjoins the imperative of "learning to see" or a "new way of seeing" and its linguistic presentation with the technology of the camera. In Dos Passos's musings on the state of poetry itself, the Camera Eye offers the possibility for the complex representation of modern life already described by Baudelaire in his essay "The Painter of Modern Life."

The "upside down image in the retina" is a reminder that the human eye is itself constructed like a camera. The body is presented as a technological apparatus, whereby the sense of sight doubles the mechanical production of images. And it is clear that the material surface of this inscription is not secondary to the subjective interiority of the author's thoughts, but is rather a primary event. The first notation on the Camera Eye makes explicit the temporality of the technique of recording. It is immediate, instantaneous; the observer is present to the event observed. As Rilke evoked through his poem, "The Panther," the image goes straight to the optic nerve, without the filter of intellectual reflection. However, this notion of immediacy is, at the same time, negated: "immediately out of color/shape/remembered bright and dark rebuilds the city." Immediately/Remembered suggests that the present can only be experienced as a moment just past, as an engram of memory that takes on the function of a storehouse of negatives, "bright and dark." Thus the unique moments of the present are connected as elements in a temporal chain. Paul de Man has called this dual movement the paradoxical formulation of modernity: "It is a temporal experience of human mutability, historical in the deepest sense of the term in that it implies the necessary experience of any present as a *passing* experience that makes the past irrevocable and unforgettable because it is inseparable from any present or future. . . . Modernity invests its trust in the present moment as an origin, but discovers that, in severing itself from the past, it has at the same time severed itself from the present."[41] For de Man, this condition of modernity goes to the heart of the definition of literature itself, which is likewise the contradictory impulse to instantaneity and to duration, or in Dos Passos's formulations, the author's task to focus the present on the screen of the future or the camera eye as immediately/remembered. What is so interesting about Dos Passos's formulation is the manner in which a mechanical device, and a visual medium, is employed to go to the heart of the complex question of literature and narrativity. In effect, the photograph provides a privileged means by which one can think through the question of what it means to represent the present.

In "The Painter of Modern Life," Baudelaire defines modernity as "the ephemeral, the fugitive, the contingent, the half of art whose other half is the eternal and the immutable."[42] And he describes how Monsieur G. struggles with the contradictory task of its representation. Fighting with his writing implements, the painter of modern life works at a frenzied pace, as if afraid that the images he has just seen in the external world will be lost before he is able to record them. The world that emerges on Monsieur G.'s paper both duplicates and exceeds the external world as the raw material is ordered, harmonized, and idealized. This same struggle for expression is evident in Dos Passos's second note on the Camera Eye, for if the first note takes as its theme the position of the observer to the present, the second addresses its retransmission. Through the use of the analogy to photography, the raw materials of memory are presented as "old photographs in a trunk," images tossed together, locked up, until the trunk is reopened and they are resorted, rearranged in a narrative that gives evidence to "the terribly various velocities of time." In other words, like Monsieur G., the author must struggle in his attempt to duplicate the freshness of perspective, the unique and evanescent moment of discovery, with a language that cannot help but negate this originary moment, for in de Man's words, and borrowing from Nietzsche, "it knows itself to be mere repetition, mere fiction and allegory, forever unable to participate in the spontaneity of action or modernity."[43] Like the creative act of Monsieur G., or that described by Dos Passos, literature is thus in a constant state of "movement," to use de Man's term, and is continuously engaged in the "fictional narration of this movement" by which literature both is and is not itself, both is and is not "modern."[44] De Man draws attention to Baudelaire's theme of the carriages in Monsieur G.'s work as the writing of this movement—a figure that in Dos Passos's text is taken up by the "paper boats / that will indicate the swirls and / eddies of the stream." In these turbulent waters, the text traces out the pursuit of "modernity."

The image of the photographs tossed together in a drawer recalls another image, namely, Rilke's allusion to the *Notebooks* as "disordered papers in a drawer" from which "the sketch of an existence and a shadow-network of forces" arise. A good example of the provisional organization (to borrow Siegfried Kracauer's phrase from "Photography") of the photographic fragments of memory in Dos Passos's Camera Eye is presented in the twenty-eighth entry in *U.S.A.* (the first Camera Eye in the second novel of the trilogy, *1919*):

> when the telegram came that she was dying (the streetcarwheels screeched round the bellglass like all the pencils on all the slates in all the schools) walking around Fresh Pond the smell of puddlewater willowsbuds in the raw wind shrieking streetcarwheels rattling on loose trucks through the Boston suburbs   grief isnt a uniform and go shock the Booch and drink wine for supper at the Lenox before catching the Federal:
>
> *I'm so tired of violets*
> *Take them all away*
>
> when the telegram came that she was dying the bell-glass cracked in a screech of slate pencils (have you ever never been able to sleep for a week in April?)   and He met me in the grey trainshed my eyes were stinging with vermillion bronze and chromegreen inks that oozed from the spinning April hills   His moustaches were white the tired droop of an old man's cheeks   She's gone Jack grief isnt a uniform and the   in the parlor   the waxen odor of lilies in the parlor (He and I we must bury the uniform of grief)[45]

Although the two paragraphs repeat words and even whole fragments, their effect is quite different. In this manner, the text "rebuilds the city" (or in this case, rebuilds the moment of learning of his mother's death) anew with each linguistic print of the image negatives. Both Rilke's sketch and Dos Passos's paper figures (the images literally printed on photographic paper and, simultaneously, the linguistic markings inscribed in the author's manuscript) are equivalent to Monsieur G.'s own sketches, which at every step both are and are not complete.

Dos Passos, like Baudelaire, uses the figure of the child as a metaphor of the suppression of anteriority in favor of the sense of discovery implied by modernity: "To observe objectively a man has to retain something of childhood's naive and ignorant state of mind. In my experience children and illiterate people often see things more exactly than educated men. The first-rate novelist like the first-rate scientist must be obsessed by his own ignorance. This conviction of ignorance is the first step toward understanding. Astonishment strangely quickens the senses."[46] The child is the one who actively engages in "new ways of seeing" and who, with no knowledge of a past or history and no access to the literary tradition is, like the illiterate, closest to an "eyeminded" mode of being. One recalls here, as well, Malte's insistence in the *Notebooks* of not knowing how to read. His affected illiteracy is a response to this dual "movement" of literature by which the literary text is both an instantaneous, spontaneous act and always a repetition. For as Malte laments, one cannot read one book without reading them all.

The Camera Eye is, in effect, the technological equivalent of this dual impulse. For photography introduces a new mechanics of seeing and a technology of representation that only seems to avoid this contradiction. If we return to Dos Passos's statement that the Camera Eye sections are the "subjective" portions of what is otherwise purportedly an "objective" text, we might now be able to puzzle out the paradox at the core of this idea. For the Camera Eye is indeed the position of one individual observer, and perhaps that of the author himself, at various moments in his life, but foremost it is the position of one who was "present" at these moments and recorded that which was most transient and ephemeral. Dos Passos does not use the Camera Eye to tell us about a world from which it is distinct, but rather presents the world directly, by redeveloping, as it were, the storehouse of fragmented and disconnected negatives into the text—"remembered bright and dark rebuilds the city." Wlad Godzich's contrast between photography and what he calls "premodern" modes of representation is instructive on this question:

> Photography is indeed immediate; it reproduces the objects such as they are, once all issues of angle, composition, and so forth are taken care of. By giving us things the way they are, photography confers upon them an imaginary presence that no mode of representation had achieved until then. Originally, image means imitation: the image that imitates the world remains distinct from the world. We now have images that coincide so much with the given that they abolish themselves as images in order to become the given magically repeated.[47]

It is for this reason, perhaps, that Dos Passos chose to refer to his texts as "contemporary chronicles."[48] The choice of the word "chronicle" reveals how the author saw his work as a record of time. As a recording of "present" time, the present is revealed through its having been recorded, or made past, and projected on the screen of the future. The use of the term "chronicle" is again evocative of Rilke's work as well: *Aufzeichnungen* (Notebooks) can also be translated as chronicles. The *Aufzeichnungen* and Dos Passos's "chronicles" are essentially associated with the time at which they come into existence, just as Kracauer described the properties of the medium of photography. Nonetheless, neither Rilke's nor Dos Passos's work are photographs, but rather, deeply invested in questions of writing. And as Dos Passos indicated, it is only through the inclusion of the Camera Eye in *U.S.A.* that the other elements of the text (Newsreels, biographies and fictional narratives) can function. The language of the Camera Eye furthermore reveals the extent to which Dos Passos's text is inscribed in a particular configuration of alternate medial possibilities, and how these media effect the organization of the human sensorium and consciousness on the individual level. It is only in this way that we can perhaps begin to understand why it is that the most personal voice of the novel is located in and presented as a camera.

The chronicles are simultaneously a recording, however, of that which cannot be recorded. In other words, by self-consciously calling attention to their recording as text and the structure of their own composition, Dos Passos's novels indicate the threshold of print and linguistic recording and its competition with other media, much as we saw with the struggling writers in the *Kinobuch* screenplays. A passage that gives evidence to this impulse can be found in the fifth Camera Eye from *The 42nd Parallel*. Here, the observer is a young boy playing when a man comes into the house with a gramophone:

> Mr. Garnet who was still hale and hearty although so very old came to tea and we saw him first through the window with his red face and John Bull whiskers and aunty said it was a sailor's rolling gait and he was carrying a box under his arm and Vickie and Pompom barked and here was Mr. Garnet come to tea and he took a gramophone out of a black box and put a cylinder on the gramophone and they pushed back the teathings off the corner of the table   Be careful not to drop it now they scratch rather heasy   Why a hordinary sewin' needle would do maam but I ave special needles
>
>   ... and he wound it up very carefully so as not to break the spring and the needle went rasp rasp ... and he had a mariner's compass in red and blue on the back of his hand and his nails looked black and thick as he fumbled with the needle and the needle went rasp rasp and far away

a band played and out of a grindy noise in the little black horn came *God Save the King* and the little dogs howled[49]

Even with the proliferation of print and narratives, biographies and songs and headlines that are included in the text, and with the wealth of visual detail, the "rasp rasp" of the gramophone cylinder evades the medium of language, and gives evidence to the boundedness, by definition, of all modern media. The noise of the gramophone draws attention to the very letters and words of which Dos Passos's text is composed, for this sound evokes the ever present background of noise transmitted through alternate channels for which there is no linguistic encoding. Through the use of the Camera Eye and multiple references to other media throughout the pages of *U.S.A.*, Dos Passos not only points to the limits of language, but also demonstrates that his theorization of modernity and more specifically modern literature is not isolated from the logic of alternate media and data flows. The literature of the period records the effects of these other media, not just as props to identify the time period (all the phonograph records and movie theaters crowding the plots of so many novels of the early twentieth century) but as constitutive of formal elements in the construction of the text and a critical component in a host of urgent questions concerning aesthetics, narrative and non-narrative representation, and subjectivity.

POSTSCRIPT ON NEW MEDIA

In an interview conducted in 1968, Dos Passos was asked to comment on the current relationship between cinema and literary writing, given the obvious and explicit connections between his own work and the methods of cinematic montage that he admired in D. W. Griffith and Sergei Eisenstein. Surprisingly, perhaps, Dos Passos maintained that this intersection was no longer as compelling as it had been for his generation: "There is now probably less interest by writers in cinema because we have become so accustomed to this medium that it is less exciting than when it was very new."[50] In his answer, Dos Passos reveals that the author's response to film (and one could add to this list the various other media we have already discussed) is particularly a reaction to a mediascape that was very much in flux at the beginning of the century. In other words, it was while the author was still "unaccustomed" or not yet habituated to their effects that they presented to the author what Dos Passos had earlier called a "new way of seeing." The literary text circumscribed by the medium of print is revealed as just one limited possibility within a rapidly expanding mediascape. Any number of authors from Rilke to Döblin to Dos Passos himself do not merely write *about* these new technologies, but go a step further, and begin to inscribe within the techniques of writing the very assumptions expressed through their themes (namely, urban life, transportation systems, communications technologies).

Early negative criticisms of film warned that the social impact of this technology would in effect bring about the end of book culture. However, it did not spell an end but rather a complex transformation of literature within the context of perceptual dishabituation. The impact of technologies such as film, photography, radio, and transportation systems, to name just a few, altered the manner in which one began to think about writing and questions of representation. In these reformulations from the beginning of the century, one can perhaps look for answers to our ongoing concern at century's end with the complicated relationship of technology to our own lives. Just as the mechanical media emerging around 1900 resulted in new concepts of vision, perception, and consciousness, the disruption of temporal and spatial continuities, and the problematic status of memory, we might question what the effects of electronic media are around 2000. How is the "understanding" of media that emerges in the literature of the earlier period necessarily reformulated in literature emerging in the second half of the twentieth and early part of the twenty-first centuries? For if Heidegger was right, that technology prevents any experience of its own essence, it is perhaps in the pages of the literary record that one must look for a beginning to these answers.

With the invention of digital photography and the ubiquity of computerized images, we have perhaps already entered what some are calling an age of "postphotography." As images are increasingly manipulated, altered, and otherwise transformed, the legitimacy of the photographic and the cinematic image and their fundamental relationship to reality is increasingly called into question. Already the status of the photograph as evidence, or the legacy of truth that once adhered to the photographic image, is seen as the naive assumption of a more innocent past. And yet, these technologies of image production have not ceased to fascinate since their invention, when they already set into motion a host of inquiries that continue to preoccupy us to this day, inquiries concerning the nature of reality, memory, history, and temporality; the status of the image; and the relationship to one's self and to others. For photography's relationship to its referent was never as straightforward as theoreticians of new media have made it appear in hindsight. The manner in which visual and audio recordings appear to present us with everything is, in fact, a mere technical effect.

To limit our reflections to just one technical medium of reproduction—the photograph—we might ask: can we detect a difference in the stance of our group of authors from the first decades of the century vis-à-vis the new media and the way later generations of authors have addressed the production and the reception of the photographic image, and if so, in what does this difference consist? I suggest that this difference is largely on the order of a shift from an earlier preoccupation with sensorial effects and their concomitant role in subject relations to a later engagement with the politics of media in the service of a cultural and social discourse of power. The perceived immediacy of the photographic image, its seeming transparent and direct presentation of the moment in which the shutter snaps, often leads one to forget the object of the photograph itself. As Geoffrey Batchen has argued, "This is almost a perceptual necessity; in order to see what the photograph is of, we must first repress our consciousness of what the photograph is. As a consequence, in even the most sophisticated discussions, the photograph itself—the actual object being examined—is usually left out of the analysis."[51] A recognition of the importance of the material, technical, and historical aspects of the photographic process is to ask how social reality and historical memory are created, restricted, and passed down through an evolving, ubiquitous medium. The photograph is indeed a heterogeneous object: it can inform, delight, instruct, and move. Although the photograph is often less informative *quantitatively* than a written document that might provide empirical data about an event, the photograph nevertheless may appear to offer more *qualitative* information because of the perceived indexical relationship to the event pictured (that which was captured on film is what *actually* transpired before the lens). This seeming immediacy, however, is belied by a complex process of selection, framing, and printing techniques. As we have seen, an author like Döblin celebrated this so-called immediacy, whereas in the work of Dos Passos, this encounter with the photographic image as an encounter with unmediated "reality" already begins to be called into question.

As we noted earlier, Siegfried Kracauer observed the simultaneous emergence of modern photography and a new conceptualization of history—specifically, in the construction of significance, coherence, and meaning, as well as on the order of the relation to time and mortality. For this reason, Kracauer posited the "memory image" and the photographic image as mutually exclusive. For if the organizing principle of the memory image (which is associated with narrative and with writing) is that of personal signification, the organizing principle of the photograph is quite simply that which is given as a spatial condition. Thus, from the perspective of photography, memory appears full of gaps because of a selection process that filters detail, whereas according to the standards of memory, the photograph is a jumble of garbage, the exterior debris or spatial and visible continuum of a specific moment in time. This results, paradoxically perhaps, in a certain disconnect between memory and the photograph.

In works of prose narrative in the postwar period, the reproduction of or even allusion to individual photographs, their staging and later dissemination, their collection in family albums, their veracity, and even their absence often serve as ways of thinking through problems of memory, history, and knowing that form the central crisis of many of the works that interrogate media of image production. How do we come to know reality? How do narratives and images structure the way we see ourselves and how we construct our notion of self, in the present and in the past? In these works, the technology of memory is presented as a composite of what W. J. T. Mitchell has called the "image-text," in which visual and verbal relations are staged; however, this narrative structure, like memory itself, is inherently unstable. The photograph is almost never presented as an unpremeditated, reassuringly stable image in which the world can be taken at face value. In other words, although the photograph may become meaningful through certain transactions and has real effects, it can never, as John Tagg has argued, "refer or be referred to a prephotographic reality as to a truth."[52] Such works therefore problematize the very process of passing on the story, or of historiography more generally, by drawing attention to the mediation of acts of both recording (the photographer, the writer) and reception (the viewer, the reader).

In his extended essay on photography, *Towards a Philosophy of Photography,* Vilém Flusser gives this definition of the photographer: "a person who attempts to place, within the image, information that is not predicted within the program of the camera."[53] By this, Flusser underscores that photography is not an individual pursuit in which an autonomous and subjective vision is wordlessly presented, but that photographic practice specifically, and media more generally, functions within networks of social, political, and ideological concerns. Flusser goes on to argue, therefore, that a "philosophy of photography is necessary for raising photographic practice to the level of consciousness, and this is . . . because this practice gives rise to a model of freedom in the post-industrial context in general."⁵⁴ As a learned, constructive practice, photography simultaneously references its own restraints, limits, and systems of rules. For example, by calling attention to the frame, our attention is called both to what is inside and to what is outside visibility. The frame interrupts, disrupts, the perceived fluidity or transparency of easy communication. We might even call this the *crisis* of photography, in the etymological sense of the term. Originally, the word *crisis* was used in medicine to identify the point where a patient will live or die. The *crisis* marks a decision: on the part of the photographer who decides when to release the shutter of the camera, to capture an image of this moment and not that, to extend the frame here but not there, to disrupt or circumvent the technical and social norms of photography. A crisis, as well, on the part of the viewer who must decide to look, to likewise be implicated in the photograph, to take responsibility for what he or she sees. In other words, the photograph is most effective (and affective) when it disrupts our existing relationship to it as a viewer. It is the recognition of these crises—photographic, historical, political—that constitute the urgency of literary works that engage media practices at the end of the century. Although it is beyond the scope of this book to present this argument in detail, I want to conclude by touching briefly on two postwar figures: Alexander Kluge and W. G. Sebald. As both are contemporary "documentarists," it is important to think about how the intersection of literature and "traditional" (or, no longer new) media frames a new set of questions in their work.

In his analysis of Kluge's "Der Luftangriff auf Halberstadt" (The Air Raid of April 8, 1945 on Halberstadt), the second pamphlet (*Heft*) in Kluge's *Neue Geschichten* (New Stories/Histories), Sebald wrote: "The reconstruction that Kluge was able to make of the disaster . . . can be likened to the revelation of the rational structure of something experienced by millions of human beings as an irrational blow of fate."⁵⁵ A close reading of Kluge's prose work, including his extensive writing on media, especially film, and the public sphere, reveals a certain similarity between the "rational structure" that Kluge describes in "Luftangriff" and the "rational structure" of public media practices that Kluge critiques elsewhere more directly. In other words, "Luftangriff" does not only describe, in detail, the events of a specific historical date, but reflects on the confluence of military and media practices more generally. In Sebald's lectures and published texts on the near absence of, or at least neglected critical reception of, literary representations of the devastation of Germany during the war, Kluge's name appears not only as one of the few but indeed as one of the exemplary figures who approached this subject. For it is not only the fact of the descriptions of the bombing of Halberstadt that we find in Kluge's *Neue Geschichten* but the mapping of a literary methodology with which Sebald's own work shares many affinities. The *Neue Geschichten* consists of a series of pamphlets or notebooks that present German cultural, political, and social history, through a heterogeneous collection of firsthand accounts, quotations from historical documents, journalistic reportages, poems, and songs, and reproduces photographs, charts, drawings, and other material elements within its pages—seen in this way, their composition sounds very much like Döblin's or Dos Passos's work. "Luftangriff," for example, is constructed through a series of fragments that describe in either first- or second-hand accounts the harrowing experience of individual residents of the town on the day it was bombed during the last weeks of the war; the details of the military strategy of fire bombing; transcripts of postwar conferences on military objectives and consequences of the war; interviews of former military personnel who took part in the raid; and attempts on the part of firemen, doctors, bureaucrats, and others to manage the day's events. The prose is interspersed with photographs, tactical drawings, and technical charts. Although one can attempt to create a chronology of events, Kluge rejects a linear narrative, emphasizing moments of simultaneity and stressing the synchronization and continuities between past and present. Kluge's crossing of genres, combining documentary and fiction, impersonal and personal points of view, what he calls "the strategy from above" and "the strategy from below"—serve to mediate between personal experience and the public recording of and discourse on these events. In this way, as Sebald recognized, Kluge's textual practices serve as a second-order reflection not only on literary representation, but more specifically, the sociopolitical and cultural implications of the role of material practices in the construction and transmission of personal and cultural memory.

In this context Kluge elaborates two types of realism: the one is the superficial reproduction of outward reality that only confirms, and thereby affirms, the existence of what it shows and permits only passive reception; whereas the second, and the method favored by Kluge, is critical and subversive, and demands the active participation of the reader in resisting the deceptive order of things. Kluge dismisses the difference between literary or fictional and documentary texts, creating confusion in the mind of the reader over whether the documents he purports to reproduce are in fact real or imagined, in order to remind us that no form of discourse is neutral. The motivation for realism should, therefore, be to stage a protest against rather than to affirm given conditions. This protest is communicated, for example, in the fourth *Heft* of the *Neue Geschichten,* "Verschrottung Durch Arbeit" (Trashed by Work), which details the conditions at a forced labor camp outside Halberstadt during the war. As in "Luftangriff," Kluge is interested in drawing linkages between industrial, economic, and political efficiencies that are to the detriment of individuals. Specifically, he exposes the horrible paradox of the contradictory aims of the organizers and profiteers of the camps: *production goals* and *extermination goals.* In addition to criticizing the role of private industry in the crimes of National Socialism, Kluge shows how the individual is reduced to an abstract sum in the calculation of the economics of labor and death. In its construction and use of language, Kluge circumvents a traditional narrative that uses meaning and causality and at its far end would permit aesthetic pleasure even in horror. In the context of this study, with its emphasis on how prose texts of the early part of the century negotiated an expanding mediascape that privileged the recording of material effects, it may be important to ask: Is Kluge's prescription for prose writing reducible to the presence of documentary material in his work? And further, to what degree is his interrogation of media consonant with Döblin's and Dos Passos's project?

In a letter to Adorno written in 1968 (and reprinted at the beginning of Marcel Atze and Franz Loquai's collection, *Sebald: Lektüren*), Sebald appears to provide a blueprint for Kluge's (and his own) literary principles. The letter was ostensibly written to ask Adorno to write a letter of reference for Sebald's application to Cambridge, and included a very broad outline of his proposed dissertation topic: the writer, Alfred Döblin. Sebald writes, "As I see it now, this project will include an analysis of the crisis of the novel, of narrative in general. For no matter how hard Döblin tried to reinvent narrative form, he was only able to succeed in the few cases where he employed the document as his most important vehicle. I'm not yet sure how I will approach this, but I want to reconceive this necessary 'objectifization' of art as one of its last possibilities."[56] The role of the document forms perhaps *the* critical core of Sebald's own prose writing, a subject on which a large body of work has and continues to be addressed, and I will not rehearse those arguments here. It may be instructive, however, to remark briefly on Sebald's pointed criticism of Döblin's work in his eventual published thesis, *Der Mythus der Zerstörung im Werk Döblins* (The Myth of Destruction in Döblin's Work). For although Döblin, as we have seen, sought likewise to create hybrid works mixing fantasy and fact (what he called *Tatsachenphantasie*), and creating a textual montage (as Walter Benjamin wrote), the reader Sebald finds no kindred literary spirit in Döblin's voluminous writings, when he concludes that in the narrative description of violence, Döblin's novels do not resolve but are symptoms of a crisis and show where the art of writing loses its function of distance. Döblin is not able to maintain a distanced description, but rather descends into observation, fascination, and identification. The habitual mythologization of extreme social circumstances and the uncritical duplication of cinematic effects might only result in the homogenization of personal and collective catastrophe and their reiteration. Döblin's texts fail under this rubric, in other words, because the documentary aspects of the work do not produce a fully productive reader, as Kluge and Sebald seek to do, but a passive one—"excited," as Dos Passos wrote, by the then new media, even dazzled—and one onto which a prescribed social message and vision is imposed, one that ultimately reinscribes meaning and causality, and insists on an aesthetic pleasure even in horror. This, especially, in the passages directed to the narrative of Biberkopf himself, or those moments in the text where documentary effects only mask its inevitable narrative. We might think of this as one reason why the film and radio play that concentrated on this aspect of the novel were so unsuccessful. Döblin's celebratory response to media, especially image and sound recording, is frankly uncritical in its insistence on the transparent recording of reality that these media would afford, and as a result threatens to duplicate, even at its emergence, the industrialization of consciousness that writers like Kluge and Sebald (and so many others of the postwar generation) will later repudiate, taking up the call to produce truly informative works that offer the capacity not only for other ways of seeing, but other ways of thinking.

Notes

CHAPTER 1

The epigraph to this chapter is drawn from Pfemfert, "Kino als Erzieher," in Kaes, *Kino-Debatte*, 62. Unless otherwise indicated, this and all other translations in the text are my own.

1. As the work of Walter Ong has shown us, the character of literature changes historically according to the material and technical resources at its disposal. See Ong, *Orality and Literacy*.
2. McLuhan, *Understanding Media*, 158.
3. Ibid., 9.
4. See Bolz, "Die Schrift des Films," 28.
5. Jay Bolter and Richard Grusin have described the "oscillating" concepts of "immediacy" (transparency) and "hypermediacy" (opacity). See Bolter and Grusin, *Remediation*, 21–44.
6. In formulating this problem, I have been particularly influenced by conversations with and the published work of Elissa Marder. See especially Marder, *Dead Time*.
7. Brecht, "The Film, the Novel and Epic Theatre," 47.
8. Foucault, *Order of Things*, xi.
9. "Foucault, Michel, 1926– ," in Gutting, *Cambridge Companion to Foucault*, 314. Although the entry is signed "Maurice Florence," there is "good reason to think that 'Maurice Florence,' is a pseudonym and that Michel Foucault was himself the author (or involved in the authorship) of the piece; certainly, the perspective of the article is very close to that of his last published works." Gutting, *Cambridge Companion to Foucault*, viii.
10. Canguilhem, "The Death of Man, or Exhaustion of the Cogito?" in Gutting, *Cambridge Companion to Foucault*, 82. This "decoding of the grid" is what constitutes a significant part of Foucault's self-described "Archaeology of the Human Sciences."
11. "Foucault, Michel, 1926– ," 315; Kittler, *Gramophone Film Typewriter*, xxxix; Kittler, *Grammophon Film Typewriter*, 3.
12. As Kittler points out, "*The Archaeology of Knowedge*, in spite of its title, forgets to date the standardization of typewriter keyboards." Kittler, "A Discourse on Discourse," 159.
13. Kittler, *Discourse Networks*, 369.
14. See Kittler, "There Is No Software," in *Literature, Media, Information Systems*, 147–55.
15. Kittler, *Discourse Networks*, 113.
16. Novalis, *Heinrich von Ofterdingen*, in *Schriften*, 1:195.
17. Kittler, *Discourse Networks*, 114.
18. Quoted in Kittler, "Romanticism-Pyschoanalysis-Film," in *Literature, Media, Information Systems*, 90.
19. See Kittler, "The Mechanized Philosopher."
20. Quoted in Kittler, *Gramophone, Film, Typewriter*, 200.
21. Seltzer, *Bodies and Machines*, 10. The spatial and temporal dislocation between where the letters strike and where they appear results from the fact that early typewriters employed an understrike mechanism. When the typist pressed a key, the corresponding bar rose from underneath the machine and struck the paper on the underside of the typewriter roller. As a result, the typist did not see a line of type until some four or five lines after it had originally been produced.
22. Saussure, *Course in General Linguistics*, 119–20.
23. Kittler, *Discourse Networks*, 1, 175.
24. Wellbery, "Foreword," in Kittler, *Discourse Networks*, xxvi.

25. See especially Kittler, "The World of the Symbolic—A World of the Machine," in *Literature, Media, Information Systems*, 130–46.

26. Benjamin, "The Work of Art in the Age of Mechanical Reproduction," in *Illuminations*, 249.

27. Bolz, "Die Schrift des Films," 28.

28. Benjamin, "The Work of Art in the Age of Mechanical Reproduction," 222.

29. Ibid., 233 (translation modified). German: Benjamin, "Das Kunstwerk im Zeitalter seiner technischen Reproduzierbarkeit (Erste Fassung)," in *Gesammelte Schriften*, vol. 1, bk. 2, p. 458. "Das heißt: *im Filmatelier ist die Apparatur derart tief in die Wirklichkeit eingedrungen, daß deren reiner, vom Fremdkörper der Apparatur freier Aspekt das Ergebnis einer eignen technischen Prozedur, nämlich der Aufnahme durch die besonders eingestellte Kamera und ihrer Montierung mit andern Aufnahmen der gleichen Art ist.* Der apparatfreie Aspekt der Realität ist hier zu ihrem künstlichsten geworden und der Anblick der unmittelbaren Wirklichkeit zu der blauen Blume im Land der Technik." In his influential translation, Harry Zohn renders the phrase as "an orchid in the land of technology." In this version one loses the explicit reverence to Novalis and, along with it, the allusion to German romanticism.

30. Hansen, "Benjamin, Cinema, and Experience," 205.

31. Benjamin, "The Task of the Translator," in *Illuminations*, 74.

32. See Weber, *Mass Mediauras*, 83, 89–91.

33. Bolz, "Abschied von der Gutenberg-Galaxis," 151.

34. I use "image-text" here to refer to heterogeneous representational structures that alternately emphasize composite forms, gaps or thresholds, or some more complex hybrid. For an extended discussion of the term, see Mitchell, *Picture Theory*, 83–91.

CHAPTER 2

The epigraph to this chapter is drawn from Rilke and Andreas-Salomé, *Briefwechsel*, 315–16. "Paris war diesmal genau wie ich mirs versprach; schwer. Und ich komme mir vor wie eine photographische Platte, die zu lange belichtet wird, indem ich immer noch dem hier, diesem heftigen Einfluß, ausgesetzt bleibe. . . . Ich bin vor Schrecken gleich Sonntag nach Rouen gereist. Eine ganze Kathedrale thut noth, mich zu übertönen. . . . Wirst Du mirs glauben, daß der Blick einer Vorüberkommenden in einer stillen Gasse Rouens, mich so bewog, daß ich fast nichts sehen konnte hernach, mich für nichts sammeln? Allmählich war dann doch die herrliche Kathedrale da, die Legenden ihrer dichtgefüllten Fenster, wo irdisches Ereignis durchscheinend wird und man das Blut seiner Farben sieht."

1. See, for example, "Die Kathedrale": "als wäre Das Geschick, / was sich in ihnen aufhäuft ohne Maßen, / versteinert und zum Dauernden bestimmt, / nicht Das, was unten in den dunklen Straßen / vom Zufall irgendwelche Namen nimmt." Rilke, *Sämtliche Werke*, 1:497–98.

2. Rilke, *Briefe aus den Jahren 1902 bis 1906*, 44. "Sie [die Kathedralen] sind die Einsamkeit und die Stille, die Zuflucht und Ruhe im Wechsel und Wirrwarr dieser Gassen. Sie sind die Zukunft, wie sie die Vergangenheit sind; alles andere läuft, rinnt, rennt und fällt . . . sie ragen und warten."

3. Talbot, *Pencil of Nature*; Sontag, "The Image-World," in *On Photography*, 154.

4. Crary, *Techniques of the Observer*, 31–32.

5. Ibid., 73.

6. Ibid., 98.

7. Rilke, *Letters*, 1:119.

8. See Marder, "Flat Death: Snapshots of History," in *Dead Time*, 68–87.

9. Baudelaire, *The Poems in Prose*, 25. Rilke told his French translator, Maurice Betz, that *The Notebooks of Malte Laurids Brigge* consists of "excerpts of a journal, poems in prose." Engelhardt, *Materialien zu Rainer Maria Rilke*, 164. An extended and detailed comparison of these two works is outside the scope of this book, but would certainly prove extremely fruitful, particularly in terms of their shared poetics of the modern urban environment. The limited scholarship in this area includes Jackson, "Rilke et Baudelaire"; Versluys, "Three City Poets"; Segal, "Rilke's Paris"; and Stevens, "*La sensation du neuf.*"

10. Likewise, Baudelaire asserts that photography and poetry (or art, more generally) are mutually exclusive: "Poetry and progress are like two ambitious men who hate one another with an in-

stinctive hatred, and when they meet upon the same road, one of them has to give place. If photography is allowed to supplement art in some of its functions, it will soon have supplanted or corrupted it altogether, thanks to the stupidity of the multitude which is its natural ally." Baudelaire, "The Salon of 1859," 154. Baudelaire's critique of the photograph is not limited to the realistic image reproduced on the metal plate or paper, but rather the complex training of the human sensorium through such a technological device. In Baudelaire's view, technological modes of image production and reception will change the nature of aesthetics and the production of art itself for the worse.

11. See Baer, *Spectral Evidence,* and Flusser, *Towards a Philosophy of Photography.*

12. In a recent edition of Rilke's letters (his "everyday" writing), Baer takes up this idea to suggest the "usefulness" of Rilke's work to all our lives. See Baer, *Poet's Guide to Life.*

13. Rilke, *Die Aufzeichnungen des Malte Laurids Brigge,* and Rilke, *The Notebooks of Malte Laurids Brigge* (henceforth cited parenthetically in the text; all references to this work will be to the translation except where otherwise noted).

14. See, for example, Dürr, "Personal Identity and the Idea of the Novel"; Ulrich Fülleborn, "Form und Sinn der Aufzeichnungen des Malte Laurids Brigge: Rilkes Prosabuch und der moderne Roman," in Engelhardt, *Materialien zu Rainer Maria Rilke,* 175–98; Herd, "An Interpretation of *Die Aufzeichnungen des Malte Laurids Brigge*"; Ernst Fedor Hoffmann, "Zum dichterischen Verfahren in Rilkes *Aufzeichnungen des Malte Laurids Brigge,*" in Engelhardt, *Materialien zu Rainer Maria Rilke,* 214–44; Mason, *Rainer Maria Rilke;* Nivelle, "Sens et structure des *Cahiers de Malte Laurids Brigge*"; Seifert, *Das epische Werk Rainer Maria Rilkes;* and Ziolkowski, *Dimensions of the Modern Novel,* 3–36.

15. Two critics who do address the question of Rilke's urban experience and its effect on the production of the novel are Bradley, *Zu Rilkes Malte Laurids Brigge,* and Andreas Huyssen, "Paris/Childhood: The Fragmented Body in Rilke's *Notebooks of Malte Laurids Brigge,*" in Huyssen and Bathrick, *Modernity and the Text,* 113–41. Huyssen is one of the few critics who reads the novel not in terms of the relative failure or success of the poetic project but as an altogether new formulation of the project in which the terms "success" and "failure" may no longer apply.

16. Rilke articulates this problem in a letter to Lou Andreas-Salomé in August 1903, stating that he longs for a place where he can work in peace: "If only the days would come there, Lou, in which I would learn to work deeply and collectedly; if only I might find a high room, a terrace, an avenue in which no one walks, and nights without a neighbor; and if the worry about the everyday would vouchsafe me only for a little while this life for which I cry out,—then I will never again permit a complaint to escape me, whatever may come later." *Letters,* 1:132–33.

17. Paul Virilio begins *The Vision Machine,* his survey of the intersecting histories of technologies of perception, art history, and military planning, with an anecdote explaining Rodin's own aversion to photography. Rodin asserts that his sculpture, though static, appears to move, whereas a photograph can only show the paralysis of an instant and thus appears unnaturally frozen, leading Rodin (allegedly) to conclude that it is "art that tells the truth and photography that lies. For *in reality time does not stand still,* and if the artist manages to give the impression that a gesture is being executed over several seconds, their work is certainly much less conventional than the scientific image in which time is abruptly suspended." Virilio, *Vision Machine,* 2. Rodin describes here essentially a plastic version of what I am calling expansive time.

18. Rilke, *Letters,* 1:93–94.

19. Benjamin, "On Some Motifs in Baudelaire," in *Illuminations,* 179.

20. In this respect, a comparison can perhaps be made here with the first few pages of James Joyce's *Portrait of the Artist as a Young Man.* Like Rilke, Joyce employs an alter ego, Stephen Dedalus, to chart the apprenticeship and development of a writer who struggles to articulate a concept of poetic language. The first pages of the novel describe the infant Stephen's initiation into a bewildering array of perceptual stimuli.

21. Rilke, *Briefe aus den Jahren 1902 bis 1906,* 24–25.

22. Ibid., 51.

23. Simmel, "The Metropolis and Mental Life," 48.

24. Freud, *Beyond the Pleasure Principle,* 19.

25. Rilke, *Letters,* 1:124.

26. Rilke, "Rodin Book," 28.

27. Bazin, "Ontology of the Photographic Image," 14.

28. Rilke, *Letters,* 1:362.

29. See Rilke, "Briefe über Cézanne (4. Okt. 1907)," in *Werke,* 4:602–4.

30. Kracauer, "Photography," in *Mass Ornament*, 47–63; henceforth cited parenthetically in the text.

31. In their study of the remediation of older media by new media, Jay David Bolter and Richard Grusin employ the concept of "reform" in order to "express the way in which one medium is seen by our culture as reforming or improving upon another." My own use of (re)form is not meant to suggest either restoration or improvement, but rather, to emphasize how media participate in the transformation of our understanding of the world and relationship to reality. See Bolter and Grusin, *Remediation*, 59.

32. Sontag, "Melancholy Objects," in *On Photography*, 80.

33. Hansen, "Decentric Perspectives," 50.

34. The same motif appears in Rilke's poem, "Schwarze Katze" (Black Cat), from the *New Poems II* (*Sämtliche Werke*, 1:595; translation in *New Poems*, 235). The poem initially describes the manner in which one's sight is absorbed by and disappears into the thick fur of the animal, but concludes with an abrupt reversal:

Alle Blicke, die sie jemals trafen,
scheint sie also an sich zu verhehlen,
um darüber drohend und verdrossen
zuzuschauern and damit zu schlafen.
Doch auf einmal kehrt sie, wie geweckt,
ihr Gesicht und mitten in das deine:
und da triffst du deinen Blick im geelen
Amber ihrer runden Augensteine
unerwartet wieder: eingeschlossen
wie ein ausgestorbenes Insekt.

[All the glances that have ever struck her
she seems to conceal about herself
so that she can look them over,
morose and menacing, and sleep with them.
But all at once, as if awakened,
she turns her face straight into your own:
and you unexpectedly meet your gaze
in the yellow amber of her round eye-stones:
trapped there like some long-extinct insect.]

The poem artiulates multiple levels of sight: the look that becomes embedded and lost in the body of the animal, the animal that in turn is a spectator to the observer's look, and the sudden opening of the cat's eye in which the observer sees himself both as subject and object of the glance. Though the poem makes no overt reference to photographic technology, the body of the observer is captured, frozen, as if on film.

35. Barthes, *Camera Lucida*, 91.

36. Rilke to Gräfin Margot Sizzo-Noris, March 17, 1922, in *Über Dichtung und Kunst*, 105.

37. Barthes, *Camera Lucida*, 14.

38. Ibid., 12.

39. In his essay on the *Notebooks*, Huyssen first notes Malte's revision of the Lacanian mirror stage in the context of an argument about Malte's ego-weakness. Huyssen, "Paris/Childhood," 127–30.

40. In his reading of the "Mummerehlen" section of Benjamin's *Berliner Kindheit*, Eduardo Cadava reads a strikingly similar scene of the young child: "In order to be himself, he must always depart from himself. Nevertheless, the one thing to which he can never bear witness is his becoming a thing. This is why, Benjamin explains, he can never resemble his own image: such a coincidence would name the moment of his death." Cadava, *Words of Light*, 107.

41. I am indebted to Elissa Marder for bringing my attention more acutely to the significance of the contents of the perfume bottle.

42. Rilke, *Werke*, 4:699–704.

43. Kittler, *Gramophone, Film, Typewriter*, 44–45.

44. Rilke, *Werke*, 4:702–3.
45. Ibid., 704.
46. Ibid., 703.
47. See Rilke, *Letters*, 2:391.
48. Ibid., 393.
49. Adorno, "The Form of the Phonograph Record," 58.
50. Ibid., 59.
51. Benjamin, "On Some Motifs in Baudelaire," in *Illuminations*, 156.
52. Rilke, *Letters*, 1:101.
53. Rilke, "Der Panther," in *Sämtliche Werke*, 1:505; translation in *New Poems*, 63.
54. The model for the panther is also indirectly linked to Rodin, as evidenced in Rilke's letter to Clara on September 27, 1902 (Rilke, *Letters*, 1:90–91):

> Rodin has a tiny plaster cast, a tiger (antique), in his studio in the rue de l'Université, which he values very highly: c'est beau, c'est tout . . . he says of it. And from this little plaster cast I saw what he means, what antiquity is and what links him to it. There, in this animal, is the same lively feeling in the modeling, this little thing (it is no higher than my hand is wide, and no longer than my hand) has hundreds of thousands of sides like a very big object, hundreds of thousands of sides which are all alive, animated, and different. And that in plaster! And with this the expression of the prowling stride is intensified to the highest degree, the powerful planting of the broad paws, and at the same time, that caution in which all strength is wrapped, that noiselessness. . . . You will see this little thing, and we mustn't fail to pay a visit to the original either (a little bronze), which is in the medal cabinet of the Bibliothèque Nationale.

55. Ryan, "Rilke's *Dinggedichte*," 27.
56. Rilke, *Letters*, 1:124.
57. The image described evokes a photographic image of his father taken sometime before he was married. Rilke is said to have carried the daguerreotype with him at all times. One version of the story maintains that Rilke once tried to clean the object but erased the image almost entirely when he removed the protective glass cover. See Leppmann, *Rilke*, 13.
58. Rilke, "Jugend-Bildnis meines Vaters," in *Sämtliche Werke*, 1:522; translation in *New Poems*, 105.
59. Although Martina Kurz reads the poem as a poetic portrait to be compared with Cézanne's practice of portraiture, I would stress here that Rilke studies Cézanne not to imitate his artistic *practice* but to find a model for artistic *process*. In other words, the poem directly addresses the question of poetic art and is only secondarily a portrait of the father. This reading also puts me at odds with Stefan Schank's psychobiographical interpretation of the poem. See Kurz, *Bild-Verdichtungen*, 257–61, and Schank, "Rilkes Vater und Rilkes Vaterbild," 81–111.
60. Benjamin, "On Some Motifs in Baudelaire," 194. In the essay, we will recall that Benjamin thinks through this problem of *Erlebnis* with particular reference to the act of photography: "Of the countless movements of switching, inserting, pressing, and the like, the 'snapping' of the photographer has the greatest consequences. A touch of the finger now sufficed to fix an event for an unlimited period of time. The camera gave the moment a posthumous shock, as it were" (174–75).
61. Rilke, *Letters*, 1:119.
62. Rilke, "Briefe über Cézanne," 625; translation from Baer, *Poet's Guide to Life*, 17–18.

CHAPTER 3

The epigraph to this chapter is drawn from "Neuland für Kinematographentheater," in Kaes, *Kino-Debatte*, 41.

> Über alles und jedes stürzt sich das sehende Objektiv-Auge des Aufnahme-Apparates, betrachtet es lange und eindringlich, bewahrt es in seinem Innern, konserviert das Geschaute aufs Filmband, und immer, wenn wir es wollen, können wir es wieder betrachten. Ich glaube, durch den Kino haben wir jetzt erst das Sehen gelernt. Die Freude am Schauen ist geweckt.

Wir wollen nicht mehr nüchterne Buchstaben zu Worten zusammensetzen, die beim Buchstabieren und Sinn-Erfassen den Geist anstrengen, sondern leicht und flüchtig die bildliche Lektüre genießen. . . . Das trockene Buch ist vom Publikum ad acta gelegt; die Zeitung wird flüchtig durchblättert, und abends wird der Bilderhunger im Kino befriedigt.

1. Anthologies in which a portion of this material can be found include Greve, Pehle, and Westhoff, *Hätte ich das Kino!*; Kaes, *Kino-Debatte;* Kaes, *Weimarer Republik,* 219–39; Kaes, Jay, and Dimendberg, *Weimar Republic Sourcebook,* 617–35; and Schweinitz, *Prolog vor dem Film.*
2. See Gunning, "Cinema of Attractions."
3. See Greve, Pehle, and Westhoff, *Hätte ich das Kino!* 21ff., and Berg-Ganschow and Jacobsen, *Film Stadt Kino Berlin,* 117ff.
4. "Neuland für Kinematographentheater," in Kaes, *Kino-Debatte,* 41.
5. In my translation, I borrow from W. J. T. Mitchell's notion of an "image-text"—a work in which verbal and visual relations are staged. It is the early recognition of the tension or gap between image and text that is one of the primary components of early writings on film. See Mitchell, *Picture Theory.*
6. "Neuland für Kinematographentheater," in Kaes, *Kino-Debatte,* 41.
7. In 1912, the three largest associations in German theater—the Bühnenverein, the Genossenschaft Deutscher Bühnenangehöriger, and the Verband Deutscher Bühnenschriftsteller—recommended a total boycott: their members were neither to work in nor to frequent the movies. See Berg-Ganschow and Jacobsen, *Film Stadt Kino Berlin,* 120ff.
8. In his introduction to the 1963 edition of the *Kinobuch,* Pinthus wrote: "Bassermann's unexpected appearance in a film had the result that for the first time all of Berlin's theater critics went to the cinema that they held in such disdain (Cines-Palast am Nollendorfplatz)—and the grand gestures of Bassermann's filmic presentation were ripped to shreds as degrading" [Bassermanns unerwartetes Auftreten im Film bewirkte, daß zum ersten Mal die gesamte Theaterkritik Berlins ins verachtete Kino ging (Cines-Palast am Nollendorfplatz)—und des grandiosen Mimen filmische Darstellung als entwürdigend verriß]. "Vorwort zur Neu-Ausgabe," in Pinthus, *Das Kinobuch,* 14.
9. Faktor, "Die stumme Premiere: Mit Lindau und Bassermann im Kientopp," in Schweinitz, *Prolog vor dem Film,* 349. "Eigentlich aber war man gekommen, weil Bassermann spielte. Erstens aus Schadenfreude: um zu sehen, wie einer, der sich jahrelang gegen eine photographische Aufnahme sträubte, nun stundenlang in effegie hingleitet, und zweitens selbstverständlich auch aus Interesse."
10. Ibid., 347. In *Der sichtbare Mensch,* Balázs repeats a version of this paradoxical formulation that film actors speak for the eyes and theater actors speak for the ears. Balázs, *Der sichtbare Mensch,* 35. In his afterword to the recent Suhrkamp edition of Balázs's book, Helmut Diederichs provides numerous examples of early film theories by other authors that were later picked up in Balázs's work. Diederichs's intention is not to demote the importance of Balázs's accomplishment, but rather to demonstrate that the book did not emerge from an intellectual vacuum but is a vital component of a larger discourse on film from the beginning of the century. See Diederichs, "'Ihr müßt erst etwas von guter Filmkunst verstehen.'"
11. Quoted in Schlüpmann, "First German Art Film," 10.
12. See Hart, "Der Atlantis-Film," in Schweinitz, *Prolog vor dem Film,* 395–401.
13. Diederichs, "The Origins of the *Autorenfilm,*" in Usai and Codelli, *Before Caligari,* 396.
14. Häfker, "Der Ruf nach Kunst," in Schweinitz, *Prolog vor dem Film,* 92. "Aber man kam jetzt auf den Weg, diejenigen Sinneseindrücke, die durch 'Wellen' physikalischer Natur erzeugt werden, dadurch festzuhalten und zu vertausendfachen, daß man diese Wellen—die optischen und die akustischen—sich selbst in festem Stoffe fangen und 'aufschreiben' ließ."
15. Kittler, *Gramophone, Film, Typewriter,* 9.
16. Musil, "Ansätze zu neuer Ästhetik," 1138.
17. Zglinicki, *Der Weg des Films,* 309. "Allerdings waren diese ersten bodenständigen Filmtheater mehr als dürftig. Ein leerstehender Laden, ein paar aufgestellte Stuhlreihen, eine schwankende Leinwand, marktschreierische Plakate—und fertig war der Kintopp. Mutter saß an der Kasse, Vater riß die Karten ab und sorgte für Ordnung, der Sohn spielte drinnen Klavier oder zog das Grammophon auf."
18. See Berg-Ganschow and Jacobsen, 119.

19. Greve, Pehle, and Westhoff, *Hätte ich das Kino!* 92. "Das Kinobuch, halb ein preziöser Scherz, halb ein ernstliches Bemühen, dem Kino neue Stoffe und Motive zu geben, bietet eine Galerie von Films, die ohne schon vorhandene Erzählungen zu benutzen, eigens von Schriftstellern und Schriftstellerinnen für das Kino erdacht sind. . . . Jeder Autor hat sich bemüht, kinematographische zu sehen und irgendeine knappe literarische Form für seine Kinoidee zu finden. Das Kinobuch ist ein abwechslungsreiches Kinotheater, von jedermann in der Tasche zu tragen und jederzeit zu genießen."

20. Quoted in Hake, *Cinema's Third Machine*, 71.

21. The response to the *Kinobuch* has not been much better in the decades that followed, even after the book was reissued in 1963. Most contemporary studies that analyze the discourse surrounding the early decades of film history refer to it only briefly. Generally, it is acknowledged as a particularly interesting example of the way in which young literary authors reacted to film, but these studies perform only scant analyses of Pinthus's formulations of a nascent film theory (an important development in the turn that film was to take before the war) and usually neglect the specifics of the screenplays themselves. Typically, the individual screenplays are dismissed because they are considered neither literary enough, that is they do not contribute anything significant to an appreciation of the literary historical period, nor cinematic enough, in that they do not reveal any real comprehension of film techniques and they do not contribute to any fundamentally new direction for cinema. The screenplays are thus prematurely dismissed as mere amateurish attempts that are not to be taken seriously, ignoring the stakes for both cinematic and literary production articulated in their scenarios. Some works that devote more than a few sentences to the *Kinobuch* include Estermann, *Die Verfilmung literarischer Werke*, 206–12; Hake, *Cinema's Third Machine*, 70–72; Heller, *Literarische Intelligenz und Film*, 67–79; and Zmegac, *Tradition und Innovation*, 227–28.

22. Pinthus, "Einleitung: Das Kinostück (1913)," in Pinthus, *Das Kinobuch*, 21. "Bevor also das Wesen des Kinostücks entschält werden kann, muß man sich wieder auf das fast vergessene urtümliche Wesen des Kinos besinnen."

23. See Pinthus, "Quo vadis—Kino? Zur Eröffnung des Königspaviollon-Theaters," in Schweinitz, *Prolog vor dem Film*, 366–69.

24. According to Friedrich Zglinicki's historical account, Pinthus's review was not particularly well received: "Back then, to write about cinema in a respectable newspaper was so contemptible that many readers protested, and Pinthus's older acquaintances reproached him for his shameful behavior" [In einem respektablen Blatt über das Kino zu schreiben, war damals so verächtlich, daß viele Leser protestierten und sich die älteren unter Pinthus' Bekannten sich seiner vorwurfsvoll schämten]. Zglinicki, *Der Weg des Films*, 382.

25. Quoted in Hake, *Cinema's Third Machine*, 118. I take up the question of the distinctions and resonances between the German and the American discourse on film in Chapter 5.

26. See Kanehl, "Kinokunst," in Kaes, *Kino-Debatte*, 50–53.

27. Pinthus, *Das Kinobuch*, 21. One of the earliest attempts at documenting the makeup of the German film audience is Emilie Altenloh's 1914 doctoral dissertation, *Zur Soziologie des Kino*. Based on questionnaires that include sex, age, marital status, profession, religious denomination, and political affiliation, her typical moviegoer (in distinction to Pinthus's and Kracauer's accounts) is a young, single, male factory worker with limited funds. See Altenloh, *Zur Soziologie des Kino*; Kracauer, "The Little Shopgirls Go to the Movies," in *Mass Ornament*, 291–304; and Hake, *Cinema's Third Machine*, 45–49.

28. Brecht, "The Film, the Novel and Epic Theatre," 47.

29. Pinthus, *Das Kinobuch*, 27–28. "Während bisher die geschriebenen Entwürfe der Kinostücke unbekannt geblieben sind, versuchte jeder der Autoren dieses Buches irgendeine literarische Form zu finden, die dem Kino irgendwie adäquat ist. Da diese Form weder die Novelle noch das Drama sein durfte—denn das Drama ist aufgezeichnetes Theater, die Novelle aufgezeichnete Erzählung—, so mag es ergötzlich und unterhaltsam sein, zu sehen, wie die Schriftsteller eine Form suchen, die in etwas aufgezeichnetes Kino ist. Knappste, zusammengedrängteste Formen des Kinostücks haben wir erstrebt; wir bemühten uns, kinematographisch zu sehen, jede Situation verfilmbar zu erfinden."

30. Greve, Pehle, and Westhoff, *Hätte ich das Kino!* 95. "Die allergewöhnlichste literarische Delikatesse verbietet mir daher über das Buch zu schreiben. Indessen ist das Buch so wichtig oder könnte so wichtig sein, daß alle literarische Delikatesse, selbst die allergewöhnlichste, das heuchlerische Maul zu halten hat."

31. Pinthus, *Das Kinobuch*, 28. "Und vielleicht spiegelt sich in dieser unwirklichen (im Kino aber verwirklichten) Welt mehr ab von unserer wirklichen Erdenwelt als wir zu glauben vermeinen."

32. Bermann, "Leier und Schreibmaschine," in Pinthus, *Das Kinobuch*, 29–33.

33. Berman's second contribution to the *Kinobuch*, "Galeotto," submitted under the pseudonym Arnold Höllriegel, updates the story of the doomed lovers Paolo and Francesca, setting its love story in a movie theater so that a film, rather than a book, is the catalyst for their adulterous passion. See Pinthus, *Das Kinobuch*, 127–31. Dante's final line from the Galeotto episode (canto 5 of *The Divine Comedy*) is also echoed in Berman's "Lyre and Typewriter" at the close of the film within the film. The happy ending for the poet and typist is punctuated by the line: "That day they typed no further." Pinthus, *Das Kinobuch*, 33.

34. Pinthus, *Das Kinobuch*, 29. "Also das war einmal ein Film, der klar beweist, wie wichtig wir Stenotypistinnen sind—wir, die wir Euere Gedichte abschreiben, aber manchmal auch verursachen."

35. Ibid., 33. "Der Film wird die geistigen Gefahren der Schreibmaschine enthüllen. Denn glaubst du, die tüchtigen Manuskripte dieses Dichters sind *gut* gewesen? Gut war das Kauen und der Diwan. Aber das werdet Ihr Berufsfrauen niemals verstehn."

36. Both *dichten* and *diktieren*, the verb forms of *Dichtung/Dichter* and *Diktat*, are derived from the Latin *dictare*, meaning to recite something to be written down, which in turn is a derivation of *dicere*, to say or speak. The word *Dichter* first came into use in the German language in the twelfth century although it was not frequently used; broader use of *Dichter* began in the eighteenth century as a replacement for *Poet*, presumably from the French. See Kluge. *Etymologisches Wörterbuch der deutschen Sprache*, 178 and 181.

37. "'Artistic observation,' [Paul Valéry] says in reflections on a woman artist whose work consisted in the silk embroidery of figures, 'can attain an almost mystical depth. The objects on which it falls lose their names. Light and shade form very particular systems, present very individual questions which depend upon no knowledge and are derived from no practice, but get their existence and value exclusively from a certain accord of the soul, the eye, and the hand of someone who was born to perceive them and evoke them in his own inner self.' With these words, soul, eye, and hand are brought into connection. Interacting with one another, they determine a practice. We are no longer familiar with this practice. The role of the hand in production has become more modest, and the place it filled in storytelling lies waste. . . . That old co-ordination of the soul, the eye, and the hand which emerges in Valéry's words is that of the artisan which we encounter wherever the art of storytelling is at home." Benjamin, "The Storyteller," in *Illuminations*, 107–8.

38. Ernst, "Möglichkeiten einer Kinokunst," in Kaes, *Kino-Debatte*, 123.

> Es ist eben doch so, daß zur Kunst zunächst Geist gehört, und Geist findet sich nun eben nicht im Tatsächlichen. Wenn ein Albrecht Dürer mit wissenschaftlicher Genauigkeit ein Rasenstück malt, dann haben wir ein Kunstwerk, denn das kleine Aquarell ist aus seinem Gehirn und seinem Herzen hervorgegangen; wenn das Kino uns eine im Wind bewegte Wiesenfläche vorführt, dann haben wir kein Kunstwerk, trotzdem für den rohen Betrachter die Filmvorführung sicher eindrucksvoller ist als das unscheinbare Bildchen. . . . Im Kino wird der Versuch gemacht, die höchste Betätigung des Menschen, die Kunst, durch Maschinenbetrieb herzustellen. Daß der Versuch scheitern muß, ist ja klar; daß er aber gemacht werden kann, das ist einer der schlimmsten Zeichen der Verwilderung unsere Zeit.

The extreme case perhaps for the so-called degeneracy of the age is the case of Thomas Rücker who murdered a man in a Hamburg commuter train in 1906. Because he could give no credible motive for his actions, his murderous impulses were eventually blamed on his addiction to the movies. Film thus becomes a cause of mental illness and delinquency. See Lorenz, "Der kinematographische Un-Fall der Seelenkunde."

39. Polgar, "Das Drama im Kinematographen," in Schweinitz, *Prolog vor dem Film*, 163.

> Die Wiese im Kinematographentheater duftet besser als die auf der Bühne, weil ja der Kinematograph eine wirkliche, echte Wiese zeigt, der ich den Duft ohneweiters zutraue und ihn nun so vollkommen, als die durch nichts gestörte Phantasie sich ihn erträumt, meiner Nase suggeriere. Sie duftet aber auch besser als die natürliche, lebende Wiese, weil diese niemals so lieblich und unvermischt Extrakt duften kann wie meine blühende Wiese, die ist

und doch nicht ist. . . . Nur im Traum und im Kinematographen gibt es eine Wirklichkeit ohne Schlacken. Für beide sind die Naturgesetze aufgehoben, die Schwerkraft erloschen, das Dasein ohne Bedingtheit.

40. "Kino und Buchhandel [Antworten auf eine Umfrage des Börsenblatts für den Deutschen Buchhandel—eine Auswahl]," in Schweinitz, *Prolog vor dem Film*, 277. "Die Adaptierung dichterischer Werke scheint auch mir vom Übel, da das Wort und damit die geistige Bedeutung durch die Beschränkung auf das bloß Mimische ausgeschaltet wird und die Neigung des Volkes zum Bilderbesehen neue Nahrung erhält."

41. "Umfrage der *Frankfurter Zeitung:* 'Vom Werte und Unwerte des Kinos," in Kaes, *Kino-Debatte*, 66. "Kunst hat mit Vergnügen nichts zu tun. Kunst bereichert die Seele, Vergnügung täuscht sie über ihre Armut hinweg." On the subject of film and the print or theatrical market, a tandem argument is that the degenerate nature of film may actually prove a benefit since it provides an outlet for unworthy themes and entertainments, thereby freeing literature and the theater to pursue loftier goals.

42. Kanehl, "Kinokunst," in Kaes, *Kino-Debatte*, 51. "Keiner Kunstform ist das *Wort* so unentbehrlich wie dem Kunstroman, und der wortlose, gemimte Kinoroman wird bei den kühnsten Hoffnungen *technischer* Vervollkommnung nur ein physisch wirksames, anreizendes, aufregendes und ewig kunstarmes Geschöpf bleiben" (italics in original).

43. See Georg Lukács, "Gedanken zu einer Ästhetik des Kinos," in Kaes, *Kino-Debatte*, 112–18. In this essay, Lukács maintains that the fundamental distinction between theater and film is not of a linguistic order, but a function of the presence or absence of the actor on the stage. Lukács argues that the essence of the theatrical effect has nothing to do with the words and gestures of the actor or with the individual elements of the plot, but lies in the power with which the living will of a person on stage can flow into another living person in the exchange between actor and audience. The film may present the gestures and actions of humans, but not the human itself. Lukács does not necessarily view this as a deficiency of film, only a limit or boundary. For this reason, it is a mistake in Lukács's view to attempt to classify film through existing artistic conventions, for it is something radically new, introducing alternate temporal and spatial categories.

44. Friedell, "Prolog vor dem Film," in Schweinitz, *Prolog vor dem Film*, 205. "Aber ich glaube, wir werden heutzutage nicht mehr so geneigt sein, dem Wort eine so absolute Hegemonie einzuräumen. Man darf vielleicht eher sagen, daß Worte für uns heutzutage schon etwas Überdeutliches und dabei etwas merkwürdig Undifferenziertes haben. Das Wort verliert allmählich ein wenig an Kredit."

45. Ewers, "Der Film und ich," in Kaes, *Kino-Debatte*, 104. "Aber das war es ja gerade, was mich reizte: die Möglichkeit endlich, endlich einmal des '*Wortes*' entraten zu können, dieses 'Wortes,' das dem Dichter bisher alles war und ohne welches er gar nicht denkbar schien. Des 'Wortes'—das dennoch für alle *tiefste* Empfindung nur ein vages und nie voll ausschöpfendes Surrogat war!"

46. Benjamin, "The Work of Art in the Age of Mechanical Reproduction," in *Illuminations*, 250.

47. Hofmannsthal, "Der Ersatz für Träume," in Kaes, *Kino-Debatte*, 149–52.

48. Ibid., 149. "Was die Leute im Kino suchen, sagte mein Freund, mit dem ich auf dieses Thema kam, was alle die arbeitenden Leute im Kino suchen, ist der Ersatz für die Träume. Sie wollen ihre Phantasie mit Bildern füllen, starken Bildern, in denen sich Lebensessenz zusammenfaßt; die gleichsam aus dem Innern des Schauenden gebildet sind und ihm an die Nieren gehen."

49. Ibid., 149.

50. Freud, *Interpretation of Dreams*, 571–88.

51. Ibid., 582.

52. Hofmannsthal, "Der Ersatz für Träume," 152.

53. Münsterberg, *Photoplay*, 35. For a detailed account of the relationship between information machines and psychoanalysis, specifically the relationship between the media technologies of film and the gramophone and Freud's theories of the unconscious, see Kittler, "Romanticism-Psychoanalysis Film," and Kittler, "The World of the Symbolic—A World of the Machine," in *Literature, Media, Information Systems*, 85–100, and 130–46.

54. Freud, *Interpretation of Dreams*, 154n.

55. Hofmannsthal, "Letter of Lord Chandos," 133; original in Hofmannsthal, *Ausgewählte Werke in zwei Bänden*, 2:341.

56. Hofmannsthal, "Letter of Lord Chandos," 131–32.
57. Ibid., 134.
58. Ibid., 134–35.
59. See Saussure, *Course in General Linguistics*.
60. Hofmannsthal, "Letter of Lord Chandos," 140.
61. Rilke, *Notebooks*, 6.
62. Hofmannsthal, himself, is known for his renunciation of lyric poetry around 1900, despite his early success in this genre. After the turn of the century, he turned his attention to the theater (including collaborations with Max Reinhardt), the opera (writing librettos), and essay writing.
63. In his essay on Baudelaire, Benjamin also describes the French poet as both last in one tradition of European poetry and first in another. See Benjamin, "On Some Motifs in Baudelaire," in *Illuminations*, esp. 155–57, 192–94.
64. Hofmannsthal, "Letter of Lord Chandos," 133–34.
65. Hofmannsthal, "Der Ersatz für Träume," in Kaes, *Kino-Debatte*, 151. "Eine dunkle Ecke, ein Anhauch der Luft, das Gesicht eines Tiers . . . der dunkle Raum hinter der Kellerstiege, ein altes Faß im Hof, halbvoll mit Regenwasser, eine Kiste mit Gerümpel. . ."
66. Hofmannsthal, "Letter of Lord Chandos," 133–34.
67. See Faber, "Hofmannsthal and the Film"; Furthman-Durden, "Hugo von Hofmannsthal and Alfred Döblin"; and Greve, Pehle, and Westhoff, *Hätte ich das Kino!* 144–47 and 190–97.
68. Brod, "Ein Tag aus dem Leben Kühnebecks, des jungen Idealistin," in Pinthus, *Das Kinobuch*, 71–75. Unfortunately, the play on Kühnebeck's name becomes lost in translation. The adjective *kühn* means bold; *Kühnheit* is boldness, a quality that the young hero displays in abundance.
69. Brod, "Kinematographentheater," in Kaes, *Kino-Debatte*, 39–41.
70. Brod, "Ein Tag aus dem Leben Kühnebecks," 71.
71. Karl May (1842–1912) was a prolific German author specializing in adventure stories of the American West. His works were read by both children and educated adults (and were said to be a favorite of Albert Einstein, Albert Schweitzer, and Hermann Hesse). Over 100 million copies of his works have been sold globally.
72. Weber, "Deus Ex Media," in *Mass Mediauras*, 157.
73. See Greve, Pehle, and Westhoff, *Hätte ich das Kino!* 24–26.
74. Ibid., 176: "Sprechfilm mich selbst gesehen. Abscheu empfunden. Eitelkeit. Ich sah einen Menschen den ich kaum kannte. Sein Organ war mir fremd und also neu. Er gefiel mir nicht. Ein Zug von Unstattischem Sonderlinswesen haftet ihm an. Eine krähende Überheblichkeit. Er hatte Mundbewegungen wie ein Zahnloser. Er hatte einen Klos im Winkel zwischen den rechten Kiefern. . . . War ich das? Das ein Text von mir?"
75. Kittler, "Romanticism-Pyschoanalysis-Film," in *Literature, Media, Information Systems*, 92.
76. Behne, "Die Stellung des Publikums zur modernen Literatur," in Kaes, *Weimarer Republik*, 220. "Das Buch ist doch nichts Andres als ein Transportmittel, ist nichts als eine Form der Mitteilung. In demselben Augenblick, da wir eine intensivere Form, ein besseres Transportmittel haben, ist das Alte zum Untergang verurteilt. Buch-Kultur kommt mir vor wie Kultur der Hieb- und Stichwaffe im Zeitalter des Lewisits."
77. Ibid., 220. "Der Film ist einfache, grade und legitime Fortsetzung des Buches—Edison der neue Gutenberg. Jenen kleinen Heften, die wir als Schulbuben hatten, deren Seiten bei flinkem Anglättern ihre Figürchen zu Phasen eines primitiven Films werden ließen, kommt die Bedeutung eines wichtigen Überganges zu. Sobald die Folge der Seiten im Buche nicht mehr nur räumlich, sondern auch zeitlich ausgenutzt wird, entsteht der Film."
78. One of Brod's novels was in fact eventually adapted for film. In 1929, Kurt Bernhardt directed *Die Frau, nach der man sich sehnt*, adapted from Brod's 1927 novel and starring Fritz Kortner and Marlene Dietrich. Brod was not happy with the final product. Indeed, he submitted an open letter to the *Berliner Tageblatt* highly critical of the director for changing the tone of the book and for leaving him out of the production process altogether. See Gandert, *Der Film der Weimarer Republik*, 220.
79. Mann, "Über den Film," in Kaes, *Kino-Debatte*, 164–66; translated as "On the Film," by H. T. Lowe-Porter, in Geduld, *Authors on Film*, 129–32.
80. Mann, "On the Film," 129.
81. Ibid., 130.
82. Ibid., translation modified.

83. See McLuhan, *Understanding Media*, 22–32.

84. Geoffrey Winthrop-Young is one of the few critics to have read Mann's novel in the context of the media technologies that it describes, claiming that the novel is "nothing less than a prewar *Gravity's Rainbow*, an early postindustrial epic that may have more important things to say about life under electric conditions than about any of the traditional items Mann is famous for—such as love and humanity, art and life, *Bildung* and decline, irony and identity, or whatever else serious German literature is supposed to be about." Winthrop-Young, "Magic Media Mountain," 30. Winthrop-Young's engaging essay primarily discusses Mann's allusions to x-rays and phonograph records, without addressing the very important role that film plays in the novel.

85. Mann, *Magic Mountain*, 310–11.

86. Ibid., 311.

87. Mann, "On the Film," 131.

88. Mann, *Magic Mountain*, 671.

89. Ibid., 180.

90. Winthrop-Young, "Magic Media Mountain," 49.

91. Mann, *Magic Mountain*, ix.

92. Pinthus, "Die verrückte Lokomotive, oder Abenteuer einer Hochzeitsfahrt," in Pinthus, *Das Kinobuch*, 77–86.

93. Ibid., 78–79.

94. Hasenclever, "Nachwort," in *Sämtliche Werke*, 5:645. Hasenclever's contribution to the *Kinobuch*, "The Wedding Night" (Die Hochzeitsnacht), portrays a woman who sells herself into the harem of an unscrupulous eastern European aristocrat in order to secure the funds necessary for her painter-boyfriend to travel to Italy to be cured of a serious illness. Eventually the boyfriend learns of the true reason for her disappearance and contrives to rescue her. The film combines several media of representation, including film, dance, painting, and dreams. Hasenclever's other forays into film include a full-length screenplay, *Die Pest* (The Plague), published in 1920; he also wrote some of the dialogue in the German version of the film *Anna Christie* (1930), starring Greta Garbo. See Hasenclever, *Sämtliche Werke*, 5:393–415.

95. Pinthus, "Verrückte Lokomotive," 80.

96. Pinthus, "Einleitung: Das Kinostück," in Pinthus, *Das Kinobuch*, 22–23.

97. Friedell, "Prolog vor dem Film," in Schweinitz, *Prolog vor dem Film*, 204. "Das Kino hat etwas Skizzenhaftes, Abruptes, Lückenhaftes, Fragmentarisches. Das ist im Sinne des modernen Geschmacks ein eminenter künstlerischer Vorteil. Die Erkenntnis der Schönheit des Fragmentes beginnt sich allmählich in allen künsten Bahn zu brechen, schließlich ist ja alle Kunst nichts anderes als ein geschicktes und bisweilen geniales Auslassen und Zwischengliedern."

98. See Barry Salt, "Early German Film: The Stylistics in Comparative Context," in Elsaesser, *Second Life*, 225–36.

99. Ibid., 236.

100. Hake, *Cinema's Third Machine*, 243.

101. See Diederichs, *Anfänge deutscher Filmkritik*, 169.

102. Frank Thiess to Paul Wegener, May 12, 1921, in Greve, Pehle, and Westhoff, *Hätte ich das Kino!* 275. "Denn Sie sind nicht mehr ein Enkel jener Generation, die um Kunst rang und für die Kunst starb, sondern ein Kind jener späten Sprößlinge des künstlichen Lichts, die eine Bogenlampe der Sonne vorziehen, weil sie sie jederzeit abdrehen können."

103. McLuhan and Fiore, *The Medium Is the Massage*, 75.

104. Wegener, "Neue Kinoziele," in Greve, Pehle, and Westhoff, *Hätte ich das Kino!* 118.

105. Wegener, "Von den künstlerischen Möglichkeiten des Wandelbildes," in Schweinitz, *Prolog vor dem Film*, 336. "Der eigentliche Dichter des Films muß die *Kamera* sein. Die Möglichkeiten, Großes klein und Kleines groß, übereinander und ineinander zu photographieren, die Möglichkeit des ständigen Standpunktwechselns für den Beschauer, die zahllosen Tricks durch Bildteilung, Spiegelungen und so fort, kurz: die *Technik* des Films muß bedeutsam werden für die Wahl des Inhalts" (italics in the original).

106. Ibid., 337. "In erster Linie ist der Film eine *visuelle* Angelegenheit. Der Filmdichter muß vom Bild ausgehen, in Bildern denken, und Stoffe wählen, die bildhaft auszudrücken sind." In a later essay, "Schauspielerei und Film," published in the *Berliner Tageblatt* in January 1915, Wegener would retract the use of the term "Filmdichter" (film-poet), saying it "doesn't sound right" (klänge falsch). See Greve, Pehle, and Westhoff, *Hätte ich das Kino!* 116.

107. See Balázs, *Der sichtbare Mensch*, 9–15.
108. Ibid., 17. "Die ganze Menschheit ist heute schon dabei, die vielfach verlernte Sprache der Mienen und Gebärden wieder zu erlernen. Nicht den Worteersatz der Taubstummensprache, sondern die visuelle Korrespondenz der unmittelbar verkörperten Seele. *Der Mensch wird wieder sichtbar werden*" (italics in the original).
109. Ibid., 18. "Die Kultur der Worte ist eine entmaterialisierte, abstrakte, verintellektualisierte Kultur, die den menschlichen Körper zu einem bloßen biologischen Organismus degradiert hat."
110. Musil, "Ansätze zu neuer Ästhetik," 1138.
111. Goll, "Das Kinodram," in Kaes, *Kino-Debatte*, 137. "Basis für alle neue kommende Kunst ist das Kino. Niemand wird mehr ohne die neue Bewegung auskommen, denn wir rotieren alle in einer anderen Geschwindigkeit als bisher." In 1914, Goll published a selection of poems under the title *Films*.

CHAPTER 4

The epigraph to this chapter is drawn from Schuster and Bode, *Alfred Döblin im Spiegel der zeitgenössischen Kritik*, 14. "Der Wortfilm rollt. Der Kinematograph wird nie und nimmer Literatur vermitteln können, aber die Literatur muß von der Kinematographie lernen. Und sie hat schon von ihr gelernt. Es ist nun einmal keine Zeit für schleppende Handlungen, Postkutschenstil und psychologische Kleinarbeit. . . . Die Einfahrt eines D-Zuges ist spannend, aber langweilig sind die Ullstein-Bücher die man zum Preise von einer Mark kaufen kann. . . . Das Döblinsche Werk hat das Tempo unseres Lebens."

1. See Schivelbusch, *Railway Journey*.
2. Schivelbusch, "Railroad Space and Railroad Time," 34.
3. See Sebald, *Der Mythus der Zerstörung im Werk Döblins*, 120.
4. Döblin concluded his open letter to the Italian futurist F. T. Marinetti, published in *Der Sturm* in March 1913, with the declaration: "Cultivate your futurism. I will cultivate my Döblinism." Döblin, "Futuristische Worttechnik: Offener Brief an F. T. Marinetti," in *Schriften zu Ästhetik, Poetik und Literatur*, 119.
5. Döblin, "An Romanautoren und ihre Kritiker. Berliner Programm," in *Schriften zu Ästhetik, Poetik und Literatur*, 121–22. "In höchster Gedrängtheit und Präzision hat "die Fülle der Gesichte" vorbeizuziehen. Der Sprache das Äußerste der Plastik und Lebendigkeit abzuringen. Der Erzählerschlendrian hat im Roman keinen Platz; man erzählt nicht, sondern baut. Der Erzähler hat eine bäurische Vertraulichkeit. Knappheit, Sparsamkeit der Worte ist nötig; frische Wendungen. Von Perioden, die das Nebeneinander des Komplexen wie das Hintereinander rasch zusammenzufassen erlauben, ist umfänglicher Gebrauch zu machen. Rapide Abläufe, Durcheinander in bloßen Stichworten; wie überhaupt an allen Stellen die höchste Exaktheit in suggestiven Wendungen zu erreichen gesucht werden muß. Das Ganze darf nicht erscheinen wie gesprochen sondern wie vorhanden."
6. Goethe, *Faust*, in *Sämtliche Werke*, vol. 7, bk. 1, p. 38.
7. Döblin, "An Romanautoren und ihre Kritiker," 119. "Gewisses ist unverrückbar in der Zeit; Homer läßt sich noch genießen: Kunst konserviert; aber die Arbeitsmethode ändert sich, wie die Oberfläche der Erde, in den Jahrhunderten; der Künstler kann nicht mehr zu Cervantes fliehen, ohne von den Motten gefressen zu werden. Die Welt ist in die Tiefe und Breite gewachsen; der alte Pegasus von der Technik überflügelt, hat sich verblüffen lassen und in einen störrischen Esel verwandelt. Ich behaupte, jeder gute Spekulant, Bankier, Soldat ist ein besserer Dichter als die Mehrzahl heutiger Autoren."
8. Döblin's rejection of the term, *Dichtkunst*, is in itself very revealing in terms of his own theory of literature as elaborated in this chapter. In a letter written in December 1927, two months before he was voted into the Academy, Döblin wrote: "By the way, why did they call it the Academy or Section 'for poetic art'? They must have known that a 'poet' is a ridiculous thing; weren't they aware of the words 'writer' and 'writings'?" *Alfred Döblin, 1878–1978*, 322. Döblin rejected the term *Dichter*, "poet," in favor of the more literal job description, *Schriftsteller*, the one who produces or sets down writing. In other words, he rejects the German term that became increasingly prominent in the eighteenth century, in favor of a word that more clearly presented his particular work as a media technician. This dichotomy between *Dichter* and *Schriftsteller* likewise captures the central

plot of Richard Bermann's "Lyre and Typewriter" in *Das Kinobuch*. "Warum hat man à propos die Akademie oder Sektion 'für Dichtkunst' genannt? Man hätte doch wissen müssen, daß ein 'Dichter' eine komische Sache ist; kannte man die Worte 'Schriftsteller' und 'Schrifttum' nicht."

9. Döblin, "Literatur und Rundfunk," in *Schriften zu Ästhetik, Poetik und Literatur*, 254.

10. Ibid., 253–54. "Das Großteil unserer Literatur also steht unter dem Zeichen der Drucktype, und das Organ, durch das diese Literatur in unsere Köpfe dringt—wir wollen das gut festhalten—, sind die Augen. . . . Die Literatur baut mit der Sprache, welche an sich ja noch immer ein akustisches Element ist. Wenn seit der Erfindung der Buchdruckerkunst fortschreitend die Literatur in unserer Zeit zu einem stummen Gebiet geworden ist, so braucht das nicht unbedingt ein Vorteil zu sein. Ja, es ist bestimmt für die Literatur und die Sprache ein Nachteil. Der Buchdruck, die Drucktype hat, um es ruhig auszusprechen, die Literatur und uns alle in einer unnatürlichen Weise zu Stummen gemacht."

11. Ibid., 258. Walter Benjamin makes a similar claim in his 1936 essay, "The Storyteller": "What distinguishes the novel from the story (and from the epic in the narrower sense) is its essential dependence on the book. The dissemination of the novel became possible only with the invention of printing." Benjamin, "The Storyteller," in *Illuminations*, 87. Both men, of course, anticipate similar arguments made by Marshall McLuhan and Walter Ong. See McLuhan, *Understanding Media*, and Ong, *Orality and Literacy*.

12. Sara Danius's book *The Senses of Modernism* also takes up the question of the relationship between literature and technology in the early twentieth century. However, her detailed analyses of three seminal modernist works focus primarily on where technology is taken up thematically in the works, and with the exception of the chapter on Joyce, pay scant attention to formal considerations of the texts.

13. See Döblin, "Epilog," in *Aufsätze zur Literatur*, 390.

14. Döblin, "Der Geist des Naturalistischen Zeitalters," in *Schriften zu Ästhetik, Poetik und Literatur*, 174. "Es ist freilich schon heute ein Unfug, eine Säule von Phidias anhimmeln zu lassen und die Untergrundbahn ein bloßes Verkehrsmittel zu nennen."

15. For just two examples, see Bance, "Alfred Döblin's *Berlin Alexanderplatz* and Literary Modernism," 53, and Ziolkowski, *Dimensions of the Modern Novel*, 107.

16. For critical reviews from the *Linkskurve*, see Prangel, *Materialien zu Alfred Döblin "Berlin Alexanderplatz,"* 86–100. Also see Reid, "Berlin Alexanderplatz—A Political Novel," and Muschg, "Nachwort," in Döblin, *Berlin Alexanderplatz: Die Geschichte vom Franz Biberkopf*, 423–24. Döblin and his wife Erna both converted to Catholicism in 1941 while living in the United States.

17. See Martini, *Der Wagnis der Sprache*, 336–72, and Zimmermann, "Benjamin and *Berlin Alexanderplatz*," 262. In "Expressionism and Döblin's *Berlin Alexanderplatz*," Zimmermann explores the relationship of the novel to specific literary movements, identifying the portrayal of Biberkopf as an example of naturalism and that of the city as an example of expressionism.

18. See Ziolkowski, *Dimensions of the Modern Novel*, 99–137.

19. See Scherpe, "Ausdruck, Funktion, Medium." Scherpe distinguishes three phases in the development of "literature of the city": (1) narrative description of a city; (2) production (*Herstellung*) of a city through parallel forms; and (3) postwar and contemporary simulations of reality. See also Scherpe, "The City as Narrator: The Modern Text in Alfred Döblin's *Berlin Alexanderplatz*," in Huyssen and Bathrick, *Modernity and the Text*, 162–79; Klotz, *Die erzählte Stadt;* and Haas, "Bemerkungen zu Alfred Döblins Roman *Berlin Alexanderplatz*," in Prangel, *Materialien zu Alfred Döblin "Berlin Alexanderplatz,"* 78–86.

20. Scherpe, "The City as Narrator," 173.

21. See Benjamin, "Krisis des Romans: Zu Döblins *Berlin Alexanderplatz*," in *Gesammelte Schriften*, 3:232. Harald Jähner even brings in geometry, distinguishing between the "line" of the narrative text and the "plane" of the montage-text. See Jähner, "City as Megaphone." In a theoretical move with echoes of McLuhan, Dietrich Scheunemann calls this shift from linearity to montage equivalent in significance to the shift from the traditional printing press to electronic media. See Scheunemann, "'Collecting Shells' in the Age of Technological Reproduction."

22. Benjamin, "Krisis des Romans," 232. "Kurz, dieser 'roman pur' ist eigentlich reines Innen, kennt kein Außen, und somit äußerster Gegenpol zur reinen epischen Haltung, die das Erzählen ist. Gides Ideal des Romans ist—so läßt er sich im strengen Gegensatz zu Döblin darstellen—der reine Schreibroman."

23. Ibid., 232–33. "Stilprinzip dieses Buches ist die Montage. Kleinbürgerliche Drucksachen, Skandalgeschichten, Unglücksfälle, Sensationen von 28, Volkslieder, Inserate schneien in diesen Text. Die Montage sprengt den 'Roman,' sprengt ihn im Aufbau wie auch stilistisch, und eröffnet neue, sehr epische Möglichkeiten. Im Formalen vor allem. Das Material der Montage ist ja durchaus kein beliebiges. Echte Montage beruht auf dem Dokument. Der Dadaismus hat sich in seinem fanatischen Kampf gegen das Kunstwerk durch sie das tägliche Leben zum Bundesgenossen gemacht. Er hat zuerst, wenn auch unsicher, die Alleinherrschaft des Authentischen proklamiert. Der Film in seinen besten Augenblicken machte Miene, uns an sie zu gewöhnen. Hier ist sie zum ersten Male für die Epik nutzbar geworden. Die Bibelverse, Statistiken, Schlagertext sind es, kraft deren Döblin dem epischen Vorgang Autorität verleiht. Sie entsprechen den formelhaften Versen der alten Epik."

24. The phrase first appears in an article on Russian film published in *Die literarische Welt* in March 1927. See Benjamin, "A Discussion of Russian Filmic Art and Collectivist Art in General," in Kaes, Jay, and Dimendberg, *Weimar Republic Sourcebook*, 626, or Benjamin, "Eine Diskussion über russische Filmkunst und kollektivistische Kunst," in Kaes, *Weimarer Republik*, 224. Readers may be more familiar with its reappearance in the essay "The Work of Art in the Age of Mechanical Reproduction" almost ten years later: "Then came the film and burst [*sprengt*] this prison-world asunder by the dynamite of the tenth of a second, so that now, in the midst of its far-flung ruins and debris, we calmly and adventurously go traveling." Benjamin, "The Work of Art in the Age of Mechanical Reproduction," in *Illuminations*, 236; Benjamin, "Das Kunstwerk im Zeitalter seiner technischen Reproduzierbarkeit (Zweite Fassung)," in *Gesammelte Schriften*, vol. 1, bk. 2, pp. 499–500.

25. In "On Some Motifs in Baudelaire," Benjamin states: "Thus technology has subjected the human sensorium to a complex kind of training. There came a day when a new and urgent need for stimuli was met by the film. In a film, perception in the form of shocks was established as a formal principle." Benjamin, "On Some Motifs in Baudelaire," in *Illuminations*, 175.

26. Bolz, "Abschied von der Gutenberg-Galaxis," 143.

27. See Kaes, Jay, and Dimendberg, *Weimar Republic Sourcebook*, 641–43.

28. See Stenzel, "Mit Kleister und Schere." For photographs of the manuscript with newspaper cuttings pasted in, see *Alfred Döblin, 1878–1978*, 242–43.

29. Döblin, "Der Bau des epischen Werks," in *Schriften zu Ästhetik, Poetik und Literatur*, 226. "Und es ist mir so gegangen, als ich dies oder jenes historische Buch schrieb, daß ich mich kaum enthalten konnte, ganze Aktenstücke glatt abzuschreiben, ja ich sank manchmal zwischen den Akten bewundernd zusammen und sagte mir: besser kann ich es jadoch nicht machen."

30. Alfred Döblin, "Krise des Romans?" in *Schriften zu Ästhetik, Poetik und Literatur*, 274–75. "Eine kleine Zahl Autoren ist besonders fein, hat Spezialitäten, etwa besonderes Naturgefühl oder Sinn für Technik, Sinn für Soziales, Sinn für Seelisches. Die hamstern draußen im Leben Kenntnisse, Eindrücke und tragen sie in den Roman hinein. Solch Roman hat schon ein anderes Gesicht als der Gebrauchsroman. Aber es ist der alte Roman geblieben. Die Herren sind steckengeblieben. Sie haben etwas zu sagen, aber gießen es in den alten Schlauch. Die empfinden schon einen gewissen Jammer: ihnen paßt der alte Schlauch meist auch nicht; aber was tun?"

31. For a detailed analysis of the aesthetic and thematic differences among the novel, radio-play, and film versions of *Berlin Alexanderplatz* within the context of the end of Weimar culture and the rise of Nazism, see Jelavich, *Berlin Alexanderplatz*.

32. Herbert Ihering, "Döblins Heimkehr: *Berlin Alexanderplatz*," in Prangel, *Materialien zu Alfred Döblin "Berlin Alexanderplatz*," 73; Friedrich Muckermann, in Prangel, 104; Wilhelm Michel, in Prangel, 107. The Muckermann and Michel essays are reprints of untitled articles.

33. See Kaemmerling, "Die filmische Schreibweise."

34. Sabine Hake makes a similar criticism of the vast body of critical literature on Döblin's novel in "Urban Paranoia in Alfred Döblin's *Berlin Alexanderplatz*," which draws on the writing of Deleuze and Guattari to perform a "schizo-analysis" of the novel.

35. Benjamin, "The Work of Art in the Age of Mechanical Reproduction," in *Illuminations*, 222.

36. Hermann Kienzl, "Theater und Kinematograph," quoted in Petro, *Joyless Streets*, 6–7.

37. Döblin, "Der Geist des naturalistischen Zeitalters," in *Schriften zu Ästhetik, Poetik und Literatur*, 173. "Physiologisch werden in der neuen Epoche andere Organsysteme und Gehirnteile beschäftigt. Die ermüdeten alten Teile erholen sich. Muskeln, Augen, Ohren und ihre nervöspsychischen Projektionen treten jetzt in den Vordergrund. Man will sich fortbewegen, sehen, hören.

Man hatte vorher seine Kraft nur gelegentlich in Kriegen entladen; jetzt kommt es zur Technik: das ist Dauerkrieg, permanente Eroberung der Welt, die ja grenzenlos ist."

38. Döblin, "'Ulysses' von Joyce," in *Aufsätze zur Literatur*, 287–88. "Man muß wissen, daß Kunstformen zusammenhängen mit einer gewissen Denkweise und einem allgemeinen Lebensmilieu. Darum werden Formen dauernd überholt. . . . In den Rayon der Literatur ist das Kino eingedrungen, die Zeitungen sind groß geworden, sind das wichtigste, verbreitetste Schrifterzeugnis, sind das tägliche Brot aller Menschen. Zum Erlebnisbild der heutigen Menschen gehören ferner die Straßen, die sekündlich wechselnden Szenen auf der Straße, die Firmenschilder, der Wagenverkehr. . . . Der Fabuliersinn und seine Konstruktionen wirken hier naiv. Dies ist der Kernpunkt der sogenannten Krisis des heutigen Romans. Die Mentalität der Autoren hat sich noch nicht an die Zeit angeschlossen."

39. Döblin, "Literatur und Rundfunk," in *Schriften zu Ästhetik, Poetik und Literatur*, 254.

40. Döblin, "'Ulysses' von Joyce," in *Aufsätze zur Literatur*, 290.

41. Bolz, "Abschied von der Gutenberg-Galaxis," 144.

42. See Kaes, "The Debate About Cinema," and Kaes, "Einführung," in Kaes, *Kino-Debatte*, 1–36.

43. Furthman-Durden, "Hugo von Hofmannsthal and Alfred Döblin," 443.

44. Döblin's contemporaries similarly ignored the broader aims of his literary project when they hastily proclaimed Döblin's novel a descendent of James Joyce's *Ulysses*, published in 1922. The first German translation of *Ulysses* did not appear until 1927. Defending his novel against this comparison, Döblin wrote in a letter to Professor Julius Petersen, "The comparison with Joyce would have to include what, to my mind, the writer does not yet know of my earlier works. A stylistic analysis of my earlier work would make very clear both the similarities and the contrasts with Joyce." Prangel, *Materialien zu Alfred Döblin "Berlin Alexanderplatz,"* 42. "Bei der Gegenüberstellung mit Joyce wäre zu ergänzen, was dem Verfasser, glaub ich, aus meinen früheren Arbeiten doch noch unbekannt ist. Eine stilistische Analyse meiner früheren Sachen würde manches aus der Anähnlichung an Joyce und der Unterscheidung sehr klar ergeben."

45. Döblin, "Bermerkungen zum Roman," in *Schriften zu Ästhetik, Poetik und Literatur*, 124. "Der Roman hat mit Handlung nichts zu tun. . . . Vereinfachen, zurechtschlagen und -schneiden auf Handlung ist nicht Sache des Epikers. Im Roman heißt es schichten, häufen, wälzen, schieben; im Drama, dem jetzigen, auf die Handlung hin verarmten, Handlungsverbohrten: 'voran!' Vorwärts ist neimals die Parole des Romans."

46. Eisenstein, "The Montage of Film Attractions," in *Selected Works*, 1:40.

47. Ibid., 41.

48. Eisenstein, "The Dramaturgy of Film Form (The Dialectical Approach to Film Form)," in *Eisenstein Reader*, 95.

49. Eisenstein, "Beyond the Shot," in *Eisenstein Reader*, 82.

50. Ibid., 87.

51. Gunning, "Cinema of Attractions," 59.

52. Döblin, "Der Bau des epischen Werks," in *Schriften zu Ästhetik, Poetik und Literatur*, 236. "Dieser Abfluß vor unseren Augen hat auch den Vorteil, daß er gleichmäßig und gleichzeitig Autor und Hörer von Überraschung zu Überraschung und ungezwungen von Reiz zu Reiz führt. Er hat den Vorteil, daß jede Situation ungezwungen die nächste gebiert."

53. Döblin, *Berlin Alexanderplatz* (English translation), 1; henceforth, this work will be cited parenthetically in the text.

54. Döblin, "Das Theater der kleinen Leute," in Schweinitz, *Prolog vor dem Film*, 153–55.

55. In the preface to his screenplay *Die geweihten Töchter*, Döblin advocates the use of split screens or films within films to project a parallel fantastic universe alongside the "actual" or "naturalistic" events of the exterior frame. See Döblin, "Die geweihten Töchter: Vorbemerkung," in *Drama Hörspiel Film*, 325. The screenplays of the *Kinobuch* also show a disproportionate number of framed film stories, further evidence of their self-reflexive preoccupations. Döblin's screenplays will be discussed later in detail.

56. Döblin, "Das Theater der kleinen Leute," 154. "Drin in dem stockdunklen, niedrigen Raum glänzt ein mannshohes Leinwandviereck über ein Monstrum von Publikum, über eine Masse, welche dieses weiße Auge mit seinem stieren Blick zusammenbannt."

57. Döblin, "An Romanautoren und ihre Kritiker. Berliner Programm," in *Schriften zu Ästhetik, Poetik und Literatur*, 121. "Mit einem Kopfschütteln, Achselzucken für das Weitere und das 'Warum' und 'Wie.' Die sprachlichen Formeln dienen nur dem praktischen Verkehr. 'Zorn,' 'Liebe,' 'Verach-

tung' bezeichnen in die Sinne fallende Erscheinungskomplexe, darüber hinaus geben diese primitiven und abgeschmackten Buchstabenverbindungen nichts."

58. Ibid., 121.

59. Ibid., 123. "Mut zur kinetischen Phantasie und zum Erkennen der unglaublichen realen Konturen! Tatsachenphantasie! Der Roman muß seine Wiedergeburt erleben als Kunstwer[k] und modernes Epos."

60. Döblin, "Die Zeitlupe," in *Die Zeitlupe*, 100–106, 265. Other responses were submitted by Georg Hermann, Mechthilde Lichnowsky, Peter Panter, Carl Zuckmayer, and Herbert Eulenberg.

61. Benjamin, "The Work of Art in the Age of Mechanical Reproduction," 233.

62. Döblin, "Der Bau des epischen Werks," in *Schriften zu Ästhetik, Poetik und Literatur*, 227. "*Der wirkliche Dichter war zu allen Zeiten selbst ein Faktum*. Der Dichter hat zu zeigen und zu beweisen, daß er ein Faktum und Stück Realität ist und noch immer so gut und faktisch wie die gute Erfindung des Triergon oder wie die [K]aroluszelle."

63. The *Tri-ergon* (literally, "work of three") refers to the development of a sound-on-film system developed by Hans Vogt, Josef Engl, and Joseph Massole. Their invention first appeared in 1922/23 and involved a recording lamp that transformed the vibrating electric current in the rhythm of the sound waves emitted by the sound source into a luminous patch on the filmstrip. This system was later employed throughout Germany. August Karolus, a physicist, first began working on television in 1923 while at the University of Leipzig. The "Karolus-Zelle" is the light valve he developed in 1925 to improve image size and clarity. See Neale, *Cinema and Technology*, 67, and Fischer and Fisher, *Tube*, 195–98.

64. Döblin, "Der Bau des epischen Werks," in *Schriften zu Ästhetik, Poetik und Literatur*, 219. "Ich brauche nicht noch besonders zu sagen, daß die Erreichung dieser exemplarischen und einfachen Sphäre den epischen Künstler von dem Romanschriftsteller trennt, welche Romanschriftstellerei eine solid bürgerliche nützliche gewerbliche Beschäftigung ist. Sie imitiert, ohne in die Realität einzudringen oder gar zu durchstoßen, einige Oberflächen der Realität. Der wirklich Produktive aber muß zwei Schritte tun: er muß ganz nahe an die Realität heran, an ihre Sachlichkeit, ihr Blut, ihren Geruch, und dann hat er die Sache zu durchstoßen, das ist seine spezifische Arbeit."

65. Benjamin, "The Work of Art in the Age of Mechanical Reproduction," 233–34.

66. Döblin, "Der Bau des epischen Werks," in *Schriften zu Ästhetik, Poetik und Literatur*, 223.

67. Ibid., 235. "Alle epischen Werke haben es mit dem Werden und Geschehen zu tun, und so, möchte ich sagen, ist es auch in der Ordnung, daß der epische Bericht nicht fertig vorgelegt wird und angeschwirrt kommt, aus der Pistole geschossen, sondern der Leser erlebt ihn in statu nascendi."

68. Münsterberg, *Photoplay*, 9.

69. Similarly, Siegfried Kracauer will emphasize "editing" as the most general and indispensable property of the film and claim that truly cinematic films are those films "which incorporate aspects of physical reality with a view to making us experience them." Kracauer, *Theory of Film*, 29, 40. Rudolf Arnheim will also make the point that film as art must employ montage, even if "it must be admitted that most film directors do not make much original use of the artistic means at their disposal. They do not produce works of art but tell the people stories. They and their employers and audiences are not concerned with form but with content." Arnheim, *Film as Art*, 133.

70. Balázs, *Theory of the Film*, 47, 120.

71. Alfred and Erna Döblin first left Berlin for Paris, where they lived from the end of 1934 through 1939. After Germany invaded France, Döblin (like many European authors) contracted a deal with a Hollywood film company to obtain the work papers necessary for emigration to the United States. Döblin's contract with Metro-Goldwyn-Mayer was dated October 8, 1940, to October 7, 1941. For his writing services, Döblin was paid a salary of $1 per week. Relative to his European contemporaries in Hollywood, Döblin was fairly successful at MGM, although he did not share this opinion. See Erich Kleinschmidt, "Nachwort," in Döblin, *Drama Hörspiel Film*, 662–69.

72. Döblin's six screenplays from this period include the following: *Die Enteisung Grönlands* (The Thaw of Greenland, November/December 1941); *Bergromance* (Mountain Romance, December 1940 / January 1941); *Mrs. Miniver* (November 1940); *Random Harvest* (Summer 1941); *Staatsanwalt Fregus* (District Attorney Fregus, March-September 1941); and *Der Ausreißer* (The Runaway, 1941). The screenplay for *Die Enteisung Grönlands* was adapted from Döblin's novel *Berge Meere und Giganten* (1923). Döblin was part of a team of writers on the script for *Mrs. Miniver*, and his contribution (one lengthy scene) did appear in the final film with some modification. Screenplay

credit went to Arthur Wimperis, George Froeschel, James Hilton, and Claudine West. The film was produced in 1942 and won an Oscar, and the screenplay was included in John Gassner and D. Nichols's *Twenty Best Film Plays* (1943). The screenplay for *Random Harvest* was based on James Hilton's best-selling novel of the same name published in January 1941. Döblin was brought on the writing team to work on the psychiatrist's scene because of his own medical experience. Screenplay credit went to Claudine West, George Froeschel, and Arthur Wimperis. The film was produced in 1942 and was a financial success. It was distributed in Germany after the war under the title *Die verlorenen Jahre* (The Lost Years). See Erich Kleinschmidt, "Editorische Nachweise," in Döblin, *Drama Hörspiel Film*, 569–77.

73. Döblin, "Vorbemerkung: Die geweihten Töchter," in *Drama Hörspiel Film*, 325. "Das zusammenhangslose Hintereinander von Scenen wird prinzipiell vermieden. Es werden Scenengruppen gebildet im Sinne eines Romankapitels und Abschnittes. Ein Filmabschnitt bringt ein gewisses Stück der Handlung; Verwandlungen verbinden die Szenen untereinander. Bei der Verwandlung verschwimmt oder verschwindet auf dem Filmstreifen das Milieu oder einzelne Träger der Handlung; die führende Figur oder Figuren bewegen sich durch den ganzen Abschnitt."

74. Ibid., 325. "Prinzip des Films muss sein: keine oder ein Minimum von Worten—in diesem Film finden sich im Ganzen zwei Sätze und zwei Überschriften. Völliges optisches Denken und Phantasieren, nicht aber in dem Sinne, daß die wesentlichen seelischen Vorgänge der Gebärdenkraft des Schauspielers überlassen werden, sondern wirkliches optisches Ausdrücken mit den eigenen Mitteln der optischen Phantasie."

75. Greve, Pehle, and Westhoff, *Hätte ich das Kino!* 222. "Alfred Döblin hat einmal ein Filmmanuskript geschrieben, das nie gedreht wurde. Wir geben hier einzelne Szenen wieder, vor allem wegen der merkwürdigen bildhaften Assoziationstechnik Döblins . . . die, in ihrer irrationalen Lockerung, schon wie eine Vorstufe zu der Technik des 'Alexanderplatz' anmutet."

76. Friedell, "Prolog vor dem Film," quoted in Petro, *Joyless Streets*, 44.

77. See Schivelbusch, *Railway Journey*, 65–66.

78. A similar scene of cinematic confusion plays out later in an actual movie theater. In this example, however, the spectator does not confuse reality with a film but the other way around: "In the third act when the noble hero is apparently killed by a bandit, Eva sighs. And when Herbert looks her way, she's just about to slide off her seat, and she faints, imagine it. Afterwards they walk silently arm-in-arm through the street. Herbert is astonished: 'Your old man is goin' to have lots of fun if you act like this.' 'He shot him, did you see that, Herbert?' 'That wasn't real, it was only a trick, didn't you spot that? Why, you're still trembling'" (499).

79. Döblin, "Literatur und Rundfunk," in *Schriften zu Ästhetik, Poetik und Literatur*, 258. "Für diese Ausdehnung sind die Augen die Schnellreiter und die D-Züge, und sie ermöglichen, das zu fassen, was man Spannung nennt."

80. Manovich, *The Language of New Media*, 225.

81. As Benjamin instructs us, "The history of every art form shows critical epochs in which a certain art form aspires to effects which could be fully obtained only with a changed technical standard, that is to say, in a new art form." Benjamin, "The Work of Art in the Age of Mechanical Reproduction," 237.

82. Kittler, *Gramophone, Film, Typewriter*, 3.

83. Ibid., 4.

84. See Saussure, *Course in General Linguistics*. In *Discourse Networks*, Kittler points out that Saussure's linguistic theory is not unrelated to early twentieth-century technologies and scientific experimentation, stating for example that "Saussure systematized, at the price of a methodological phonocentrism, the countless scriptural facts that experiments circa 1900 produced and let stand in their facticity." Kittler, *Discourse Networks*, 254. Saussure's theory is, therefore, supported by the "discourse network" of 1900.

85. Culler, *Ferdinand de Saussure*, 45.

86. Foucault, *Order of Things*, xxiv.

87. Saussure, *Course in General Linguistics*, 14.

88. I have employed the term "jeopardize" here to resonate with Foucault's critique of a so-called mastery of discourse, as articulated in his essay, "The Order of Discourse." Foucault argues here that the prioritization of the institution or system of language as a homogeneous and limited condition of possibility of all acts of speaking is merely a strategic fiction: "Prohibitions, barriers,

thresholds and limits [have] been set up in order to master, at least partly, the great proliferation of discourse, in order to remove from its richness the most dangerous part, and in order to organise its disorder according to figures which dodge what is most uncontrollable about it. It is as if we had tried to efface all trace of its irruption into the activity of thought and language." Foucault, "Order of Discourse," 66. Döblin makes a similar challenge in his effort to introduce time into the narrative event.

89. Döblin, "Bermerkungen zum Roman," in *Schriften zu Ästhetik, Poetik und Literatur*, 124.

90. Döblin, "Bau des epischen Werks," in *Schriften zu Ästhetik, Poetik und Literatur* 240. "Ich möchte von einem Spannungsnetz, von einem dynamischen Netz sprechen, das sich allmählich über das ganze Werk ausdehnt, an bestimmten Konzeptionen befestigt wird, und in dieses Netz werden Handlungen und Personen eingebetten. Und Sie erkennen hier, daß epische Werke dieser Art weder gleichen dem grenzenlosen alten epischen Typ, noch dem schlechten modernen dramatischen Romantyp." This comparison is made even more explicit in Döblin's 1922 essay, "Berlin und die Künstler" (Berlin and the Artists): "Berlin is wonderful. The horse-trams fizzled out, electrical wires were strung over the street, the city lay under a vibrating, charged net" [Berlin ist wundervoll. Die Pferdebahnen gingen ein, über die Straßen wurden elektrische Drähte gezogen, die Stadt lag unter einem schwingenden, geladenen Netz]. Döblin, "Berlin und die Künstler," in Prangel, *Materialien zu Alfred Döblin "Berlin Alexanderplatz,"* 10.

91. "Ihre glänzenden Augen irrten flackernd im Dunkeln umher, und ihre Lippen bebten, Doppelpunkt, Gänsefüßchen, Lore, Gedankenstrich, Gedankenstrich, Lore, Gedankenstrich, Gänsefüßchen, Gänsebeinchen, Gänseleber mit Zwiebel." Döblin, *Berlin Alexanderplatz,* 64.

92. Döblin, *Drama Hörspiel Film,* 657. "Dann sah ich auch, daß ein Theaterstück sich nicht aus Alexanderplatz formen ließ. Denn die Schicksalslinie Biberkopfs, besser gesagt, die Schicksalsmelodie war nicht in die Bühnenform zu pressen. In die Bühnenform, deren Form vorschreibt—Aufteilung in Szenen und in Aktschlüsse und in einen Schluß, eiserner Vorhang herunter—das ging nicht. Es konnte nur ein Rundfunk-Hörspiel oder ein Film werden. Gerade die Mittel des Films, die der Tonfilm dem Drama voraus hat, konnten hier helfen. Die Photographie—die unverändert die Atmosphäre, das Lokalkolorit des Alexanderplatz-Viertels spiegelt, zweitens die Sprache, die Franz Biberkopf unmittelbar sprechen läßt und daher akustische echter als jeder Roman sein kann, und dann drittens—die Begleitmusik, die besonders wirksam das ewig Gleitende in diesem Biberkopfschicksal unterstützt und ausdrücken kann."

93. Quoted in *Alfred Döblin, 1878–1978,* 253–54. "Der Fall ist umso lehrreicher, als Döblins Buch die Chance bot, einen Film zu schaffen, der Zustände episch vermittelt. Man hat diese Gelegenheit versäumt, und das lockere Assoziationsgewebe des Romans . . . zu einer geschlossenen Unterweltsfabel verengt, wie sie nun einmal üblich ist. . . . Kurzum, eine Reihe von Zugeständnissen verdirbt hier das Konzept, und rein durch die macht der Verhältnissen wird aus einer Dichtung, die sich dem Film zuneigt, ein Film, der sich von ihr abwendet, ohne sich selber damit zu nützen."

94. Ihering, "Der *Alexanderplatz* Film," in Prangel, *Materialien zu Alfred Döblin "Berlin Alexanderplatz,"* 241–42. "Berlin Alexanderplatz kann dieser Film, nach Döblins Roman, kaum heißen. . . . In Döblins Roman ist die Filmform vorgezeichnet. Er war, übertrieben gesagt, ein geschriebener Film. . . . Unbegreiflicherweise setzte sich Alfred Döblin mit Hans Wilhelm zusammen, um aus dem Roman Berlin Alexanderplatz den Film *Heinrich George als Franz Biberkopf* zu machen. . . . Es fehlt das Entscheidende: die Bindung zu einer filmischen Form."

95. Eggebrecht, "Zu Döblins Erfolg," 210. "Außerordentlich ist die optische Beobachtungskraft Döblins. Hätten wir eine unternehmungslustige Filmindustrie, sie müßte sich um dies Buch reißen. Ruttmanns mutiger Berlin-film, in dem der Mensch Berlins hinter lauter Montagen der Technik und des Verkehrs verloren ging, würde wie eine kleine Vorstudie dazu wirken." As is evident in my own reading of the novel, traffic and movement on the street are intrinsic components of its composition, particularly as they relate to the influences of other media on the text itself. For this reason, I do not take up here Rainer Werner Fassbinder's film adaptation of *Berlin Alexanderplatz* produced for German television, which engages an entirely changed media aesthetic in postwar Germany. Further, with some important exceptions, Fassbinder's film is largely composed of interior shots (of courtyards, apartments, bars, stores, and the like), and as a result does not deal overtly with questions of media as does Ruttmann's film. A prominent exception to this is found in Part One when Franz walks into a doorway with a red, blinking "Kino" sign over his head. This red light flashing on and off frequently shines into Franz's apartment as well. In Fassbinder's film, the confu-

sion of urban experience is largely conveyed through sounds that penetrate the interior spaces into which the characters seek refuge from the city. In this fashion, the film portrays the psychological or "inner urbanization" of Franz and the other characters. See Fassbinder, *Die Anarchie der Phantasie*, 148–49, and 183.

96. Döblin, "Bau des epischen Werks," in *Schriften zu Ästhetik, Poetik und Literatur*, 240. "Fragt man, wem dann diese Werke, Werke mit diesen Formgesetzen ähneln, so hat die bisherige Zergliederung es schon gezeigt: symphonischen Werken."

97. Kracauer, "Cult of Distraction," in *Mass Ornament*, 326.

98. For a detailed and exemplary reading of the surfaces of modernity (architecture, advertising, film, and shop windows), see Ward, *Weimar Surfaces*.

99. Natter, "The City as Cinematic Space," 218.

100. Kracauer, *From Caligari to Hitler*, 187–88.

CHAPTER 5

The epigraph to this chapter is drawn from Dos Passos, "The Writer as Technician," in *John Dos Passos: The Major Nonfictional Prose*, 169.

1. John Dos Passos, "The Writer as Technician," in *John Dos Passos: The Major Nonfictional Prose*, 169.

2. Dos Passos, "Grosz Comes to America," in *John Dos Passos*, 173.

3. Ibid., 174.

4. Despite the theoretical confluence of these statements, Crary's discussion of photography dates to a nineteenth-century discourse, whereas Dos Passos is clearly referring to the twentieth century (as is evident in the generation gap between his parents and himself). This temporal distinction does not, however, negate their similarity, for Dos Passos views European artists as having begun to formulate the terms of this problem much earlier than those in the United States.

5. Dos Passos, "Grosz Comes to America," in *John Dos Passos*, 177.

6. Dos Passos's analogy of the modern artist to the doctor also recalls Benjamin's analogy between the surgeon and the filmmaker in his essay, "The Work of Art in the Age of Mechanical Reproduction." See Benjamin, "The Work of Art in the Age of Mechanical Reproduction," in *Illuminations*, 233–34.

7. Dos Passos, "Translator's Foreword to *Panama; or, The Adventures of My Seven Uncles*," in *John Dos Passos*, 134.

8. "Prolog vor dem Film," in Schweinitz, *Prolog vor dem Film*, 202.

9. Dos Passos, "Contemporary Chronicles," in *John Dos Passos*, 33.

10. Dos Passos, *Manhattan Transfer*, 12; henceforth, this work will be cited parenthetically in the text.

11. For a study that addresses the "multilinear" composition common to both novels, see Komar, *Pattern and Chaos*, 15–56.

12. Dos Passos, "What Makes a Novelist," in *John Dos Passos*, 272.

13. Joris Duytschaever, "Joyce—Dos Passos—Döblin: Einfluß oder Analogie?" in Prangel, *Materialien zu Alfred Döblin "Berlin Alexanderplatz,"* 144.

14. Hans Sochaczewer, "Der neue Döblin," in Prangel, *Materialien zu Alfred Döblin "Berlin Alexanderplatz,"* 56–57. "Dieser Roman wird die verblüffen, die mit der neuen amerikanischen Literatur nicht vertraut sind; Einflüsse formaler Natur machen sich geltend, wie sie noch in keinem deutschen Roman zu finden gewesen sind."

15. See, for example, Duytschaever, "Joyce—Dos Passos—Döblin," in Prangel, *Materialien zu Alfred Döblin "Berlin Alexanderplatz,"* 136–49; Mitchell, *James Joyce and the German Novel*, 131–50; Mitchell, "Joyce and Döblin"; and Zalubska, "Parallelen der Erzähltechnik."

16. Excerpts of the "Hades" chapter of Joyce's *Ulysses* were published June 17, 1927, in *Die Literarische Welt*, with an introduction by Ivan Goll titled, "Der Homer unserer Zeit" (The Homer of Our Age). The German translation of *Ulysses* was published by Rhein-Verlag in late October 1927. In July 1927, excerpts from the German translation of Dos Passos's *Manhattan Transfer* appeared in *Die Neue Rundschau;* the issue also featured a review of Döblin's novel, *Manas*. In October 1927, a ten-page excerpt of the German translation of *Manhattan Transfer* appeared in *Almanach 1928*

along with selections from Döblin's *Das Ich über der Natur* and *Manas*. The German translation of *Manhattan Transfer* was published by Fischer Verlag in October 1927; the German translation of *The 42nd Parallel* was published in 1930. As far as Joyce's influence on Dos Passos is concerned, we have Dos Passos's statement from his autobiography, *The Best Times*: "Coming through Paris I bought an early copy of *Ulysses* and even shook the limp hand of a pale uninterested man in dark glasses sitting beside the stove in the back room of Shakespeare and Company whom Miss Beach claimed was James Joyce. I read the book at one gulp while laid up with a bout of flu in a tiny inside cabin way down in the third class of one of the big transatlantic liners: parts I found boring and parts I found magnificent. If *Ulysses* didn't accomplish anything else—for me at least—it disposed of the current theory that the English novel was dead." Dos Passos, *The Best Times*, 131.

17. Dos Passos went to Hollywood in July 1934 to work on the screenplay for director Josef von Sternberg's *The Devil Is a Woman*, starring Marlene Dietrich. In a letter to Ernest Hemingway written soon after his arrival in California, Dos Passos claimed he was "taking a look at the world's greatest bullshit center . . . but it's all very educational I suppose." At the time, Dos Passos was working on the final book of his *U.S.A.* trilogy, *The Big Money*, and as he went on to explain to Hemingway, "I need some of this stuff in my business and the best way to get it is to see it from the inside." As Dos Passos soon learned, however, only his name and not his ideas were being used. In a letter to Edmund Wilson dated shortly before his departure from Hollywood in October of the same year, Dos Passos wrote: "I was merely in the position of Queen Marie endorsing a vanishing cream. It turns out that all the while a young man, whose name I believe is Nertz, was writing the real screen play behind the scenes. I'm darn sorry I wasn't able to stagger round the studios some more. It was interesting there, though the horrid stalking of intangibles makes it more nerve-wracking, I imagine, than the average industrial plant." Ludington, *Fourteenth Chronicle*, 437, 443.

18. Dos Passos, "John Dos Passos," in *John Dos Passos*, 247. Although Dos Passos may already have been familiar with Eisenstein's ideas and was certainly acquainted with the term "montage," he could not have seen *Potemkin* before writing *Manhattan Transfer*. Eisenstein's work was not released in the United States until 1926, and his articles on montage did not appear in American journals until after 1927. See Spindler, "John Dos Passos and the Visual Arts," 402–3. Dos Passos met Eisenstein in 1928 while traveling in Russia. At the time, he was writing *The 42nd Parallel*, the first novel of his *U.S.A.* trilogy. He also discussed his admiration for the filmmaker in his autobiography: "Eisenstein had a curt aphoristic way of talking. We agreed thoroughly about the importance of montage. He may have already been suffering from a damaging amount of conceit as a result of the adulation which surrounded him, but he had one of the most brilliantly synthesizing minds I ever ran into. If he'd been a mathematician, he would have skipped the early stages and started out with calculus and logic." Dos Passos, *The Best Times*, 180–81.

19. The relationship between Dos Passos's writing and film has a long history, beginning with Sinclair Lewis's and D. H. Lawrence's reviews of the novel in 1925 and 1927. See Maine, *Dos Passos*, 67–72, 74–77. Later studies include Astre, *Thèmes et structures*, 1:156–200; Foster, "John Dos Passos' Use of Film Technique"; Lowry, "The Lively Art of *Manhattan Transfer*"; and Spindler, "John Dos Passos and the Visual Arts."

20. Eisenstein, "Beyond the Shot," in *Selected Works*, 1:145.

21. Eisenstein, "The Dramaturgy of Film Form (The Dialectical Approach to Film Form)," in *Selected Works*, 1:177.

22. Ibid., 177.

23. Ibid., 178.

24. Dos Passos, "Contemporary Chronicles," in *John Dos Passos*, 239; Dos Passos, "What Makes a Novelist," in *John Dos Passos*, 272.

25. Quoted in Maine, *Dos Passos*, 75.

26. Ibid., 65.

27. Dos Passos, "What Makes a Novelist," in *John Dos Passos*, 272.

28. In his study of the novel, Craig Carver identifies many of the newspaper sources of events and images presented in the novel. See Carver, "The Newspaper and Other Sources of *Manhattan Transfer*."

29. See Kittler, "The City Is a Medium."

30. Dos Passos, "Writer as Technician," in *John Dos Passos*, 169.

31. Dos Passos, "John Dos Passos [Interview July 2, 1962]," in *John Dos Passos*, 247.

32. Dos Passos, "Introductory Note to *The 42nd Parallel*," in *John Dos Passos*, 179.

33. Dos Passos, "An Interview with John Dos Passos [1968]," in *John Dos Passos*, 283.
34. Dos Passos, "John Dos Passos [Interview July 2, 1962]," in *John Dos Passos*, 247.
35. See Westerhoven, "Autobiographical Elements in the Camera Eye."
36. Pizer, "The Camera Eye in *U.S.A.*," 429.
37. Foster, "John Dos Passos' Use of Film Technique," 190. For his part, Vertov maintained that his filmmaking methods had an indirect influence on certain writers, including Dos Passos. See Vaughan, "The Man with the Movie Camera," 53.
38. Dos Passos, *U.S.A.*, 13.
39. Dos Passos, "The Duty of the Writer," in *John Dos Passos*, 205.
40. Quoted from Dos Passos's collected papers at the University of Virginia, in Ludington, *John Dos Passos*, 259–60.
41. De Man, "Literary History and Literary Modernity," 246–47.
42. Baudelaire, "The Painter of Modern Life," 13.
43. De Man, "Literary History and Literary Modernity," 262.
44. Ibid., 260.
45. Dos Passos, *U.S.A.*, 368–69.
46. Dos Passos, "What Makes a Novelist," in *John Dos Passos*, 274.
47. Godzich, "Languages, Images, and the Postmodern Predicament," 367–68.
48. Dos Passos, "Contemporary Chronicles," in *John Dos Passos*, 238.
49. Dos Passos, *U.S.A.*, 55–56.
50. Dos Passos, "An Interview with John Dos Passos [1968]," in *John Dos Passos*, 288.
51. Batchen, *Each Wild Idea*, 59–60.
52. Tagg, *Burden of Representation*, 3.
53. Flusser, *Towards a Philosophy of Photography*, 84.
54. Ibid., 81.
55. Sebald, "Between History and Natural History," 98.
56. Atze and Loquai, *Sebald*, 15–16.

Bibliography

Adorno, Theodor W. "The Form of the Phonograph Record." Translated by Thomas Y. Levin. *October* 55 (Winter 1990): 56–61.
Alfred Döblin, 1878–1978. Ausstellung des deutschen Literaturarchivs. Marbach am Neckar: Schiller-Nationalmuseum, 1978.
Alighieri, Dante. *The Divine Comedy*. Bk. 1, *Inferno*. Translated by John D. Sinclair. New York: Oxford, 1939.
Altenloh, Emilie. *Zur Soziologie des Kino: Die Kino-Unternehmung und die sozialen Schichten ihrer Besucher*. Jena: Diederichs, 1914.
Arnheim, Rudolf. *Film as Art*. Berkeley and Los Angeles: University of California Press, 1957.
Astre, Georges-Albert. *Thèmes et structures dans l'oeuvre de John Dos Passos*. Vol. 1. Paris: Lettres Modernes, 1956.
Atze, Marcel, and Franz Loquai, eds. *Sebald. Lektüren*. Eggingen: Isele, 2005.
Baer, Ulrich, ed. and trans. *The Poet's Guide to Life: The Wisdom of Rilke*. New York: Modern Library, 2005.
———. *Spectral Evidence: The Photography of Trauma*. Cambridge, Mass.: MIT Press, 2002.
Balázs, Béla. *Der sichtbare Mensch oder die Kultur des Films*. Frankfurt am Main: Suhrkamp, 2001.
———. *Theory of the Film*. Translated by Edith Bone. New York: Roy, 1953.
Bance, A. F. "Alfred Döblin's *Berlin Alexanderplatz* and Literary Modernism." In *Weimar Germany: Writers and Politics*, edited by A. F. Bance, 53–64. Edinburgh: Scottish Academic Press, 1982.
Barnouw, Dagmar. *Critical Realism: History, Photography and the Work of Siegfried Kracauer*. Baltimore: Johns Hopkins University Press, 1994.
Barthes, Roland. *Camera Lucida: Reflections on Photography*. Translated by Richard Howard. New York: Hill and Wang, 1981.
Batchen, Geoffrey. *Each Wild Idea: Writing, Photography, History*. Cambridge, Mass.: MIT Press, 2001.
Baudelaire, Charles. *Baudelaire. The Complete Verse*. Edited and translated by Francis Scarfe. Vol. 1. London: Anvil, 1986.
———. "The Painter of Modern Life." In *The Painter of Modern Life and Other Essays*, translated and edited by Jonathan Mayne, 1–40. New York: Da Capo, 1964.
———. *The Poems in Prose, with La Fanfarlo*. Edited and translated by Francis Scarfe. Vol. 2. London: Anvil, 1989.
———. "The Salon of 1859: The Modern Public and Photography." In *Art in Paris, 1845–1862. Salons and Other Exhibitions Reviewed by Charles Baudelaire*, translated and edited by Jonathan Mayne, 149–53. London: Phaidon, 1965.
Bazin, André. "The Ontology of the Photographic Image." In *What Is Cinema?* trans. Hugh Gray, 9–16. Berkeley and Los Angeles: University of California Press, 1967.

Benjamin, Walter. *Gesammelte Schriften.* Edited by Rolf Tiedemann and Hermann Schweppenhäuser. Vol. 1, bk. 2. Frankfurt am Main: Suhrkamp, 1974.
———. *Gesammelte Schriften.* Edited by Hella Tiedemann-Bartels. Vol. 3. Frankfurt am Main: Suhrkamp, 1972.
———. *Illuminations.* Edited by Hannah Arendt. Translated by Harry Zohn. New York: Schocken, 1968.
———. "A Small History of Photography." In *One-Way Street and Other Writings,* trans. Edmund Jephcott and Kingsley Shorter, 240–57. London: New Left Books, 1979.
Berg-Ganschow, Uta, and Wolfgang Jacobsen, eds. *Film Stadt Kino Berlin.* Berlin: Argon, 1987.
Bolter, Jay David, and Richard Grusin. *Remediation: Understanding New Media.* Cambridge, Mass.: MIT Press, 2000.
Bolz, Norbert. "Abschied von der Gutenberg-Galaxis: Medienästhetik nach Nietzsche, Benjamin und McLuhan." In *Armaturen der Sinne: Literarische und technische Medien 1870 bis 1920,* edited by Jochen Hörisch and Michael Wetzel, 139–56. Munich: Fink, 1990.
———. "Die Schrift des Films." In *Diskursanalysen 1: Medien,* edited by Friedrich A. Kittler, Manfred Schneider, and Samuel Weber, 26–34. Opladen: Westdeutscher Verlag, 1987.
Bolz, Norbert, and Willem van Reijen. *Walter Benjamin.* Frankfurt am Main: Campus, 1991.
Bradley, Brigitte. *Zu Rilkes Malte Laurids Brigge.* Bern: Francke, 1980.
Brecht, Bertolt. "The Film, the Novel and Epic Theatre." In *Brecht on Theatre: The Development of an Aesthetic,* edited and translated by John Willett, 47–51. New York: Hill and Wang, 1964.
Cadava, Eduardo. *Words of Light: Theses on the Photography of History.* Princeton: Princeton University Press, 1997.
Carver, Craig. "The Newspaper and Other Sources of *Manhattan Transfer.*" *Studies in American Fiction* 3, no. 2 (Autumn 1975): 167–79.
Clarke, D. S., Jr. *Sources of Semiotic: Readings with Commentary from Antiquity to the Present.* Carbondale: Southern Illinois University Press, 1990.
Crary, Jonathan. *Techniques of the Observer: On Vision and Modernity in the Nineteenth Century.* Cambridge, Mass.: MIT Press, 1990.
Culler, Jonathan. *Ferdinand de Saussure.* Rev. ed. Ithaca: Cornell University Press, 1986.
Danius, Sara. *The Senses of Modernism: Technology, Perception, and Aesthetics.* Ithaca: Cornell University Press, 2002.
De Man, Paul. "Literary History and Literary Modernity." In *In Search of Literary Theory,* edited by Morton W. Bloomfield, 239–67. Ithaca: Cornell University Press, 1972.
Derrida, Jacques. "Freud and the Scene of Writing." In *Writing and Difference,* trans. Alan Bass, 196–231. Chicago: University of Chicago Press, 1978.
———. *Of Grammatology.* Translated by Gayatri Chakravorty Spivak. Corrected ed. Baltimore: Johns Hopkins University Press, 1997.
Diederichs, Helmut. *Anfänge deutscher Filmkritik.* Stuttgart: Fischer + Wiedleroither, 1986.
———. "'Ihr müßt erst etwas von guter Filmkunst verstehen': Béla Balázs als Filmtheoretiker und Medienpädagoge." In *Der sichtbare Mensch oder die Kultur des Films,* edited by Béla Balázs, 115–47. Frankfurt am Main: Suhrkamp, 2001.
Doane, Mary Ann. *The Emergence of Cinematic Time.* Cambridge, Mass.: Harvard University Press, 2002.
Döblin, Alfred. *Aufsätze zur Literatur.* Edited by Walter Muschg. Olten: Walter, 1963.

———. *Berlin Alexanderplatz: Die Geschichte vom Franz Biberkopf.* Edited by Walter Muschg. Olten: Walter, 1961.

———. *Berlin Alexanderplatz: The Story of Franz Biberkopf.* Translated by Eugene Jolas. New York: Continuum, 1992.

———. *Drama Hörspiel Film.* Edited by Erich Kleinschmidt. Olten: Walter, 1983.

———. *Schriften zu Ästhetik, Poetik und Literatur.* Edited by Erich Kleinschmidt. Olten: Walter, 1989.

———. *Die Zeitlupe: Kleine Prosa.* Olten: Walter, 1962.

Dos Passos, John. *The Best Times: An Informal Memoir.* New York: New American Library, 1966.

———. *John Dos Passos: The Major Nonfictional Prose.* Edited by Donald Pizer. Detroit: Wayne State University Press, 1988.

———. *Manhattan Transfer.* Boston: Houghton Mifflin, 1953.

———. *U.S.A.* New York: Library of America, 1996.

Dürr, Volker. "Personal Identity and the Idea of the Novel: Hegel in Rilke." *Comparative Literature* 39, no. 2 (Spring 1987): 97–114.

Eggebrecht, Axel. "Zu Döblins Erfolg." *Die Weltbühne,* February 4, 1930, 208–11.

Eisenstein, Sergei. *The Eisenstein Reader.* Edited by Richard Taylor. Translated by Richard Taylor and William Powell. London: BFI, 1998.

———. *Selected Works.* Vol. 1, *Writings, 1922–34.* Edited and translated by Richard Taylor. London: BFI, 1988.

Elsaesser, Thomas, with Michael Wedel, ed. *A Second Life: German Cinema's First Decades.* Amsterdam: Amsterdam University Press, 1996.

Engelhardt, Hartmut, ed. *Materialien zu Rainer Maria Rilke: Die Aufzeichnungen des Malte Laurids Brigge.* Frankfurt am Main: Suhrkamp, 1974.

Estermann, Alfred. *Die Verfilmung literarischer Werke.* Bonn: Bouvier, 1965.

Faber, Marion. "Hofmannsthal and the Film." *German Life and Letters* 32 (1978–79): 187–95.

Fassbinder, Rainer Werner. *Die Anarchie der Phantasie: Gespräche und Interviews.* Edited by Michael Töteberg. Frankfurt am Main: Fischer, 1986.

Fischer, David E., and Marshall Jon Fisher. *Tube: The Invention of Television.* Washington, D.C.: Counterpoint, 1996.

Flusser, Vilém. *Towards a Philosophy of Photography.* Translated by Anthony Mathews. London: Reaktion, 2000.

Foster, Gretchen. "John Dos Passos' Use of Film Technique in *Manhattan Transfer* and *The 42nd Parallel.*" *Film Literature Quarterly* 14, no. 3 (1986): 186–94.

Foucault, Michel. "The Order of Discourse." Translated by Ian McLeod. In *Untying the Text,* edited by Robert Young, 48–77. Boston: RKP, 1981.

———. *The Order of Things: An Archaeology of the Human Sciences.* New York: Hill and Wang, 1964.

Freedman, Ralph. *Life of a Poet: Rainer Maria Rilke.* New York: Farrar, Straus and Giroux, 1996.

Freud, Sigmund. *Beyond the Pleasure Principle.* Translated by James Strachey. New York: W. W. Norton, 1961.

———. *The Interpretation of Dreams.* Translated by James Strachey. New York: Avon, 1965.

———. *Die Traumdeutung.* In *Gesammelte Werke,* vol. 2/3, edited by Anna Freud et al. Frankfurt am Main: Fischer, 1942.

———. "The 'Uncanny.'" In *The Standard Edition of the Complete Psychological Works of Sigmund Freud,* edited and translated by James Strachey, 17:218–52. London: Hogarth, 1955.

Frisby, David. *Fragments of Modernity: Theories of Modernity in the Work of Simmel, Kracauer and Benjamin.* Cambridge, Mass.: MIT Press, 1986.

Furthman-Durden, Elke C. "Hugo von Hofmannsthal and Alfred Döblin: The Confluence of Film and Literature." *Monatshefte* 78, no. 4 (1986): 443–55.

Gandert, Gero, ed. *Der Film der Weimarer Republik: Ein Handbuch der zeitgenossischen Kritik.* Berlin: Walter de Gruyter, 1993.

Geduld, Harry M., ed. *Authors on Film.* Bloomington: Indiana University Press, 1972.

Gibson, William. *Neuromancer.* New York: Ace, 1984.

Gide, André. *Les faux-monnayeurs.* Paris: Gallimard, 1925.

Godzich, Wlad. "Languages, Images, and the Postmodern Predicament." In *Materialities of Communication,* edited by Hans Ulrich Gumbrecht and K. Ludwig Pfeiffer, translated by William Whobrey, 355–70. Stanford: Stanford University Press, 1994.

Goethe, Johann Wolfgang von. *Faust: Part One.* Translated by Martin Greenberg. New Haven: Yale University Press, 1992.

———. *Sämtliche Werke.* Edited by Albrecht Schöne. Vol. 7, bk. 1. Frankfurt: Deutscher Klassiker, 1994.

Greve, Ludwig, Margot Pehle, and Heidi Westhoff, eds. *Hätte ich das Kino! Die Schriftsteller und der Stummfilm.* Stuttgart: Klett, 1976.

Gunning, Tom. "The Cinema of Attractions: Early Film, Its Spectator and the Avant-Garde." In *Early Cinema: Space Frame Narrative,* edited by Thomas Elsaesser, with Adam Barker, 56–62. London: BFI, 1990.

Gutting, Gary, ed. *The Cambridge Companion to Foucault.* New York: Cambridge University Press, 1994.

Güttinger, Fritz. *Der Stummfilm im Zitat der Zeit.* Frankfurt am Main: Deutsches Filmmuseum, 1984.

Hake, Sabine. *The Cinema's Third Machine: Writing on Film in Germany, 1907–1933.* Lincoln: University of Nebraska Press, 1993.

———. "Urban Paranoia in Alfred Döblin's *Berlin Alexanderplatz.*" *German Quarterly* 67, no. 3 (Summer 1994): 347–68.

Hansen, Miriam. "Benjamin, Cinema, and Experience: 'The Blue Flower in the Land of Technology.'" *New German Critique* 40 (Winter 1987): 179–224.

———. "Decentric Perspectives: Kracauer's Early Writings on Film and Mass Culture." *New German Critique* 54 (Fall 1991): 47–76.

Hasenclever, Walter. *Sämtliche Werke.* Vol. 5, *Kleine Schriften.* Edited by Chirstoph Brauer, Corinna Bürgerhausen, Klaus Mackowiak, Jörg Schläger, and Annelie Zurhelle. Mainz: Hase and Koehler, 1997.

Heller, Heinz-B. *Literarische Intelligenz und Film: Zu Veränderung der ästhetischen Theorie und Praxis unter dem Eindruck des Films 1910–1930 in Deutschland.* Tübingen: Max Niemeyer, 1985.

Herd, E. W. "An Interpretation of *Die Aufzeichnungen des Malte Laurids Brigge:* Based on an Analysis of the Structure." *Seminar* 9 (1973): 208–28.

Hofmannsthal, Hugo von. *Ausgewählte Werke in zwei Bänden.* Vol. 2, *Erzählungen und Aufsätze.* Edited by Rudolf Hirsch. Frankfurt: Fischer, 1957.

———. "The Letter of Lord Chandos." In *Selected Prose,* trans. Mary Hottinger, Tania Stern, and James Stern, 129–41. New York: Pantheon, 1952.

Huyssen, Andreas, and David Bathrick, eds. *Modernity and the Text: Revisions of German Modernism.* New York: Columbia University Press, 1989.

Jackson, John E. "Rilke et Baudelaire." *Stanford French Review* 3 (1979): 325–41.

Jähner, Harald. "The City as Megaphone in Alfred Döblin's *Berlin Alexanderplatz.*" In *Berlin: Culture and Metropolis,* edited by Charles W. Haxthausen and Heidrun Suhr, 141–51. Minneapolis: University of Minnesota Press, 1990.

Jelavich, Peter. *Berlin Alexanderplatz: Radio, Film, and the Death of Weimar Culture.* Berkeley and Los Angeles: University of California Press, 2006.

Joyce, James. *A Portrait of the Artist as a Young Man.* New York: Modern Library, 1996.

Kaemmerling, Ekkehard. "Die filmische Schreibweise: Am Beispiel Alfred Döblin: Berlin Alexanderplatz." *Jahrbuch für Internationale Germanistik* 5, no. 1 (1973): 45–61.

Kaes, Anton. "The Debate About Cinema: Charting a Controversy (1909–1929)." *New German Critique* 40 (Winter 1987): 7–33.

———, ed. *Kino-Debatte: Texte zum Verhältnis von Literatur und Film, 1909–1929.* Tübingen: Niemeyer, 1978.

———. *Weimarer Republik: Manifeste und Dokumente zur deutschen Literatur, 1918–1933.* Stuttgart: Metzler, 1983.

Kaes, Anton, Martin Jay, and Edward Dimendberg, eds. *The Weimar Republic Sourcebook.* Berkeley and Los Angeles: University of California Press, 1994.

Kittler, Friedrich A. *Aufschreibesysteme, 1800/1900.* Munich: Wilhelm Fink, 1985.

———. "The City Is a Medium." Translated by Matthew Griffin. *New Literary History* 27, no. 4 (Autumn 1996): 717–29.

———. *Discourse Networks, 1800/1900.* Translated by Michael Metteer, with Chris Cullins. Stanford: Stanford University Press, 1990.

———. "A Discourse on Discourse." *Stanford Literature Review* 3, no. 1 (1986): 157–66.

———. *Grammophon Film Typewriter.* Berlin: Brinkmann and Bose, 1986.

———. *Gramophone, Film, Typewriter.* Translated by Geoffrey Winthrop-Young and Michael Wutz. Stanford: Stanford University Press, 1999.

———. "Literatur und Literaturwissenschaft als Word Processing." In *Germanistik—Forschungsstand und Perspektiven. Vorträge des Deutschen Germanistentages, 1984,* edited by Georg Stötzel, 410–19. Berlin: Walter de Gruyter, 1985.

Kluge: Etymologisches Wörterbuch der deutschen Sprache. 23rd expanded ed. Berlin: Walter de Gruyter, 1995.

Knilli, Friedrich. "Massenmedien und Metropolen." In *Medien Metropole. Berlin, Paris, New York,* edited by Friedrich Knilli and Michael Nerlich, with Heino Maß. Heidelberg: Carl Winter, 1986.

Komar, Kathleen. *Pattern and Chaos: Multilinear Novels by Dos Passos, Döblin, Faulkner and Koeppen.* Columbia, S.C.: Camden House, 1983.

Kracauer, Siegfried. *From Caligari to Hitler: A Psychological History of the German Film.* Princeton: Princeton University Press, 1947.

———. *The Mass Ornament: Weimar Essays.* Translated and edited by Thomas Y. Levin. Cambridge, Mass.: Harvard University Press, 1995.

———. *Theory of Film: The Redemption of Physical Reality.* Princeton: Princeton University Press, 1997.

Kurz, Martina. *Bild-Verdichtungen: Cézannes Realisation als poetisches Prinzip bei Rilke und Handke.* Göttingen: Vandenhoeck and Ruprecht, 2003.

Leppmann, Wolfgang. *Rilke: Sein Leben, seine Welt, sein Werk.* Bern: Scherz, 1981.

Lorenz, Thorsten. "Der kinematographische Un-Fall der Seelenkunde." In *Diskursanalysen 1: Medien,* edited by Friedrich Kittler, Manfred Schneider, and Samuel Weber, 108–28. Opladen: Westdeutscher Verlag, 1987.

Lowry, E. D. "The Lively Art of *Manhattan Transfer.*" *PMLA* 84, no. 6 (October 1969): 1628–38.

Ludington, Townsend, ed. *The Fourteenth Chronicle: Letters and Diaries of John Dos Passos.* Boston: Gambit, 1973.

———. *John Dos Passos: A Twentieth-Century Odyssey.* New York: Dutton, 1980.

Maine, Barry, ed. *Dos Passos: The Critical Heritage.* London: Routledge, 1988.

Mann, Thomas. *The Magic Mountain*. Translated by John E. Woods. New York: Knopf, 1995.

Manovich, Lev. *The Language of New Media*. Cambridge, Mass.: MIT Press, 2001.

Marder, Elissa. *Dead Time: Temporal Disorders in the Wake of Modernity (Baudelaire and Flaubert)*. Stanford: Stanford University Press, 2001.

Martini, Fritz. *Der Wagnis der Sprache. Interpretationen deutscher Prosa von Nietzsche bis Benn*. Stuttgart: Ernst Klett, 1954.

Mason, Eudo. *Rainer Maria Rilke. Sein Leben und sein Werk*. Göttingen: Vandenhoeck and Ruprecht, 1964.

Mast, Gerald, Marshall Cohen, and Leo Bruady, ed. *Film Theory and Criticism*. New York: Oxford University Press, 1992.

McLuhan, Marshall. *Understanding Media: The Extensions of Man*. Cambridge, Mass.: MIT Press, 1994.

McLuhan, Marshall, and Quentin Fiore. *The Medium Is the Massage*. New York: Touchstone, 1967.

Mitchell, Breon. *James Joyce and the German Novel, 1922–1933*. Athens: Ohio University Press, 1976.

———. "Joyce and Döblin: At the Crossroads of *Berlin Alexanderplatz*." *Contemporary Literature* 12 (1971): 173–87.

Mitchell, W. J. T. *Picture Theory: Essays on Verbal and Visual Representation*. Chicago: University of Chicago Press, 1994.

Münsterberg, Hugo. *The Photoplay: A Psychological Study*. New York: Arno, 1970.

Musil, Robert. "Ansätze zu neuer Ästhetik: Bemerkungen über eine Dramaturgie des Films." In *Gesammelte Werke*, vol. 2, edited by Adolf Frisé, 1137–54. Reinbek bei Hamburg: Rowohlt, 1978.

Natter, Wolfgang. "The City as Cinematic Space: Modernism and Place in *Berlin, Symphony of a City*." In *Place, Power, Situation, and Spectacle: A Geography of Film*, edited by Stuart C. Aitken and Leo E. Zonn, 203–27. Lanham, Md.: Rowman and Littlefield, 1994.

Neale, Steve. *Cinema and Technology: Image, Sound, Colour*. London: BFI, 1985.

Nietzsche, Friedrich. "On Truth and Lie in an Extra-Moral Sense." In *The Portable Nietzsche*, edited and translated by Walter Kaufmann, 42–47. New York: Viking, 1954.

Nivelle, Armand. "Sens et structure des *Cahiers de Malte Laurids Brigge*." *Revue d'esthétique* 12 (1959): 5–32.

Novalis. *Schriften*. Vol. 1, *Das dichterische Werk*. Edited by Paul Kluckhohn and Richard Samuel, with Heinz Ritter and Gerhard Schulz. Stuttgart: Kohlhammer, 1960.

Ong, Walter J. *Orality and Literacy: The Technologizing of the Word*. London: Routledge, 2002.

Petro, Patrice. *Joyless Streets: Women and Melodramatic Representation in Weimar Germany*. Princeton: Princeton University Press, 1989.

Pinthus, Kurt, ed. *Das Kinobuch*. Zürich: Arche, 1963.

———. *Menschheitsdämmerung: Ein Dokument des Expressionismus*. New ed. Hamburg: Rowohlt, 1964.

Pizer, Donald. "The Camera Eye in *U.S.A.*: The Sexual Center." *Modern Fiction Studies* 26, no. 3 (Autumn 1980): 417–30.

Prangel, Matthias. *Materialien zu Alfred Döblin "Berlin Alexanderplatz."* Frankfurt am Main: Suhrkamp, 1975.

Reid, James H. "Berlin Alexanderplatz—A Political Novel." *German Life and Letters* 21, no. 3 (April 1968): 214–23.

Rilke, Rainer Maria. *Die Aufzeichnungen des Malte Laurids Brigge*. Frankfurt am Main: Insel, 1982.

———. *Briefe aus den Jahren 1902 bis 1906*. Edited by Ruth Sieber-Rilke and Carl Sieber. Leipzig: Insel, 1930.
———. *Letters of Rainer Maria Rilke*. Vol. 1, *1892–1910*. Translated by Jane Bannard Greene and M. D. Herter Norton. New York: W. W. Norton, 1945.
———. *Letters of Rainer Maria Rilke*. Vol. 2, *1910–1926*. Translated by Jane Bannard Greene and M. D. Herter Norton. New York: W. W. Norton, 1947.
———. *New Poems*. Selected and translated by Edward Snow. New York: North Point, 2001.
———. *The Notebooks of Malte Laurids Brigge*. Translated by Stephen Mitchell. New York: Vintage, 1990.
———. "The Rodin Book: First Part." In *Rodin and Other Prose Pieces*, trans. G. Craig Houston, 1–43. London: Quartet, 1986.
———. *Sämtliche Werke*. Vol. 1, *Gedichte*. Frankfurt am Main: Insel, 1955.
———. *Über Dichtung und Kunst*. Edited by Hartmut Engelhardt. Frankfurt am Main: Suhrkamp, 1974.
———. *Werke*. Vol. 4, *Schriften*. Edited by Horst Nalewski. Frankfurt am Main: Insel, 1996.
Rilke, Rainer Maria, and Lou Andreas-Salomé. *Briefwechsel*. Edited by Ernst Pfeiffer. Zürich: Niehans, 1952.
Ryan, Lawrence. "Rilke's *Dinggedichte*: The 'Thing' as 'Poem in Itself.'" In *Rilke-Rezeptionen / Rilke Reconsidered*, edited by Sigrid Bauschinger and Susan L. Cocalis, 27–35. Tübingen: Francke, 1995.
Saussure, Ferdinand de. *Course in General Linguistics*. Edited by Charles Bally and Albert Sechehaye, with Albert Riedlinger. Translated by Wade Baskin. New York: McGraw-Hill, 1959.
Schank, Stefan. "Rilkes Vater und Rilkes Vaterbild." In *Rilke heute. Der Ort des Dichters in der Moderne*, edited by Vera Hauschild, 81–111. Frankfurt am Main: Suhrkamp, 1997.
Scherpe, Klaus. "Ausdruck, Funktion, Medium: Transformationen der Großstadterzählung in der deutschen Literatur der Moderne." In *Literatur in einer industriellen Kultur*, edited by Götz Grossklaus and Eberhard Lämmert, 139–61. Stuttgart: Cotta, 1989.
Scheunemann, Dietrich. "'Collecting Shells' in the Age of Technological Reproduction: On Storytelling, Writing and Film." In *Orality, Literacy and Modern Media*, edited by Dietrich Scheunemann, 79–94. Columbia, S.C.: Camden House, 1996.
Schivelbusch, Wolfgang. "Railroad Space and Railroad Time." *New German Critique* 14 (1978): 31–40.
———. *The Railway Journey: The Industrialization of Time and Space in the 19th Century*. Berkeley and Los Angeles: University of California Press, 1986.
Schlüpmann, Heide. "The First German Art Film: Rye's *The Student of Prague* (1913)." Translated by Jan-Christopher Horak. In *German Film and Literature: Adaptations and Transformations*, edited by Eric Rentschler, 9–24. New York: Methuen, 1986.
Schuster, Ingrid, and Ingrid Bode, eds. *Alfred Döblin im Spiegel der zeitgenössischen Kritik*. Bern: Francke, 1973.
Schweinitz, Jörg, ed. *Prolog vor dem Film: Nachdenken über ein neues Medium, 1909–1914*. Leipzig: Reclam, 1992.
Sebald, Winfried Georg. "Between History and Natural History: On the Literary Description of Total Destruction." In *Campo Santo*, edited by Sven Meyer, translated by Anthea Bell, 68–101. London: Hamish Hamilton, 2005.
———. *Der Mythus der Zerstörung im Werk Döblins*. Klett: Stuttgart, 1980.

Segal, Naomi. "Rilke's Paris: 'Cité plein de rêves.'" In *Unreal City: Urban Experience in Modern European Literature and Art*, edited by Edward Timms and David Kelley, 97–110. New York: St. Martin's, 1985.

Seifert, Walter. *Das epische Werk Rainer Maria Rilkes*. Bonn: Bouvier, 1969.

Seltzer, Mark. *Bodies and Machines*. New York: Routledge, 1992.

Simmel, Georg. "The Metropolis and Mental Life." In *Classic Essays on the Culture of Cities*, edited by Richard Sennett, 47–60. New York: Appleton-Century-Crofts, 1969.

Sokel, Walter. "The Devolution of the Self in *The Notebooks of Malte Laurids Brigge*." In *Rilke: The Alchemy of Alienation*, edited by Frank Baron, Ernst S. Dick, and Warren R. Maurer, 171–90. Lawrence: Regents Press of Kansas, 1980.

Sontag, Susan. *On Photography*. New York: Farrar, Straus and Giroux, 1977.

Spindler, Michael. "John Dos Passos and the Visual Arts." *Journal of American Studies* 15, no. 3 (December 1981): 391–405.

Stenzel, Jürgen. "Mit Kleister und Schere: Zur Handschrift von *Berlin Alexanderplatz*." *Text + Kritik* 13/14 (June 1966): 41–44.

Stevens, Adrian. "*La sensation du neuf*: Rilke, Baudelaire und die Kunstauffassung der Moderne." In *Rilke und die Moderne: Londoner Symposion*, edited by Adrian Stevens and Fred Wagner, 226–46. Munich: Iudicium, 2000.

Tagg, John. *The Burden of Representation: Essays on Photographies and Histories*. Minneapolis: University of Minnesota, 1988.

Talbot, William Henry Fox. *The Pencil of Nature*. New York: Da Capo Press, 1969.

Usai, Paolo Cherchi, and Lorenzo Codelli, eds. *Before Caligari: German Cinema, 1895–1920 / Prima di Caligari: Cinema Tedesco, 1895–1920*. Pordenone: Edizioni Biblioteca della'Immagine, 1990.

Vaughan, Dai. "The Man with the Movie Camera." In *The Documentary Tradition*, edited by Lewis Jacobs, 53–59. 2nd ed. New York: W. W. Norton, 1979.

Versluys, Kristiaan. "Three City Poets: Rilke, Baudelaire, and Verhaeren." *Revue de Litterature Comparee* 54 (1980): 283–307.

Virilio, Paul. *The Vision Machine*. Translated by Julie Rose. London: BFI, 1994.

Ward, Janet. *Weimar Surfaces: Urban Visual Culture in 1920s Germany*. Berkeley and Los Angeles: University of California Press, 2001.

Weber, Samuel. *Mass Mediauras: Form, Technics, Media*. Edited by Alan Cholodenko. Stanford: Stanford University Press, 1996.

Westerhoven, James. "Autobiographical Elements in the Camera Eye." *American Literature* 48, no. 3 (November 1976): 340–64.

Winthrop-Young, Geoffrey. "Magic Media Mountain: Technology and the *Umbildungsroman*." In *Reading Matters: Narrative in the New Media Ecology*, edited by Joseph Tabbi and Michael Wutz, 29–52. Ithaca: Cornell University Press, 1997.

Zalubska, Cecylia. "Parallelen der Erzähltechnik in den Werken von Alfred Döblin und James Joyce." *Studia Germanica Posnaniensia* 1 (1971): 59–67.

Zglinicki, Friedrich von. *Der Weg des Films: Geschichte der Kinematographie und ihrer Vorläufer*. Berlin: Rembrandt, 1956.

Zimmermann, Ulf. "Benjamin and *Berlin Alexanderplatz*: Some Notes Towards a View of Literature and the City." *Colloquia Germania* 12, no. 3 (1979): 256–72.

———. "Expressionism and Döblin's *Berlin Alexanderplatz*." In *Passion and Rebellion: The Expressionist Heritage*, edited by Stephen Eric Bronner and Douglas Kellner, 217–34. New York: Universe Books, 1983.

Ziolkowski, Theodore. *Dimensions of the Modern Novel: German Texts and European Contexts*. Princeton: Princeton University Press, 1969.

Zmegac, Viktor. *Tradition und Innovation: Studien zur deutschsprachigen Literatur seit der Jahrhundertwende*. Vienna: Böhlau, 1993.

Index

Ackerknecht, Erwin, 55
Adler, Joseph, 95–96, 118
Adorno, Theodor, 44, 162
Altenloh, Emilie, 171n. 27
American Writers' Congress, 133
Andreas-Salomé, Lou, 21, 33, 49, 167n. 16
"An Romanautoren und ihre Kritiker" (Döblin), 97–98
architecture, 119–20
Arnheim, Rudolf, 180n. 69
L'Arrivée d'un train (Lumière), 88–89
arts. See also *individual arts*
   experience and, 92–94
   film and, 14–17, 55, 56–60, 62–67, 69–70, 71, 83–84, 89–90, 91, 92–94, 108, 115–16, 129, 142
   film criticism and, 56–58, 62–67, 69–70
   intellect and, 84
   literature and, 112–13, 115
   media and, 1–3, 8–9, 14–17
   modernity and, 134–37
   object and, 25, 68, 84
   perception and, 134–36
   photography and, 166n. 10
   poetry and, 68
   reality and, 115
   representation and, 84, 137–38
   soul and, 68, 69, 71
   space and, 17, 137
   technology and, 1–3, 8–9, 14–17, 18, 68, 69, 166n. 10
   time and, 17, 27, 33, 53, 137, 167n. 17
Ashen, 58
Atlantis, 58
aura, 44, 70
Autorenfilm, 56–68

Baer, Ulrich, 27
Balázs, Béla, 55, 59, 92–94, 116, 170n. 10
Barthes, Roland, 39–40
Basserman, Dieter, 44
Bassermann, Albert, 56–57
Batchen, Geoffrey, 158

Battleship Potemkin (Eisenstein), 91, 141
Baudelaire, Charles
   Dos Passos and, 149, 152, 153
   on modernity, 152
   on photography, 166n. 10
   Rilke and, 25–26, 45, 52–53
Bazin, André, 33
Behne, Adolf, 82–83
Benjamin, Walter
   on art, 181n. 81
   on aura, 44, 70
   on dislocation, 68
   on Döblin, Alfred, 102–3
   on experience, 29–30, 36, 45–46, 52–53
   on film, 72, 92, 103, 114
   on media, 20
   on novels, 177n. 11
   on perception, 14–16, 106
   on reality, 115
   "The Storyteller," 72
   on wishes, 29–30, 34
Berlin, Symphonie der Großstadt (Ruttmann), 128–32
Berlin Alexanderplatz (Döblin)
   film version of, 116–17, 126–32
   information and, 120–26
   Kinostil of, 103–6, 108–11, 118–20
   Manhattan Transfer (Dos Passos) compared with, 138, 139–47
   media and, 19
   as a novel, 100–106
Bermann, Richard, 62, 65–66, 67–68, 72, 177n. 8
Bernhardt, Kurt, 174n. 78
Betz, Maurice, 166n. 9
Bild und Film, 55
The Birth of a Nation, 141
"Black Cat" (Rilke), 168n. 34
Blom, August, 58
blue flower, 10, 15–16
body, 75–76, 92–93, 135
Bolter, Jay David, 165n. 5, 168n. 31
Bolz, Norbert, 14, 16, 104
Brecht, Bertolt, 5–6, 65, 66

Brod, Max, 62, 78–83
Buddenbrooks (Mann), 84

The Cabinet of Dr. Caligari, 120
Cadava, Eduardo, 168n. 40
Camera Eye, 19, 138, 147–56
camera obscura, 23–25, 135
Canguilhem, Georges, 7
cathedrals, 21–23
Cendrars, Blaise, 136–37
Cézanne, Paul, 26, 33, 53, 169n. 59
"Chandos Letter" (Hofmannsthal), 74–77
cities
    in Berlin, Symphonie der GroBstadt (Ruttmann), 128–32
    in Berlin Alexanderplatz (Döblin), 101–2, 103–4, 106, 107, 118–21, 123–24, 127–28, 128–32, 139–40, 143–47
    in Manhattan Transfer (Dos Passos), 138–40, 143–47
    Rilke and, 21–22, 25–26, 27–34, 45–50, 52–53
communications technology, 124–26
conflict, 141–42
consciousness
    experience and, 32
    film and, 16, 73–74
    knowledge and, 7
    photography and, 36, 50
    poetry and, 48, 50
    theory of, 6
    time and, 47
"Construction of the Epic Work" (Döblin), 114–15
Crary, Jonathan, 23–24, 135
criticism. See film criticism; literary criticism
Culler, Jonathan, 122

Dada, 103
Daniel Defoe (Hofmannsthal), 78
Danius, Sara, 177n. 12
Das Abenteuer der Lady Glane, 60–61
Das fremde Mädchen (Hofmannsthal), 58, 77–78
Das Kinobuch (Pinthus)
    advent of, 60–62
    introduction of, 62–67, 89
    overview of, 18–19
    screenplays in, 18–19, 62, 66–68, 72, 78–83, 88–90, 172n. 33, 175n. 94, 179n. 55
data. See information
death, 30–31
Deledda, Grazia, 58
de Man, Paul, 151–52
Der Andere (Mack), 56–57
Der Artist, 54, 55
"Der Ersatz für Träume" (Hofmannsthal), 72–74, 76–77
Derrida, 43

Der Rosenkavalier (Hofmannsthal), 78
Der sichtbare Mensch (Balázs), 59
Der Student von Prag (Rye), 57–58
Descartes, 24
The Devil Is a Woman, 184n. 17
Diederichs, Helmut, 58, 91, 170n. 10
Die Ermordung einer Butterblume und andere Erzählungen (Döblin), 95–97, 118–19
Die Frau, nach der man sich sehnt (Brod), 174n. 78
"Die geweihten Töchter" (Döblin), 116–18
Dietrich, Marlene, 174n. 78, 184n. 17
"Die verrückte Lokomotive" (Pinthus), 88–90
"Die Zeitlupe" (Döblin), 113–14
difference, 12
discourse
    film and, 5–6, 54–55, 55–58, 91, 108–11, 171n. 21
    information and, 10–11
    knowledge and, 6–8
    literature and, 5–6, 8–13, 17, 19
    media and, 7–13, 17, 19
    modernity and, 12–13
    phonograph and, 11
    photography and, 22–25, 38, 147
    poetry and, 9–11, 68
    technology and, 7–13, 90–91
Döblin, Alfred
    "An Romanautoren und ihre Kritiker," 97–98, 112–13
    Berlin Alexanderplatz, 19, 100–106, 108–11, 116–17, 118–32, 138, 139–47
    "Construction of the Epic Work," 114–15
    Die Ermordung einer Butterblume und andere Erzählungen, 95–97, 118–19
    "Die geweihten Töchter," 116–18
    "Die Zeitlupe," 113–14
    Dos Passos compared with, 137, 138
    Kinostil of, 97–98, 99, 103–6, 108–20, 140–43
    on radio, 98–100
    screenplays by, 109, 116–18, 126–32
    work of generally, 19
doppelgänger, 81
Dos Passos, John
    Camera Eye of, 19, 138, 147–56
    Döblin compared with, 137, 138
    Manhattan Transfer, 19, 138–48
    U.S.A. trilogy, 19, 138, 141, 144–45, 147–56
    on writing, 133–38, 156–57
dreams, 69–70, 72–74, 77
Dürer, Albrecht, 69, 70
Duse, Eleonora, 58
Duytschaever, Joris, 140

Edison, Thomas, 1, 8, 20
editing, 90, 91, 117–18, 180n. 69
education, 8, 10
Eggebrecht, Axel, 128

Ehrenstein, Albert, 62
Einstein, Albert, 136, 137
"Ein Tag aus dem Leben Kühnebecks, des jungen Idealisten" (Brod), 78–83
Eisenstein, Sergei, 91, 108–11, 130, 141–42, 145, 156
engineering, 133–34
Engl, Josef, 180n. 63
epistemology, 6–8, 38, 40. *See also* knowledge
Ernst, Paul, 69–70
Ewers, Hans Heinz, 57, 71–72
experience
  arts and, 92–94
  consciousness and, 32
  dreams and, 73–74
  film and, 55–56, 73–74, 77, 81, 88–90, 92–94, 116, 119–20, 128, 131–32
  knowledge and, 35–38
  literature and, 27–41, 45, 92–94, 98, 119–20, 128, 131–32, 145
  memory and, 32–41, 45
  modernity and, 28, 45–46, 52–53
  perception and, 73–74
  phonograph and, 43–45
  photography and, 27–41, 50, 149
  poetry and, 28–30, 32–34, 43–53, 60, 98
  time and, 29–31, 34, 35–40, 151–52
  vision and, 27–34

Faktor, Emil, 56–57
Fassbinder, Rainer Werner, 182n. 95
Faust (Goethe), 10
Les faux-monnayeurs (Gide), 102
film. *See also* film criticism; screenplays
  architecture and, 119–20
  arts and, 14–17, 55, 56–60, 62–67, 69–70, 71, 83–84, 89–90, 91, 92–94, 108, 115–16, 129, 142
  Autorenfilm, 56–58
  consciousness and, 16, 73–74
  development of, 8, 108
  discourse and, 5–6, 54–55, 55–58, 91, 108–11, 171n. 21
  dreams and, 69–70, 72–74, 77
  editing for, 90, 91, 117–18, 180n. 69
  experience and, 55–56, 73–74, 77, 81, 88–90, 92–94, 116, 119–20, 128, 131–32
  immediacy of, 55–56, 78, 82
  information and, 11, 92, 99–100, 116, 121–22, 122–23, 130–31
  intellect and, 84
  intertitles for, 61, 64
  knowledge and, 78
  language and, 70–74, 77–78, 95–98, 142
  in literature, 84–85
  literature and, 5–6, 17, 18–19, 54–56, 58–67, 68, 70–72, 78–88, 91–92, 92–94, 95–98, 99–100, 103–16, 118–20, 121–22, 122–23, 126–32, 140–43, 146–48, 156–57
  media and, 1–2, 14–17, 58–60, 62, 65, 70–71, 99–100
  mediascape and, 18–19, 54–56, 58–60, 87–88, 128
  medium and, 14–15
  modernity and, 106
  montage and, 103, 108–11, 116, 117–18, 129–30, 140–43
  movement and, 88–90, 95–96, 113–14, 118–20, 129–30
  music and, 129
  narrative and, 127–28
  narrators for, 60–62
  novels and, 100–107, 111, 112–13, 118–20, 126–32, 140–43
  object and, 70, 84, 89
  painting and, 129
  perception and, 16–17, 57, 69–72, 73–74, 78, 80–82, 88–90, 112, 116, 119–20, 142, 156–63
  photography of, 88–92
  poetry and, 15–16, 74–78
  reading in, 66–67, 79–80, 83
  reality and, 78–83, 112–14, 115–16, 129, 131–32
  reception and, 16–17
  reference and, 16
  representation and, 78–83, 84, 91–92, 97–98, 111, 112, 113–14, 131–32, 141–43
  slow motion in, 113–14
  soul and, 70, 71, 112
  sound for, 180n. 63
  space and, 17, 61, 63, 65, 80, 83, 87–88, 89, 91, 113–14, 128, 142
  as spectacle, 70, 83–84
  subject and, 16
  technology and, 14–17, 18–19, 54–56, 58–60, 61–62, 67–73, 87–92, 106, 108, 114
  theater and, 56–58, 62–67, 77–78, 91, 108, 116, 173n. 41, 173n. 43
  theaters for, 60–61, 108
  theory of, 65–66, 89, 91–94, 108–11, 112, 115–16, 171n. 21
  time and, 8–9, 17, 61, 63, 65, 78, 80, 83–88, 113–14, 121–22, 122–23, 128, 142
  transportation and, 88–90, 95–96, 118–20, 130, 142
  truth and, 70
  vision and, 55–56, 57
  writing in, 66–68
film criticism
  arts and, 56–58, 62–67, 69–70
  dreams in, 72–74, 77
  language in, 72–74, 76–77
  literature and, 62–67, 127–28
  mediascape and, 18–19, 54–56, 58–60
  movement in, 130

film criticism *(continued)*
  reality in, 131
  technology and, 18–19, 54–56, 58–60, 69–70
  theater and, 62–67
  time in, 83–88
Film-Kurier, 55
Flusser, Vilém, 27, 159–60
Foster, Gretchen, 148–49, 150
Foucault, Michel, 6–8, 122, 181n. 88
Freud, Sigmund, 9, 13, 32, 45, 46, 73–74
Friedell, Egon, 71, 72, 89–90, 119, 137
Froeschel, George, 181n. 72

"Galeotto" (Höllriegel), 172n. 33
Gassner, John, 181n. 72
"The Georgetown Loop," 89
Gide, André, 102
Gish, Lillian, 78
Godzich, Wlad, 154
Goethe, 10, 30, 84, 97
Goll, Yvan, 94
Griffith, D. W., 141, 156
Grosz, George, 134, 135–36
Grusin, Richard, 165n. 5, 168n. 31
Gunning, Tom, 54–55, 63

Häfker, Hermann, 58–59
Hake, Sabine, 90, 178n. 34
handwriting, 12, 68. *See also* writing
Hansen, Miriam, 15–16
Hart, Julius, 58
Hasenclever, Walter, 62, 89
Hauptmann, Gerhart, 58, 82
Heidegger, 157
Heine, Heinrich, 96
Hemingway, Ernest, 184n. 17
Heyse, Paul, 70–71
Hilton, James, 181n. 72
Hofmannsthal, Hugo von, 58, 72–78, 112, 146
Höllriegel, Arnold, 172n. 33
Houssaye, Arsène, 26
Huyssen, Andreas, 167n. 15, 168n. 39

ignorance, 153–54
Ihering, Herbert, 64, 127
imagination, 10, 43, 49–50
immediacy
  of film, 55–56, 78, 82
  of literature, 143, 151–52
  of media, 5, 6
  of photography, 47, 151–52, 154, 158
indexes, 123
information
  discourse and, 10–11
  film and, 11, 92, 99–100, 116, 121–22, 122–23, 130–31

literature and, 10–11, 28–29, 98–100, 104–5, 120–26, 143–45
media and, 3–4, 9, 10–11, 98–100, 104–5, 143–45
novels and, 120–26
phonograph and, 11
photography and, 22–23, 25, 28–29, 158
poetry and, 28–29
radio and, 98–100, 123–24
technology and, 9, 10–11
time and, 121–26
intellect, 84
The Interpretation of Dreams (Freud), 73–74
intertitles, 61, 64

Jähner, Harald, 177n. 21
journalism, 46, 114–15, 147–48
Joyce, James, 107, 140, 167n. 20, 179n. 44

Kaemmerling, Ekkehard, 105
Kaes, Anton, 108
Kanehl, Oskar, 64, 71
Karolus, August, 180n. 63
Key, Ellen, 46
Kienzl, Hermann, 106–7
Kinematograph, 55
Kinostil, 97–98, 99, 103–6, 108–20, 140–43. *See also* montage
Kittler, Friedrich
  Discourse Networks, 7–13
  on experimentation, 181n. 84
  on literature, 60, 82
  on media, 17, 135
  on poetry, 42–43, 68
  on senses, 112
  on time, 121–22
Kluge, Alexander, 160–63
knowledge. *See also* truth
  epistemology, 6–8, 38, 40
  experience and, 35–38
  film and, 78
  media and, 7–8, 14
  photography and, 35–38, 159
  of self, 27, 29, 75–76
  subject and, 7, 14
Kortner, Fritz, 174n. 78
Kracauer, Siegfried
  on *Berlin, Symphonie der Großstadt* (Ruttmann), 131
  on *Berlin Alexanderplatz*, 127
  on editing, 180n. 69
  on photography, 26, 27, 35–38, 45, 50–51, 51–52, 153, 155, 158–59
Kurz, Màrtina, 169n. 59

Lacan, 13, 40, 122
Ladenkino, 60–61

Lamprecht, Gerhard, 84
language
  dreams and, 72–74, 77
  film and, 70–74, 77–78, 95–98, 142
  in film criticism, 72–74, 76–77
  in literature, 70–72, 95–100, 111, 112–13, 139–40, 145–47, 155–56
  mastery of, 181n. 88
  mediascape and, 145–47
  medium of, 75–76
  modernity and, 155–56
  poetry and, 74–77
  sound and, 125–26
  time and, 122
  writing and, 74–78
Lasker-Schüler, Else, 62
The Last Laugh, 120
Lawrence, D. H., 142–43
"Leier und Schreibmaschine" (Bermann), 67–68, 72, 177n. 8
letters, 12, 122–23, 156
Licht-bild Bühne, 55
Liebelei (Schnitzler), 58
Lindau, Paul, 56
literary criticism, 101–6, 140. *See also* film criticism
literature. *See also* film criticism; literary criticism; novels; poetry
  architecture and, 119–20
  arts and, 112–13, 115
  body and, 92–93
  communications technology and, 124–26
  difference and, 12
  discourse and, 5–6, 8–13, 17, 19
  experience and, 27–41, 45, 92–94, 98, 119–20, 128, 131–32, 145
  film and, 5–6, 17, 18–19, 54–56, 58–67, 68, 70–72, 78–88, 91–92, 92–94, 95–98, 99–100, 103–16, 118–20, 121–22, 122–23, 126–32, 140–43, 146–48, 156–57
  film criticism and, 62–67, 127–28
  film in, 84–85
  immediacy of, 143, 151–52
  information and, 10–11, 28–29, 98–100, 104–5, 120–26, 143–45
  journalism and, 46, 114–15
  Kinostil in, 97–98, 99, 103–6, 108–20, 140–43
  language in, 70–72, 95–100, 111, 112–13, 139–40, 145–47, 155–56
  media and, 2–3, 8–14, 17–20, 58–60, 62, 66, 70–71, 98–100, 101–2, 104–5, 143–45, 155–56, 156–63
  mediascape and, 2–3, 4–6, 13–14, 17–20, 26, 58–60, 87–88, 98–100, 109, 128, 133–38, 140, 143–47, 156–63
  memory and, 45, 152–53
  in modernism, 17–18, 101–3

  modernity and, 4–6, 25–26, 45, 100–108, 133–38, 149–56
  montage in, 102, 103–4, 108–11, 140–43, 145
  movement and, 95–96, 118–21, 123–24, 143–45, 152
  narrative and, 120–26, 127–28, 138–40, 144–45, 162–63
  perception and, 27–34, 69–72, 82, 98, 103, 119–20, 142, 145, 149–57
  photography and, 18, 19, 25–41, 147–56, 157–60
  photography in, 38–39
  postmodernity and, 20, 156–63
  radio and, 98–100, 105, 107, 123–24, 127–28
  reality and, 78–83, 107, 112–15, 131–32, 161–63
  recording and, 142–43
  reference and, 5, 12
  representation and, 78–83, 97–98, 106, 112–14, 131–32, 137–38, 141–43, 145, 146–47, 154–55, 160–61
  senses and, 98, 103, 121, 125–26
  soul and, 107
  sound and, 41–45, 139–40, 155–56
  space and, 5, 6, 28, 83, 87–88, 96–97, 106, 107, 113–14, 128, 142
  technology and, 4–6, 13–14, 17–20, 26, 65, 67–68, 70–72, 87–88, 100–101, 114, 124–26, 133–34, 137–38, 140
  theater and, 126
  theory of, 65–66
  time and, 5, 6, 8–9, 25–27, 46, 78, 83, 84–88, 96–97, 106, 107, 113–14, 115, 121–26, 128, 142, 150–52, 154–55
  transportation and, 95–96, 118–21, 123–24, 130, 139, 142
  typewriter and, 67–68
  vision and, 27–34, 149–56
  writing in, 102–3
Lucidor (Hofmannsthal), 78
Lukács, Georg, 71
Lumière brothers, 88–89

Mack, Max, 56
The Magic Mountain (Mann), 84–88
Manhattan Transfer (Dos Passos), 19, 138–48
Mann, Thomas, 83–88, 94
Manovich, Lev, 120
Marder, Elissa, 25, 165n. 6, 168n. 41
Marinetti, F. T., 176n. 4
Massole, Joseph, 180n. 63
mathematics, 12–13
May, Karl, 174n. 71
McLuhan, Marshall, 2, 14, 84, 91, 112, 177n. 11
media. *See also* mediascape
  arts and, 1–3, 8–9, 14–17
  discourse and, 7–13, 17, 19

media *(continued)*
  epistemology and, 7–8
  film and, 1–2, 14–17, 58–60, 62, 65, 70–71, 99–100
  immediacy of, 5, 6
  information and, 3–4, 9, 10–11, 98–100, 104–5, 143–45
  knowledge and, 7–8, 14
  literature and, 2–3, 8–14, 17–20, 58–60, 62, 66, 70–71, 98–100, 101–2, 104–5, 143–45, 155–56, 156–63
  mathematics and, 12–13
  modernity and, 4–6
  movement and, 143–45
  narrative and, 162–63
  perception and, 3–4, 14–15
  phonograph as, 1–2
  poetry and, 9–11, 99
  postmodernity and, 156–63
  print, 103–4, 143–45
  radio and, 98–100
  reference and, 5
  representation and, 157
  space and, 5, 6
  subject and, 14
  technology and, 1–6, 7–13
  terminology of, 2, 3–4
  theater and, 99
  theory of, 3–4
  time and, 5, 6, 8–9
mediascape
  film and, 18–19, 54–56, 58–60, 87–88, 128
  film criticism and, 18–19, 54–56, 58–60
  language and, 145–47
  literature and, 2–3, 4–6, 13–14, 17–20, 26, 58–60, 87–88, 98–100, 109, 128, 133–38, 140, 143–47, 156–63
  modernity and, 133–38
  photography and, 18, 26
  poetry and, 26
  postmodernity and, 156–63
  reality and, 131–32
  technology and, 13–14, 133–34, 137–38, 140
  terminology of, 2
  vision and, 135–36
  writing and, 133–38
medium, 3–4, 13, 14–15, 75–76
memory
  Camera Eye and, 152–53
  experience and, 32–41, 45
  knowledge and, 35–38
  literature and, 45, 152–53
  perception and, 32–34
  photography and, 26, 27–28, 32–41, 52, 152–53, 158–59
  poetry and, 32–34, 45, 52

reference and, 36
Rilke and, 26, 27–28, 32–41, 42
time and, 26, 34, 35–40, 53
truth and, 36, 47
Metro-Goldwyn-Mayer, 117
Mierendorff, Carlo, 64–65
Mitchell, W. J. T., 159, 170n. 5
modernism, 17–18, 101–3
modernity
  arts and, 134–37
  Camera Eye and, 149–56
  discourse and, 12–13
  experience and, 28, 45–46, 52–53
  film and, 106
  language and, 155–56
  literature and, 4–6, 25–26, 45, 100–108, 133–38, 149–56
  media and, 4–6
  mediascape and, 133–38
  perception and, 106–7, 134–36
  photography and, 50, 138, 149–56
  poetry and, 25–26, 35, 45–46
  postmodernity, 20, 156–63
  representation and, 134, 135, 137–38
  senses and, 106–7
  soul and, 106–7
  space and, 137
  technology and, 4–6, 106–7
  time and, 25–26, 137, 150–52
  vision and, 135–36
  writing and, 133–38
Modersohn, Otto, 29
montage. *See also* Kinostil
  in film, 103, 108–11, 116, 117–18, 129–30, 140–43
  in literature, 102, 103–4, 108–11, 140–43, 145
movement. *See also* transportation
  Camera Eye and, 152
  film and, 88–90, 95–96, 113–14, 118–20, 129–30
  in film criticism, 130
  literature and, 95–96, 118–21, 123–24, 143–45, 152
  media and, 143–45
  photography and, 152
Müller, Johannes, 24
Münsterberg, Hugo, 74, 115–16
Murnau, F. W., 120
music, 129. *See also* phonograph
Musil, Robert, 59, 93–94, 136
Muther, Richard, 29

narrative, 120–26, 127–28, 138–40, 143–47, 162–63
narrators, 60–62
Natter, Wolfgang, 130
Neue Geschichten (Kluge), 160–63
New Poems (Rilke), 22, 26, 47–53, 151, 168n. 34

newsreels, 147–48
Nichols, D., 181n. 72
Nietzsche, 11, 152
The Notebooks of Malte Laurids Brigge (Rilke)
   Baudelaire compared with, 25–26
   "Chandos Letter" (Hofmannsthal) compared with, 74–75, 76
   handwriting in, 68
   overview of, 18
   photography and, 27–41
   poetry and, 45–47, 49, 50
   U.S.A. trilogy (Dos Passos) compared with, 149, 153, 154, 155
Novalis, 10, 15
novels
   film and, 100–107, 111, 112–13, 118–20, 126–32, 140–43
   information and, 120–26
   narrative and, 138–40, 143–47
   reality and, 112–13, 114–15
   technology and, 133–34, 137–38
   time and, 115, 121–26

object
   arts and, 25, 68, 84
   film and, 70, 84, 89
   photography and, 22–25, 36, 38, 40–41, 52, 158, 168n. 34
   poetry and, 48, 52, 68, 168n. 34
   technology and, 68
objectivity, 148–49, 153–54
Ofterdingen, Heinrich von, 10
Ong, Walter, 165n. 1, 177n. 11
"On the Film" (Mann), 83–88
Opus I (Ruttmann), 129

painting, 129, 152
Panama (Cendrars), 136–37
"The Panther" (Rilke), 48–50
perception. *See also* reception; senses
   arts and, 134–36
   Camera Eye and, 149–56
   dreams and, 73–74
   experience and, 73–74
   film and, 16–17, 57, 69–72, 73–74, 78, 80–82, 88–90, 112, 116, 119–20, 142, 156–63
   literature and, 27–34, 69–72, 82, 98, 103, 119–20, 142, 145, 149–57
   media and, 3–4, 14–15
   memory and, 32–34
   modernity and, 106–7, 134–36
   photography and, 22–25, 27–34, 49, 52, 149–56, 158, 168n. 34
   poetry and, 28–29, 32–34, 49, 52, 98, 168n. 34
   reading and, 70–71
   Rilke and, 22–25, 27–34, 55–56
   soul and, 106–7
   technology and, 106–7
   time and, 29–31
   vision and, 27–34
Petersen, Julius, 179n. 44
Pfemfert, Franz, 1–2, 8, 9, 20
philosophy, 10
phonograph, 1–2, 8–9, 11, 17, 41–45, 121–22, 123
photography
   arts and, 166n. 10
   Camera Eye, 19, 138, 147–56
   camera obscura and, 23–25, 135
   consciousness and, 36, 50
   digital, 157
   discourse and, 22–25, 38, 147
   Dos Passos and, 19, 138, 147–56
   epistemology and, 38, 40
   experience and, 27–41, 50, 149
   of film, 88–92
   immediacy of, 47, 151–52, 154, 158
   information and, 22–23, 25, 28–29, 158
   knowledge and, 35–38, 159
   in literature, 38–39
   literature and, 18, 19, 25–41, 147–56, 157–60
   mediascape and, 18, 26
   memory and, 26, 27–28, 32–41, 52, 152–53, 158–59
   modernity and, 50, 138, 149–56
   movement and, 152
   object and, 22–25, 36, 38, 40–41, 52, 158, 168n. 34
   perception and, 22–25, 27–34, 49, 52, 149–56, 158, 168n. 34
   poetry and, 18, 19, 25–27, 47–53, 149–51
   postmodernity and, 157–60
   reality and, 149, 157–59
   reception and, 23–24, 159–60
   recording and, 159–60
   reference and, 24, 36, 37
   representation and, 154–55
   Rilke and, 18, 21–41, 47–53, 149
   sound and, 155–56
   space and, 23–25, 37
   stained-glass windows compared with, 21–23
   subject and, 22–25, 40–41, 52, 158, 168n. 34
   technology and, 23–25, 26
   time and, 22–27, 33, 35–40, 50, 52, 150–52, 154–55, 167n. 17
   of trauma, 27
   truth and, 23–25, 36, 37–38, 51–52, 159
   vision and, 27–34, 135, 149–56
Pinthus, Kurt, 18–19, 62–67, 88–90. *See also Das Kinobuch*
poetry
   arts and, 68
   consciousness and, 48, 50

poetry *(continued)*
    discourse and, 9–11, 68
    education and, 10
    experience and, 28–30, 32–34, 43–53, 60, 98
    film and, 15–16, 74–78
    imagination and, 10, 43, 49–50
    information and, 28–29
    language and, 74–77
    media and, 9–11, 99
    mediascape and, 26
    memory and, 32–34, 45, 52
    modernity and, 25–26, 35, 45–46
    object and, 48, 52, 68, 168n. 34
    perception and, 28–29, 32–34, 49, 52, 98, 168n. 34
    philosophy and, 10
    phonograph and, 41–45
    photography and, 18, 19, 25–27, 47–53, 149–51
    Rilke and, 18, 22, 25–27, 28–30, 35, 41–45, 46–53, 60, 74–75, 76, 98, 149, 151
    senses and, 43–45, 98
    soul and, 68
    space and, 29, 50
    state and, 10
    subject and, 48, 50, 52, 168n. 34
    technology and, 9–11, 15–16, 26, 67–68, 114
    time and, 25–27, 29–31, 33, 34, 41–42, 46–53
    truth and, 51–52
    typewriter and, 67–68
    writing of, 67–68, 74–77, 176n. 8
Polgar, Alfred, 69–70, 72
"Portrait of My Father as a Young Man" (Rilke), 50–53
Portrait of the Artist as a Young Man (Joyce), 167n. 20
postmodernity, 20, 156–63
print media, 103–4, 143–45
Prussian Academy of Art and the Reichrundfunkgesellschaft, 98–99
psychoanalysis, 13
Pudovkin, Vsevolod, 110–11

Quo vadis?, 63–64

radio, 98–100, 105, 107, 123–24, 127–28
Rathenau, Walther, 71
reading, 66–67, 70–71, 79–80, 83
reality. *See also* truth
    arts and, 115
    film and, 78–83, 112–14, 115–16, 129, 131–32
    in film criticism, 131
    literature and, 78–83, 107, 112–15, 131–32, 161–63
    mediascape and, 131–32
    novels and, 112–13, 114–15
    photography and, 149, 157–59

representation and, 78–83, 112–15, 131–32
time and, 115
reception, 16–17, 23–24, 159–60. *See also* perception
recording, 142–43, 159–60
reference, 5, 12, 16, 24, 36, 37
Reinhardt, Max, 78
representation
    arts and, 84, 137–38
    film and, 78–83, 84, 91–92, 97–98, 111, 112, 113–14, 131–32, 141–43
    literature and, 78–83, 97–98, 106, 112–14, 131–32, 137–38, 141–43, 145, 146–47, 154–55, 160–61
    media and, 157
    modernity and, 134, 135, 137–38
    photography and, 154–55
    reality and, 78–83, 112–15, 131–32
    technology and, 137–38
    theory of, 69
    time and, 150–52, 154–55
    writing and, 137–38
Rilke, Clara, 22, 30, 35, 169n. 54
Rilke, Rainer Maria
    in France, 21–23, 25–26, 27–34, 41, 42, 49
    memory and, 26, 27–28, 32–41, 42
    New Poems, 22, 26, 47–53, 151, 168n. 34
    The Notebooks of Malte Laurids Brigge, 18, 25, 26, 27–41, 45, 49, 50, 68, 74–75, 76, 149, 153, 154, 155
    perception and, 22–25, 27–34, 55–56
    phonograph and, 41–45
    photography and, 18, 21–41, 47–53, 149
    poetry and, 18, 22, 25–27, 28–30, 35, 41–45, 46–53, 60, 74–75, 76, 98, 149, 151
    work of generally, 18
Rodin, Auguste, 25, 26, 29, 33, 169n. 54
romanticism, 12–13
Rücker, Thomas, 172n. 38
Ruttmann, Walter, 128–32
Ryan, Lawrence, 49
Rye, Stellan, 57

Salt, Barry, 90
Samonova, Lyda, 57
Saussure, Ferdinand de, 12, 122
Schank, Stefan, 169n. 59
Scherpe, Klaus, 177n. 19
Scheunemann, Dietrich, 177n. 21
Schivelbusch, Wolfgang, 95–96, 119
Schnitzler, Arthur, 58, 114–15
Schreber, Daniel Paul, 9
screenplays
    in *Das Kinobuch* (Pinthus), 18–19, 62, 66–68, 72, 78–83, 88–90, 172n. 33, 175n. 94, 179n. 55
    by Döblin, 109, 116–18, 126–32
    by Dos Passos, 141

sculpture, 33, 167n. 17, 169n. 54
Sebald, W. G., 96, 160, 162–63
Seltzer, Mark, 11–12
senses. *See also* perception; sound; vision
    film and, 112
    literature and, 98, 103, 121, 125–26
    modernity and, 106–7
    phonograph and, 43–45
    poetry and, 43–45, 98
    technology and, 106–7
    time and, 121
Sienkiewicz, Henryk, 63
Simmel, Georg, 32, 93
slow motion, 113–14
Sochaczwer, Hans, 140
Sontag, Susan, 22, 38
soul, 68, 69, 70, 71, 106–7, 112
sound, 31, 41–45, 125–26, 139–40, 155–56, 180n. 63
space
    arts and, 17, 137
    film and, 17, 61, 63, 65, 80, 83, 87–88, 89, 91, 113–14, 128, 142
    literature and, 5, 6, 28, 83, 87–88, 96–97, 106, 107, 113–14, 128, 142
    media and, 5, 6
    modernity and, 137
    phonograph and, 17, 44
    photography and, 23–25, 37
    poetry and, 29, 50
    private and public, 31
    technology and, 6
    as time, 30
    transportation and, 95–96
spectacle, 70, 83–84
stained-glass windows, 21–23, 34
state, 10
Sternberg, Josef von, 184n. 17
Stiller, Mauritz, 58, 77
"The Storyteller" (Benjamin), 72
Strauss, Richard, 78
Stuart, Henry Longman, 143
subject
    film and, 16
    knowledge and, 7, 14
    media and, 14
    photography and, 22–25, 40–41, 52, 158, 168n. 34
    poetry and, 48, 50, 52, 168n. 34
subjectivity, 148–49, 154
symbols, 122–23

Tagg, John, 159
Talbot, William Henry Fox, 22
Tannenbaum, Herbert, 62
technology
    arts and, 1–3, 8–9, 14–17, 18, 68, 69, 166n. 10
    communications, 124–26
    discourse and, 7–13, 90–91
    dreams and, 73
    film and, 14–17, 18–19, 54–56, 58–60, 61–62, 67–73, 87–92, 106, 108, 114
    film criticism and, 18–19, 54–56, 58–60, 69–70
    information and, 9, 10–11
    knowledge and, 7–8
    literature and, 4–6, 13–14, 17–20, 26, 65, 67–68, 70–72, 87–88, 100–101, 114, 124–26, 133–34, 137–38, 140
    media and, 1–6, 7–13
    mediascape and, 13–14, 133–34, 137–38, 140
    modernity and, 4–6, 106–7
    novels and, 133–34, 137–38
    object and, 68
    perception and, 106–7
    photography and, 23–25, 26
    poetry and, 9–11, 15–16, 26, 67–68, 114
    postmodernity and, 157
    representation and, 137–38
    senses and, 106–7
    soul and, 106–7
    space and, 6
    time and, 6
    writing and, 133–34
telegraph, 125
theater
    film and, 56–58, 62–67, 77–78, 91, 108, 116, 173n. 41, 173n. 43
    literature and, 126
    media and, 99
theaters, movie, 60–61, 108
theory
    of consciousness, 6
    of film, 65–66, 89, 91–94, 108–11, 112, 115–16, 171n. 21
    of literature, 65–66
    of media, 3–4
    of representation, 69
Therese (Schnitzler), 114–15
Thiess, Frank, 91
time
    arts and, 17, 27, 33, 137, 167n. 17
    Camera Eye and, 150–52, 154–55
    consciousness and, 47
    death and, 30–31
    experience and, 29–31, 34, 35–40, 151–52
    film and, 8–9, 17, 61, 63, 65, 78, 80, 83–88, 113–14, 121–22, 122–23, 128, 142
    information and, 121–26
    journalism and, 115
    language and, 122
    literature and, 5, 6, 8–9, 25–27, 46, 78, 83, 84–88, 96–97, 106, 107, 113–14, 115, 121–26, 128, 142, 150–52, 154–55
    media and, 5, 6, 8–9
    memory and, 26, 34, 35–40, 53

time *(continued)*
    modernity and, 25–26, 137, 150–52
    novels and, 115, 121–26
    perception and, 29–31
    phonograph and, 8–9, 17, 41–42, 44, 121–22
    photography and, 22–27, 33, 35–40, 50, 52, 150–52, 154–55, 167n. 17
    poetry and, 25–27, 29–31, 33, 34, 41–42, 46–53
    reality and, 115
    reference and, 36
    representation and, 150–52, 154–55
    senses and, 121
    space as, 30
    technology and, 6
    transportation and, 95–96
trains, 88–90, 95–96
transportation. *See also* movement
    film and, 88–90, 95–96, 118–20, 130, 142
    literature and, 95–96, 118–21, 123–24, 130, 139, 142
trauma, 27
truth. *See also* knowledge; reality
    film and, 70
    memory and, 36, 47
    photography and, 23–25, 36, 37–38, 51–52, 159
    poetry and, 51–52
typewriter, 11–12, 67–68

Ulysses (Joyce), 107, 140, 179n. 44
U.S.A. trilogy (Dos Passos), 19, 138, 141, 144–45, 147–56

Valéry, Paul, 68
Verein deutscher Schriftsteller, 108
Vertov, Dziga, 148
Viertel, Berthold, 81–82
Virilio, Paul, 167n. 17
vision, 27–34, 55–56, 57, 135–36, 149–56
Vogt, Hans, 180n. 63

Weber, Samuel, 16, 80
"The Wedding Night" (Hasenclever), 175n. 94
Wegener, Paul, 57, 91–92, 114
Welbery, David, 13
West, Claudine, 181n. 72
Wiene, Robert, 78, 120
Wiesenthal, Grete, 77
Wilhelm, Hans, 116, 126
Wilson, Edmund, 184n. 17
Wimperis, Arthur, 181n. 72
Winthrop-Young, Geoffrey, 87, 175n. 84
wishes, 29–30
World War II, 160–62
writing, 12, 66–68, 74–78, 102–3, 133–38, 176n. 8

Zglinicki, Friedrich, 61, 171n. 24
Zimmerman, Ulf, 177n. 17